Anger is Not
an Emotion

~

Jeanette Kasper

Text Copyright © 2001 by Jeanette Kasper
Calgary, Alberta, Canada

Published by **Be You Inc.**
2428 Palisade Dr SW
Calgary, Alberta, Canada T2V 3V3
Website: www.beyouinc.com

First printing, June 2001.

ISBN 0-9688009-0-4

Printed in Canada by The Printman (printman@nucleus.com)

ACKNOWLEDGEMENTS

I am so very Grateful that the Spirit of the Universe has passed to me and through me, sharing this Laughter and Learning with those whom it can heal.

Theode – a Thank you that comes from the bottom of my soul up through all of my love for you.
Brett, **Rhys**, **Gia**. My guinea pigs. Thank you for being in my life. I love each one of you so much.

Bonnie Luft – for the digital production, for taking care of the details, and for the immense support throughout all. Thank you.
Jay Winan – for helping me put the concepts together in a readable format.

To everyone who has attended one of my workshops or seminars. Thank you for your input. To everyone from whom I've learned. Your lessons were priceless. Thank you.

Introduction

Some of us are those angry people who don't seem to care who is near or where we are when we explode. We take no prisoners. We get aggressive. We attack. Some of us get incredibly nervous around angry people and our minds go blank. Two days after facing that angry person we think, "That's what I should have said!" *Anger Is Not an Emotion* gives quick tips and long-term strategies for people on both sides of the anger equation.

Anger is not an emotion, anger is our defense mechanism. Anger is our attack mechanism.

I've been a single mother on welfare, knowing that the world owed me. I was angry at the world and everyone in it. I couldn't understand, though, how could I be furiously angry with my beautiful two-year-old son. I remember him standing in front of me with a look of confusion and fear on his face, and hating that I had put it there. Yet, I couldn't stop yelling at him. I knew I wanted to change. I did not want to be an angry, attacking person. And I felt the despair—that feeling that I'm always going to be this way. I have felt the guilt and I blamed myself constantly for continuing to be that angry person. Why couldn't I stop?

I've been in situations where the rage bubbles up from inside, and spews out of my mouth, and look out to those who are standing near by. I've done the Road Rage thing. How could I be screaming mad at a driver I didn't know, and who had changed lanes safely, even though he didn't use his signal light? Why would I waste energy on that kind of situation?

I have screamed at the kids and my husband at home. How could I be so angry that I could ignore all those strangers around me, and fly into a screaming rage in a public place (and I still feel the embarrassment over those times!) With the amount of anger and attacking I have directed towards my husband, it surprised me, even at the time, that he would still be willing to work things out. We got to the point where I was so volatile that he hated coming home at the end of the day because he didn't know what he would face. I didn't know what I was facing, either. It seemed that the least little thing could send me into a rage. Afterwards, I would be so ashamed, embarrassed, and apologetic. But in the heat of the anger I felt out of control. I had no idea why or what to do about it.

I've ended best friendships because those people wouldn't do things my way or they did something to which I took offense. I remember leaving many a gathering of friends or family and the second we were closeted in the car, I would start with a litany of all the stupid and idiotic things I had heard and seen at the party. I remember listening to myself talk, knowing that I had said those exact same things before, and feeling bored with the discussion, but I truly didn't know what else to talk about.

For the seven years that I was a Customs Officer, every conversation I had with my husband, I was trying to figure out how he was lying to me. (Didn't do much for the happiness in our marriage.) But I didn't get angry on the job. No need to get defensive in that job. I had control of people's lives.

In the office jobs I had, I was totally the opposite. How could I feel so in control at home, and so much like a victim in the office? I was not assertive. I was a little 'yes' girl. I didn't know how to talk in a way that sounded mature or knowledgeable. I felt completely out of my element and had no idea what to say or how to act. If someone in the office got angry, my mind went blank. But when I got home I talked big. I was going to handle it tomorrow (always tomorrow; and tomorrow never came.)

I've been married to a wonderful man who, in far too many situations, it didn't matter what he said, didn't matter what he did, and look out if he tried to remain silent. *He was damned if he did, and damned if he didn't.* I hated that feeling of anger welling up inside of me. I hated the words that came out of my mouth. I felt constantly guilty. I hated those feelings. And I felt helpless to change.

I had a really hard time understanding why we were so busy around the house, and what we could do about it. Both my husband and I had grown up in farming communities; my husband on a farm, and I grew up in a small town in Saskatchewan, Canada. With three children, living in the middle of

Calgary, Canada, we managed to replicate the farm he had grown up on. We were busy every second of every day. We raised rabbits for food. I took home those cute little ducklings from the kindergarten class (when our children were that age), raised them in our backyard and then, yummmm (you get the picture). We were busy all of the time with little time to spend with the kids. We talked about how we seemed to spend so little time having fun with the kids, yet we still could find no extra quality time for the kids. We often got angry and resented having so many chores to do, but that was how life was. There was really no thought that we could change it. How could we keep saying that the children were the most important thing in our life, when time with them never happened because we had so many chores that had to be done? The anger, resentment, frustration, and rage that flowed out of feeling stuck in a rut in my life, not knowing how to change it, and not knowing what to change it to even if I could, were directed at my kids, my husband, and anyone else who stepped into the line of fire.

For many, many years I blamed those wonderful people who are my parents. They did it *to* me. If they had raised me differently, I would be different. I couldn't understand what my husband meant when he said that I had to make peace with my parents. I was talking to them. We spent time together. But I complained so often about the things they had done to me, and "that's why I'm like this." It took me 35 years to understand the phrase, *they did the best they could with what they had.* I blamed them for the way I was parenting because they had taught me to parent that way. Today, I'm so very happy they raised me exactly the way they did. I've learned. I've grown. I've taken responsibility for myself, and I like who I am. And I am who I am, partially, because they did exactly what they did.

I feel like I have *done it all* when it comes to anger. It has been the biggest issue in my life. Learning to control my anger has been my hardest lesson. The first realization that made a difference in my life is described in Level I: Anger is Not an Emotion. If anger is my defense mechanism of attacking others, what am I defending myself from? How can I stop attacking others? The simplest strategy in controlling my anger is physical. I calm down when I am singing or coloring with the kids. I have figured out why those two techniques work, and how to translate them into techniques that anyone can use anywhere, anytime. Level II describes the second realization that helped me calm down. I realized how The Negative Thought Cycle was keeping me focused on all the things around me that are dangerous, so I had to stay in defense-attack. I needed to be angry a lot, to stay safe.

Level III, The Golden Rule Causes Conflict, is one of the most fun, and easiest realizations I had, when thinking about what was wrong with all those other people. Why were they constantly trying to *do it to me*? Why couldn't they just change their behavior, so I could stop getting angry with them?

Level IV, Make Them Calm Down, addresses how to communicate with others. All I want is for that customer to calm down so that I can solve the problem, but every word I say makes the other person angrier. Why? And how can I talk to others so they stay calm and listen, instead of blowing up in a rage? Level V, What Can I Do About Me? examines the root of anger. Why do I feel the need to defend myself in the first place? And Level VI, Lead Your Safety Brain to Change discusses the fact that the book is just information. I want to help you in your life not just in your head. Collecting information does nothing to change us. There are specific techniques in Level VI that we can use to make it easier to actually change from being angry and attacking to being calm, peaceful, and poised.

The amazing thing is that I'm still married to the same man, and we now have an incredibly loving relationship. It's amazing, too, that my parents continue to love me, even though I've done and said many things, even as an adult, that would have justified them giving up on me. My children, who bore the brunt of my anger for a long time, have now learned that even moms can change. They are now happy, well-adjusted kids. They show high self-esteem. As a family, we now laugh together, instead of shout, scream, and yell together. It's so much better this way.

I've done the research. I've had the realizations. Then I had to make those theories and realizations work. Throughout the book I share real stories to show how the different theories and realizations work. All the names in all of the stories have been changed to protect the guilty.

I've taught this information in public seminars and in corporations for over four years to over 50,000 people in North America and the United Kingdom. They saw how easy it could be. They've made their changes. So can you.

Here is a smorgasbord. You've never read anything quite like this about anger. But once you've read it, you'll see how practical it is, and how simple making the changes can be. Life can be just as good for you. You can change. Here's your chance.

Anger is natural, it just isn't necessary.

Table of Contents

LEVEL 1

Anger is Not
an Emotion

Chapter I
Our Defense Mechanism
or The Physical Response

We do not often stop to think about what we were like before we had all of the things we have today: houses, cable TV, the Internet, cars, schools, places to go to work, electricity. Yet, these are the things that set us apart from all the other animals in the animal kingdom. We are not the strongest animals nor the fastest nor the most aggressive. Still, we are at the top of the food chain because we have weapons. We also have machinery. We have science. We use tools. We can go anywhere, do anything we want, and the rest of the animal kingdom has to tolerate us or move or die. We eat whatever we want, be it meat or vegetable. In fact, much of what we eat is processed to the point where it is difficult to recognize its origin. Humans are now at the top of the food chain because we are able to have new ideas, make choices, and implement changes. We can change ourselves and our surroundings to match new ideas. Most animals in the animal kingdom simply follow instinct and routine to survive. If anything dramatic happens in their environment the animals are as likely to die as they are to move or to adapt. That seems to be the basis of the whole theory of evolution. The strongest of a species, and the most adaptable, are the ones who survived. The human animal is the most adaptable of all. We can affect our environment in ways that no other animal can.

However, let's think back to a time before humans discovered tools. Let's take a look at how we managed in the animal kingdom before we had fire or guns or knives or clubs or spears. What were we like as the human animal?

Before we discovered tools, before we had words, before we had cars, before we had swimming pools, the human animal was not a predator. The human animal was not naturally a hunter. Physically, we had no natural body parts adapted to attacking. We did not have big, sharp teeth for tearing into our prey. We did not have long, sharp, deadly claws. We could not run very fast and we were not particularly physically strong compared to most other animals. The human animal was very naturally the prey or the hunted. We were, physically, very close to the bottom of the food chain. Physically, we still are very close to the bottom of the food chain.

As prey, we found safety in belonging to a pack or a herd. There are probably many reasons that we, as the human animal, started forming packs: for companionship, for procreation, for the efficiency of shared work. However, as with other animals in the animal kingdom, the primary reason for the human animal to come together in packs, was for survival, for safety.[1]

Other animals that are naturally hunted and form into packs or herds for safety, are, for example, the beaver, the gopher, and the deer. One gopher alone in a field will not survive very long. Two eyes cannot watch all the directions from which danger might come. So, gophers find their safety in packs with many eyes watching for danger, many ears listening for danger, and many noses sniffing for danger.

How many pocket gophers in any given field? (Too many!) When one gopher sees danger coming, how does it indicate to the rest of its pack or burrow that there is danger coming? It gives a loud, sharp whistle or chirp. All the other gophers hear the sound and dive into their holes for safety.

In North America we have the beaver. Beavers are naturally the hunted, the prey. They do not have any natural attacking tools: no long, sharp claws, no poisonous fangs. They do have long, sharp front teeth, but those teeth are for gnawing down trees. If cornered, with no way to swim away and escape, the beaver will use those teeth as best it can for protection, but it will often lose that fight and be eaten. If the beaver has any path for running or swimming away, it will naturally make that choice first. So, a pack or a colony of beavers stays together for safety. How many beavers would live in a beaver colony? Five or ten? One or two families? When one beaver sees danger coming, it indicates to the rest of the beavers that there is danger by slapping its broad tail on the water, then diving into the water and swimming away. All of the other beavers hear the sound and they all dive for safety, too.

There are many other animals that are naturally hunted and form into packs for safety. Some examples are deer, monkeys, horses, buffalo, rabbits, and geese. Any one of these animals will stand and fight if it is backed into a corner. It will fight with what it has, but it usually loses to the wolf, the hyena, the cougar, or the coyote. However, for each of these animals at the lower end of the food chain, their natural instinct is to run and hide. Most are equipped with speed or a natural camouflage (jackrabbits change color from season to season so that their coats blend with their surroundings, some lizards have skin that changes color). They can either hide effectively or run and get away.

If the human animal is like the gopher, the beaver, the deer, and all of these other hunted animals that are at the bottom of the food chain, then, we too, must have a signal, to tell the rest of our pack that there is danger. How did the human animal indicate to the rest of its pack that there was danger coming (before telephones and 911)? It either yelled or screamed. One of the pack would see danger coming and would yell loudly, or scream, so that the rest of the pack would hear the signal and run and hide.

We still react to that instinctive human danger signal today. Do you remember the last time you were out in a public place and you heard somebody yell or scream? Maybe you were passing by a park or a playground, or you were in a parking lot at a mall or the grocery store, and you heard another parent yell or scream at the kids. (So, it wasn't you this time!) What is the very first thing you did? You stopped and looked around, trying to identify where the sound was coming from. Do you also remember your heart rate speeding up as you looked around?

All stimuli, from all of our senses, the ears, the eyes, the nose, the mouth, and touch, go quickly and directly through the brain stem and are sent as messages to two different parts of the brain—the cortex and the amygdala. [2] The amygdala is a small almond-shaped part that is deep inside the brain. The amygdala is responsible for activating our defense mechanisms. The amygdala is judging whether the sound, sight, taste, feel, or smell is something that is safe, or not. The first message is sent to the amygdala. If the stimuli sent to the amygdala resemble anything that we can judge from experience as dangerous, or if they are totally new and we do not know anything about them, the amygdala will trigger our defense mechanisms.

The other message is sent from the brain stem to our cortex–the part of our brain responsible for conscious, rational thought. This is the part of our brain that is responsible for coming up with new ideas. It is also the part of our brain that does all organizing and planning. The cortex will take a look at the sight, sound, taste, feel, or smell and think about it, consciously.

Something interesting and very relevant to note about the messages sent to these two parts of the brain is that the message gets to the amygdala far, far faster than it gets to the cortex.[3] This makes sense. It is far more necessary for us to be able to react quickly to something that threatens our survival than it is for us to think about something. It is nice to be able to think things through and process them rationally and logically, but if the amygdala did not react so quickly we would be dead and unable to think about anything.

The message that goes to the amygdala is simultaneously sent to the cortex for processing. Each circuit connecting the amygdala to the cortex is a one-way street. Messages are sent one way. A message of danger is sent from the amygdala to the cortex. After the cortex thinks it through, a message is sent from the cortex to the amygdala. This is a rational thought about the stimuli. "It's not a rattlesnake. It's only a curved stick." This message does not come back to the amygdala down the same circuit. There are far more cell circuits connecting the amygdala to the cortex than there are connecting the cortex to the amygdala. The amygdala is in a position to bombard the cortex with danger messages because it can send the message through many more circuits. Messages coming back from the cortex to the amygdala simply do not have the same power because the message is sent on far fewer circuits. This ensures that the amygdala makes the first judgment, a judgment that cannot be overridden by other parts of the brain. This is probably the main reason that it is so difficult to exert conscious control over fear.[4] It is as though all of our defense systems, neurological, biological, psychological, are first hardwired to the amygdala to ensure our survival. The amygdala is then wired to the other areas of our brain, to ensure both electrical and chemical signals are getting to all parts of the brain.

As for that yell or scream in a public place, the amygdala processes the signal that there is danger and activates our defense mechanisms. The amygdala processes the signals so quickly, Joseph LeDoux proved the sound messages reach the amygdala in 12 milliseconds,[5] that in the split second it perceives danger, it tells the body to release adrenaline into the system. In fact, two of the chemicals released by the adrenal gland, corticosteroid and norepinephrine (adrenaline) trigger most of the physiological changes we feel when we are scared and think we are in danger.[6] Our heart starts to race. Our blood pressure goes up. Our palms get sweaty. Our mouth gets dry. We might feel the need to urinate. And our minds go blank.

The neurobiological systems within our bodies are very complex. Scientists are only now starting to discover what is happening neurologically and biologically when we receive signals through our senses. There are over ten billion neurons (receptors of electrical impulses) within our brains alone. Scientists who have studied the brain for years do not fully comprehend how everything works with the different stimuli we receive. And, of course, scientists from different areas of study are in total disagreement over almost every single theory proposed. However, the understanding that when we judge something to be unsafe we release adrenaline to activate our defense mechanisms within our bodies is a well-accepted fact. The intricacies of exactly which chemicals and neurons are released from where, in exactly what order, and why and how, are far more detailed than we need to learn in order to discuss and control our anger. If you would like further information about how the body processes signals neurobiologically, there is some absolutely fascinating reading in the area of neuroscience.

When we perceive something as being unsafe, we release adrenaline to activate our defense mechanisms. The adrenaline releases fat into our blood stream.[7] That fat in the blood stream is the extra energy needed for the fight or flight response. That adrenaline in our system is our defense mechanism, our safety mechanism. As soon as we judge something to be unsafe—it takes only a split second—we release the adrenaline into our system. We are now completely in defense mode, ready to defend ourselves. We have activated our safety brain, the amygdala, and shut off access to our thinking brain, the cortex.[8] Daniel Goleman, in *Emotional Intelligence*, describes this as a hijacking.[9] Our bodies get hijacked and our thinking brain is now out of the loop, as our safety brain takes over and we concentrate completely on defending ourselves and surviving.

The thinking brain is the rational, cognitive, thinking, logical part of our brains. We are aware of our thoughts from the thinking brain. This is the part of our brain that comes up with new ideas. It is the part of your brain that helped you to buy this book. You bought the book because your thinking brain decided that *Anger Is NOT an Emotion* might have some new ways of looking at anger. It might help you manage your anger, give you some ideas on helping those around you to calm down, or at least you could stay calm when those around you go ballistic.

The willingness to do something different in order to have a better life comes from our thinking brain. And a willingness to do something different is a willingness to change. Change is such an integral part of our lives. We often think, "I could have said something different yesterday, instead of blowing up," or "I could use different words so that Jane, at work, stays calmer," or "If I had more money I would be happier," or "I should look around for a new job, where I'd be challenged more," or "Next time, I'm not going to take even one bite of that cheesecake; instead, I'm going to lose those 5 pounds." All of these thoughts indicate that you are willing to change. And all of these thoughts come from our thinking brain, the part of our brain that sees how we could change and what would make us happier, and helps us achieve our goals. Change is a good thing. Changing little and big things in our lives can lead us to living the life we want, a life that we are happier living. The ability to change even the small things comes from the thinking brain.

The safety brain is the part of our brain that is constantly looking for danger and trying to keep us safe. The safety brain's only goal is to keep us safe. The safest thing is to keep us doing everything the same way that we have always done it. Any change would be unsafe because if something changes, we cannot know the consequences of the change. Fear of the unknown. We must remain exactly the way we are right now, doing everything exactly the way we are doing it right now, and the way we did it yesterday and the day before that, until we die. That would be the safe thing to do. And that is the goal of our safety brain. Stay the same. Stay safe.

How much of the time, in any given day, is our thinking brain in control, and how much of the time is our safety brain in control? We've all heard the studies that we use anywhere from 1% to 10% of our brains. What is the rest of our brain doing? Sitting around like a slug all day, doing nothing. We've heard these studies often enough that we believe them. In fact, the idea that we use between 1% to 10% of our brain, is an urban myth.[10] There is absolutely no research backing these studies.

Most of us use all of our brain, all the time. For people who have brain damage, either from birth or because of accidents or surgery, they may have some impaired function because of the brain damage; however, they are fully using what is there to use. If we only used 10% of our brain, we would be dead. We need our full brain at all times. The brain runs the body and the mind.

However, much of the time we are not consciously thinking about what we are doing. We are simply doing it. I wonder if we are making conscious decisions about what we are doing only 10% the time? I've done no research on this, but let's take a casual look at the first hour of an average day, and see how much is devoted to thinking consciously, and how much we do just because we are used to doing it that way.

- Alarm goes off at 6:30 a.m. It's always set at 6:30 a.m. – *Habit*
- You turn off the alarm without even looking at it. – *Habit*
- You snuggle back under the covers for a few more minutes. Why? Because that's what you always do. – *Habit*
- 10 minutes later your eyelids fly open, and you look at the clock, have you overslept? Nope. Just that usual 10 minutes. – *Habit*
- You get out of bed. Why do you get out on that side everyday? – *Habit*
- You stumble off to the bathroom. Why do you go there first? – *Habit*
- Back in the bedroom, you get dressed. Why did you pick that outfit? You probably gave it a bit of thought. – *Thought*
- Why did you pick that color? Because it's the right color. It feels good today. Why does it feel good? Because a long time ago you learned that when you wear this color you feel good. – *Habit*
- Head to the kitchen to make breakfast. Why there next? – *Habit*
- What's for breakfast? Why do you always have that for breakfast? – *Habit*
- Do you clean up after yourself or not? – *Habit*
- Where is the usual stuff you grab on your way out the door? – *Habit*
- Overcoat, raincoat, light jacket, or no jacket at all? Probably heard the weather forecast and made a conscious decision. – *Thought*
- When it's that temperature, or that forecast, how do you know to wear that for outdoors? – *Habit*

We could go into a lot more detail about each step we take, each thing we touch, and each thought or non-thought we have as we go through our routines of the day. Most of our day is, however, routine. Most of our day is governed by our safety brain, simply taking us through decisions and actions that we always make and take because those are the ones that we have proven, through experience, are the safe decisions and actions to make and take. Is routine and habit 90% or 95% of our day? For our purposes, the actual figure does not matter. What does matter is the understanding that our safety brain runs most of our lives in the effort to keep us safe.

Reading this book is a habit run by your safety brain. How long ago did you learn to read? Do you remember learning to read? Remember how hard it was to sound out the letters and the words? I do not remember for myself, but we are currently working with our six-year-old daughter as she learns to read, and we can see how difficult it is to learn this skill. Learning a new skill requires the activity of the thinking brain. Yet, now, reading this book, each word, each syllable, each paragraph and page flow by your eyes. Reading is a habit, and you do not have to think about how to do it. You just read. Habit. Run by our safety brain.

Once we have learned to do something (and learning something new, of course, comes from the thinking brain), and made it into a habit, then we store the habit in our safety brain, and the safety brain keeps us doing things the habitual, routine way because that is safe.

Think of learning to drive a car. I remember learning to drive a car, and learning how to do a shoulder check. Over which shoulder was I supposed to check? It was so awkward. And it still is awkward. Think, now, of the last time you drove somewhere, got out of the car, headed into a building, and then stopped to think, "How did I get here?"

Once we learned to drive, the mechanics of driving became a habit. Sometimes when we drive, we are conscious of our driving, but on some trips our safety brain takes over and gets us to where we are going seemingly without the assistance of our thinking brains. "How did I get here?" Habit. Everything we learn is made into a habit, and then our safety brain takes over, helping us to do things the same, old way so we can be safe.

Some common habits that we try to change are the following:

Smoking: When I feel (good, bad, indifferent, stressed, hungry, angry) I light up a cigarette.

Eating: How many meals I eat. What I like to eat. When I eat. How much I eat.

Sleeping: How many hours I need. When I go to sleep. How well I sleep.

Watching TV: I always watch _____ (fill in the blank).

Procrastinating: I always avoid _____ (fill in the blank).

Yelling at the kids: I get home from work, the kids get home, and that time of day is the witching hour.

Getting to work: I always take the same route (the same bus) to work.

Shopping: I always shop at the same grocery store; or, I always shop when I'm feeling down.

We hate it when they change the aisles at the grocery store. Why do we hate it? Because we have to relearn whether the grocery store is safe. The changes make it unsafe. How many of us have stopped shopping at a store or a mall that has changed its aisles or done a major renovation? The danger factor was big enough that we actually stopped using those services. One reason is that, if they will make it unsafe once, they might make it unsafe again. Another reason is that we have been forced to go do our shopping at a different store, and we have found the new store to be safe, so we continue going to the safe store.

Recently, after a meal, I grabbed a piece of gum to sweeten my breath. The next day, after supper, I grabbed a piece of gum, again. The third day, I popped in a piece of gum after lunch, and then again after supper. After a week of this, having established a new habit, I was finding myself buying the multipacks of gum. Once I realized that I was starting to need a piece of gum after every meal, it was time to stop chewing gum. I did not want to get dependent upon gum.

It is so easy to begin a habit. And many of your habits are as small and insignificant as this. But they are habits. First, you have to become aware of the habit, and then you have to break it. How easy is it to break these habits? Often, it is not easy. The need for a piece of gum after every meal is coming from my safety brain, and my safety brain is ready to fight to keep me chewing gum because it is the safe action.

Listen to the words you use when you are talking to yourself about things you would like different in your life. You say to yourself, "I should quit smoking." That would be your thinking brain talking. Then you hear the words, "I don't need to smoke. I want to smoke." *Need* and *want* are good words to indicate that your safety brain is in control. Your safety brain is exerting persuasion and pressure to keep you doing your life the safe way. It is strange to think of smoking as being safe. Yet it is safe in that it has become a habit. Psychologically and physically you have become dependent upon the action of smoking, and the chemicals you are inhaling. Smoking might not be a safe activity in terms of how long you will live, but it is a safe activity to your safety brain because it fulfills both physical and psychological needs. Our safety brain keeps us performing our habits.

If it is so easy to start a new habit, like chewing a piece of gum after each meal, why isn't it as easy to quit smoking, lose weight, stop yelling at the kids, or quit arguing with your spouse? Starting a brand new habit is a lot easier than quitting an old habit. In fact, chewing a piece of gum after every meal was, for me, restarting an old habit I thought I had broken. I like my sugar or sweets. Eating sweets is an old habit. Chewing a piece of gum after each meal was easy because it was restarting an old habit.

Dr. Tom Miller has an audiocassette learning program called *Self Discipline and Emotional Control.*[11] In it he talks about the safety brain as being a horse and our thinking brain as being the rider. In this learning program, Dr. Miller concentrates a lot on the rider, and getting the rider to take control of the horse. Dr. Miller's analogy is excellent, but we are going to concentrate on the horse.

Horses are stronger than riders. If the rider decides that it wants the horse to do something that the horse does not want to do, and the horse does not have on a bridle, saddle, or halter for the rider to exert pressure, who wins? The horse.

The last time I took my six-year-old daughter riding at a dude ranch northwest of Calgary, I was on a large horse, and Gia was on a Shetland pony. Shetland ponies are notorious for being stubborn little beasts. The first challenge we faced was getting that Shetland pony to follow my horse out of the barn. That pony was not interested in leaving the barn because the barn is safe. The barn is cool and dim. The barn has oats. It is the same for your horse, your safety brain. Your horse is not interested in leaving the barn and doing anything new because staying where it is right now is safe.

We finally got that Shetland pony to follow my horse and once we had gotten through two gates, about 700 yards from the barn, I decided it was time for Gia to show that horse who was boss. I wanted her to turn her horse in a full circle to the left and face towards me again. How easy was it for her to turn that horse half way around and face the barn again? Really easy. How easy was it for her to get her horse to turn the rest of the way around and face away from the barn towards me? Difficult. It is the same with your horse. Once you start doing something in a new way, if your safety brain, your horse, sees even the smallest opportunity to get you back to doing things the old way, getting you back to the barn, it will try every trick it can to ensure that you go back to doing things the old way. That's why we hear about people on the dieting roller coaster. They lose weight. They gain weight. They lose it. They gain it. They lose it. They gain it. They lose it. They gain it. We hear about people who quit smoking. Start again. Quit smoking. Start again. Quit smoking. Start again. Quit smoking. Start again.

Establishing new habits and breaking old habits is like leading your horse to a meadow. If there are no pathways already going through the grass, you can get that horse to go in any direction through the grass with little resistance. Once the horse has gone through the meadow once, you can see a faint trail through the grass. Bring the horse to that meadow again and the horse wants to follow that faint trail through the grass. If it sees the path, it will want to follow that path. The trail becomes more obvious each time the horse follows it. Get the horse to follow that same path a few more times, and pretty soon the path is actually carved into the ground. This is what we are like. We have all kinds of pathways going through our meadows that are really deeply carved. Some of our patterns have been carved into the dirt since birth. We grew up with parents and siblings and friends all doing and saying things, and we learned to respond in certain ways. Now, today, we are going to lead our horse to the meadow, and we want it to step off the pathway into the grass. Have you ever gone hiking? How easy is it, as a hiker, to step off a trail into the woods. I have found that it is not very easy. I have a tendency to want to stay on the trail. It is obviously safe because so many people have walked it that they have carved it into the dirt. That is what it is like when we try to change something in our lives. It is extremely difficult to get our horses to step off the pathway and start doing things a new way. The habits are set. The safety brain does not overwhelm the thinking brain, but it can leave the thinking brain out of the loop. It can shut off access to the thinking brain, so we continue doing life the same, old, safe way.

The safety brain does not form habitual behavior all by itself. The thinking brain sees something it wants to try and persuades the safety brain to go along with the attempt, because it might be good for us, or maybe it is more dangerous for us to not try the new activity in the safety brain's judgment. Often this is the case with children. It is safer to try the new activity—learning the alphabet, doing up their own shoes, eating the spinach, trying a new sport, trying alcohol or drugs, than it is to disappoint a parent, teacher, coach, or peer.

The first time we engage in the new activity we find it to be safe. Either the activity in and of itself is safe or pleasant or we gain acceptance into a pack or greater acceptance from an existing pack. Either way, this new activity is safe. So, we do it again and again and again. How many times do we have to perform that same activity before it becomes a new habit? Brian Tracy, author of *The Psychology of Achievement*,[12] indicates through his research that it takes 21 days to change a habit. I know from personal experience that three weeks straight of performing a new activity every day, leads me to continue that activity indefinitely, as a habit. It's probably not exactly 21 days for everyone. Try 28 days. Try 40 days. Maybe for younger children it takes fewer days because they are not fighting against old habits or maybe it takes more time because they have no experience to draw on. Sometimes, in trying to stop old habits, it takes months or even years because the old habit fits so many of our needs and helps us to feel safe on so many different levels. Sometimes, an old habit that has been pleasurable suddenly becomes totally unsafe, and just one incident is enough to form the new habit of never again engaging in that particular activity. The length of time to start or stop a habit changes. What does not change is the fact that starting a new habit or stopping an old habit engages both the thinking brain and the safety brain. And the safety brain, if it judges something to be unsafe, wins. We do not change.

Many of us have set the goal that we were going to lose weight. Even a simple change like being thinner is dangerous. The safety brain's reasoning in this is it does not know what life will be like if we are 10 pounds lighter. What else could change? How will people treat us if we are 10 pounds lighter? How will we have to act if we are 10 pounds lighter? What kinds of strange foods will we have to eat if we are 10 pounds lighter? How will we have to dress if we are 10 pounds lighter? Our safety brain does not know. So, the safety brain helps us to keep weighing the same so it can keep us safe. Change is not good. Change is dangerous. We have to keep weighing the same amount.

Let's say that we have decided to lose some weight. We are going on a diet—a pure thinking brain idea. The best way to lose the weight will be to stop eating that piece of cake for dessert every day. How does our safety brain trick us into eating the cake so that we keep weighing the same weight?

- A little voice keeps telling us that just one bite won't hurt.
- We promise ourselves that we will start tomorrow.
- We tell ourselves we will exercise it off later.
- We make dinner plans with friends, and everyone knows how fattening those dinners are.
- We have to eat it, or we'll insult the cook.
- We deserve it. Today was a hard day, and we deserve a treat.
- It tastes so good. Our safety brains have us actually salivating in anticipation.
- We forget we even set the goal until after the last bite of cake slides down our throat.

All of these are safety brain tricks to keep us eating exactly the way we do for the rest of our lives until we die. No changes.

All information we encounter goes into the safety brain first, so that it can judge whether each thing is safe or not. Everything we touch, taste, smell, hear, think, and feel goes into our safety brain first. If the safety brain judges something to be safe, then it will permit us to continue. If the safety brain judges the information to be unsafe, then it releases adrenaline into the system. The adrenaline basically shuts off access to our thinking brain, and we go completely into our safety brain, triggering all of our defense mechanisms so we can get to safety.

Have you ever been in a situation where, in a public place, maybe in the office, you were faced with an angry person? This person in front of you is spitting mad, and you can't think of anything to say! This is exactly what happens: when we judge a situation to be unsafe, we shut off access to our thinking brain. *You couldn't think of anything to say.* Our instinct in this situation is to run and hide because that is one of our top safety techniques. If we can get away, and the predator (angry person) cannot find us, we are safe. Many of us used this technique as children when our parents were angry.

Think about being faced with an angry coworker. The coworker's anger means that adrenaline has interfered with his or her thinking brain. Our coworker has judged something to be unsafe and has activated the safety brain. Are we sure we want to continue the conversation with this coworker? Many of us have. We continued the conversation, trying to get them to calm down, and every word we said, our coworker (or spouse or friend or client or family member) got angrier and angrier and angrier. If we try to continue a conversation with someone when they are showing the least little bit of anger, understand that they have no access to their thinking brains. If we try to continue the conversation, we are basically talking to their horse's butt. We are having a discussion with the animal part of them that has absolutely no access to rational thought. We are arguing with their defenses. They won't be logically thinking about solutions but will be blaming, criticizing, or raging! That is the defense mode. Attack. When someone is angry, they are on the defensive. They have no access to their thinking brain. And they are in attack mode.

If the other person gets irritated, angry, annoyed, frustrated, or in a downright rage, it is time to end the discussion. He or she does not have access to the thinking brain anymore. We know that it is impossible to have a calm, rational discussion with someone's safety brain. Instead, find a non-confrontational way to end the discussion with words like, "I can't think straight right now. Can we talk about it after dinner," or "I need to think this through. Let's meet again at 2:00 p.m. to finish talking about it." The discussion does need to be finished, but at a later time. Do not leave it hanging unresolved forever. Set a time to finish the discussion when you are both calmed down, with full access to your thinking brains, ready to look at solutions.

Think about yourself. If you get the least little bit irritated, angry, annoyed, frustrated, or in an outright rage, and you try to continue the conversation with that other person, your horse's butt is doing the talking. I've certainly done it. When I get angry, I'm a yapper. I have to yap, yap, yap until I get that other person to engage. My defenses are talking, and I dig myself some pretty deep holes if I let myself yap when I am angry. We no longer have access to our thinking brains when we get angry. So, end the conversation and come back to it when you are calm and able to use rational thought to work out a good solution.

It is possible to train our safety brains to not take over in situations that we judge to be unsafe. Firefighters, lawyers, police, top military units, SWAT teams, stockbrokers, top executives have all been trained (or trained themselves) to maintain control when that adrenaline hits their systems or to withhold the adrenaline from their systems in situations that the rest of us would definitely judge to be dangerous. *G.I. Jane*,[13] starring Demi Moore, had an excellent scene demonstrating this point. In *G.I. Jane*, Demi Moore is the first and only female to be accepted into training for one of the top U.S. military units. At one point the candidates are tied down and have water poured onto their faces at such a rate that they are struggling to keep from drowning. The reasoning behind the training was that the trainees and G.I. Jane would be able to stay alive in water, regardless of the circumstances. In combat situations, these people retain their ability to use their thinking brains because they have been trained to do so. Firefighters and police officers have similar, rigorous training. They need to be able to think and function in situations where the rest of us panic.

We are able to train ourselves to control our defense mechanisms and to think once we have released the adrenaline into our systems. We can release adrenaline into our systems, without then becoming angry or freezing or running and hiding. However, there cannot be anger without adrenaline.

We have explored the fact that once we judge something to be unsafe, we activate our defense systems and turn over full control to our safety brains. Our absolute primary defense mechanism is to run and hide. That is our instinct, but that is not anger. That is passivity. That is giving in to the other person so that the other person does not escalate his or her attack.

A yell or a scream, a loud voice, even a loud noise is something that we all instinctively recognize as a sign of danger. How many parents talk in a loud voice around the house, in just regular conversation? We yell, "Come for dinner," or "Turn off that TV," or "Get your homework done." If a yell is the human animal's danger signal, and we shut off access to our thinking brains when we hear a yell, what are we doing to our children? When we yell around the house, our children automatically release adrenaline into their systems and slam that gateway shut. They no longer have access to their thinking brains.

This can often be the case until we train the kids that a loud voice from mom and dad does not necessarily mean danger. It is like the water training for the military. After a while they are able to think, even though they hear the loud sound. The kids become desensitized to their parents yelling at them to do something. How many of us would say that our kids deliberately refuse to cooperate with us? Are we sure? Or is the fault partly our own because we are giving them the signal to activate their defense mechanisms?

Start talking in a lower voice. Walk to where your kids are, and make your requests in a calm, even, quieter voice than you usually use. Watch the amazing results you will get! Share this information with your family, and get everyone's commitment to use "indoor voices" indoors. Everyone will stay calmer. In the office and at meetings, do people keep their voices calm and quiet, or noisy and loud? When you hear a loud person in the office, do you just want to leave? Give this piece of information to those people around the office, and get everyone on the quieter track. The office and your meetings will become far more productive.

Chapter 2
When Do We Attack?

Part I: When will we attack?

The human animal is not naturally a fight animal. The human animal is naturally a flight animal. Our first inclination, in any situation, is to run away and hide. The first part of defense-attack is to judge a situation to be unsafe. Once we have judged the situation to be unsafe, our safety brain needs to decide instantly what is the best way to stay safe. Do we freeze, thinking that the predator cannot find us? Do we run and hide, so it cannot get to us? Or do we become angry and attack?

Anger is not an emotion, anger is one of our primary defense mechanisms. Once our safety brain has decided that the situation is unsafe, whether we are dealing with a boss, a stupid driver, a three-month-old child, a grizzly bear, a store clerk, or a mother-in-law, the anger comes from the safety brain's decision that the best way to stay safe is to attack. What is that decision to attack based on? In what situations will we stand and fight? In what situations will we become angry? There are three situations when any naturally hunted animal in the food chain will stand and fight.

1. When an animal is cornered and there is no way out, it will try to fight its way to safety. (In which case it usually ends up as lunch.)

Think of anyone who you would consider to be weaker than you—your children, a coworker, a friend, or your spouse. If these people consider you to be stronger than they are, then they probably do not get angry with you very often. When they do, it is probably because they feel cornered. They have no other option. This holds true for you, as well. Can you remember a situation with a person, maybe a parent, where you finally felt that you absolutely had to stand up for yourself? That is exactly the feeling of being cornered and getting angry so you could free yourself. Some of us may have approached that person in a rational, reasonable, reasoning way. But the feeling of being cornered and having no way out is the feeling that you have tried everything. You have tried reasoning, you have tried telling that person to stop, you have tried everything, and the only way left is to force them to stop, to attack and make them stop.

2. A naturally hunted animal will stand and fight when it is protecting a weaker member of the pack.

Within many human packs we see that children are especially protected. Children are naturally the weakest members of the pack. Come on you moms and dads, how many of you have stood up for your children, or other children, at school, at a store or mall, or at the playground, when the children were being chastised by another adult? We will stand up for our children in circumstances where, if we were the ones being chastised in that same way, we would not protect ourselves.

We will also protect a weaker adult who belongs to our pack. Have you ever stood up for a coworker or a boss, or someone else on a committee, who does not usually speak up for himself or herself? "Let's hear what Ed has to say." Very simple words that are actually trying to protect Ed's rights. Did you ever stand up for one of your siblings, or for a friend at a restaurant? "Sheila's steak is overcooked and her whole dinner is cold. We need to have it replaced." Why did you not simply leave it up to Sheila to speak up for herself? Because you felt that Sheila would not stand up for herself. You have the perception that she would rather give in and go along with what is happening than to make waves. Speaking up for someone else, even in this very simple situation, is protecting someone who is weaker. Standing up for someone like this is not attacking. However, many parents will find themselves getting angry with, i.e., attacking, the other parent for the way they have spoken to, or disciplined, the children. Many people will find themselves becoming angry with someone in the office, maybe a boss, who has treated a coworker in a way that we find absolutely appalling. We will get angry when we feel a friend has been mistreated by other friends or a partner or spouse. We become angry when our parents dealt unfairly, or even disciplined, our brothers and sisters. The anger, in these instances, came from that need to protect someone who was unable or unwilling to protect themselves. We consider ourselves to be stronger than the other person. Often, we do not act on the anger. We do not actually have a conversation with our parents, the boss, or our friend's spouse, but we do release the adrenaline into our system, activate our defense mechanisms, and then decide that attack is the best way to deal with the situation. We might not actually attack, but we get angry, readying ourselves for the possibility of attacking. Have you ever then found yourself angry at the person you wanted to protect? Once that adrenaline is released into our system, and our attack systems have been activated, we can turn that attack on anyone who is present. Remember, it is your safety brain that now has control.

3. A naturally hunted animal will attack another in its pack when vying for position in the pack.

In the herd or the pack, animals will naturally fight for position. Who is the alpha male? Who is the alpha female? In the animal kingdom, male animals fight for position to establish which male will have the right to mate with the females in the pack. Who is at the bottom of the pack? The males posturing and fighting each other are simply vying for position in the pack. For both males and females, fighting for position is determining who is stronger, who is weaker, who gets to set the rules, and who has to live by the rules that others set. Sometimes, in the animal kingdom, when a new male challenges the dominant male in an existing pack, the new male takes over with no fight at all. The existing leader of the pack decided on the spot to simply give up its position and leave. This is true within human packs as well. Sometimes when we are challenged, we do not fight back. We simply give in. A new boss starts in the office, and we all simply cooperate. No one challenges the new ways.

We know that the strongest person is in control, and we never challenge. Sometimes children will challenge their parents for position on certain issues. A five-year-old will say, "No, I'm not going to bed now." One look from the parents has that child heading off to bed. There are many, many challenges between people where nobody gets angry. Yet, in looking at the three situations in which people get angry, challenging for position is very common. If we can get angry in such a way that the other person perceives us to be stronger, then they back down and we get our way.

My 12-year-old was very good at this for a number of years, until my husband and I realized that our son too often came out on top after he had gotten angry over an issue. He had the position, almost, of running the family on different issues. (Or maybe it was me realizing that I had been giving in. I think my husband realized a long time ago that, for all my bluster and noise, I was a soft touch when it came to issues with the kids.) I have learned to look my 12-year-old in the eye and say, "Do you think there is anything you can say, right now, that would get me to change my mind?" or "This is non-negotiable." Our 12-year-old rarely gets angry anymore over issues of position. He now knows that he will not gain control if he attacks. So, he does not even try, or at least not often, and not by going into a rage as he had in the past.

If we look at other people and know them to be weaker, a judgment made by our safety brains in a split second, or if we even think we have a chance of proving that we are stronger than they are, we will challenge them. Sometimes we challenge by becoming angry and attacking or confronting them. When they back down, or if they back down, we have gained position. We are in control.

So, anger is defense-attack. From here-on-in we will use the words "anger" and "defense-attack" interchangeably. We need to internalize this understanding of anger. If we only use the old term, "anger," we have a tendency to fall back into the old understanding. So, anger is defense-attack. New term—new understanding.

Part II: How do we know we are stronger?

Of the three situations in which the human animal will go to defense-attack, fighting for position is Number One. In order to fight for position, we have to judge that we have a good chance of succeeding. We would never fight someone who is obviously bigger, stronger, or more aggressive than we are, just for position. We might fight this person if we feel cornered, or even to protect someone else, but not just for position. In order to fight for position, first we have to have decided that we have a winning chance.

There are three areas of strength: physical, emotional, and intellectual. Physical strength is just that: bigger, taller, fitter, stronger physical size and ability. Emotional strength is shown through people's confidence in themselves. Confidence is demonstrated in a number of obvious and subtle ways. People show confidence in themselves by allowing others to have their say. Confidence is shown through the ability to laugh at ourselves. Confidence is shown through poised, calm, and relaxed behavior in most situations. Intellectual strength is shown when someone has great knowledge in a specific area, or a true understanding of how things work—whether those things are machines, authors, children, or eggs. Our safety brain judges how much stronger the other person is in each of those three areas before deciding whether we should attack or not. Depending upon what the rules of the pack are, and what position we are vying for, in order to attack we need to feel stronger than the other person in one or more of these areas.

The Number One element that will inform us whether we are stronger than the other person is body language. Body language is between 55%- 80% of communication,[1] depending upon which study you read. That means that, before you open your mouth and say anything, you have already communicated over half of who you are. The power of the message given through body language is irrefutable.

I am often invited to give keynote speeches at conventions and training programs in corporations based on the information in this book. At one location, at lunch time, I walked across the street to a grocery store. I was dressed in a very formal, navy blue skirt suit. I was alone. My purse was on my shoulder. I was walking at a good pace. I was looking down, thinking about something that had come up in the morning training session. There was a lady standing on the boulevard near the grocery store. As I reached the other side of the street, she said something to me. I didn't particularly want to engage with her, so I flashed her a smile and went back to my thoughts. As I got a couple of steps past her, she asked, "Are you a teacher?" Adult education is teaching. I responded, "Yes," with a smile, and continued walking.

And she started swearing at me. Loudly! She was even using the "f" word!

Why would she consider me to be a safe person to attack? Remember, we are governed by our safety brain. In every situation we have safety in the actions we take, and the words we use. We never say or do anything unless our safety brain has said that's it O.K. to do so. Our lives are governed by the need to stay safe. So she had to have judged me a safe person to attack in order to have done what she did.

Why did she consider me to be a safe person to attack? She didn't know anything about me. We had no history. She was not a participant from the workshop. The only things she knew about me, she got in less than 10 seconds of contact and only three words. She read from my body language that I was weaker than she was, that I was a safe person to attack. What led her to believe that?

- I did not engage in a casual conversation. Maybe she thought that I would not engage in a conflict, either.
- I smiled at her. I am a safe person. I am not interested in fighting.
- I was looking down. In the animal kingdom, the dominant animal makes eye contact, the rest avoid eye contact unless they are willing to fight. I did not make eye contact; therefore, it might be a natural assumption that she was the dominant person in this situation.
- I was past her by about 15 feet before she started to attack. I probably would not turn around to confront. Maybe she even judged that I was running away from her as I was well beyond her and walking at a good pace.
- My shoulders were slightly slumped because I was looking down. Poor posture indicates a weak body. Anyone who is physically fit has excellent posture, because the muscles are strong.
  Poor posture = a weak body = a weak person, physically.
- I am a smaller person—about 5'3" (on a good day) and not overweight.

From my body language alone, she was able to make all of these assumptions. She assumed that I was weaker than she was and, therefore, a safe person to attack. That she was absolutely wrong in that assumption does not negate the lesson in the story!

In reading the rest of the book and finding different phrases and different words to use in the conflicts that you face, IF YOU DON'T CHANGE YOUR BODY LANGUAGE, DON'T BOTHER CHANGING YOUR WORDS. If body language is 55% of communication,[2] and people are taking in all of that information from your body language alone, you need to change your body language in order for people to judge, on a nonverbal level, that you are not a safe person to attack. Body language is 55% of the message. Consciously use your body language to give the message that you want to give.

Tonality (the way you say the words) is 38% of communication.[3] Say this statement, "I love that outfit," six times. Each time you say it, use a different tone of voice to give a different message. You can give a genuine compliment. You can use sarcasm, suggesting that it is, in fact, a horrid outfit. You can use a tone of voice that suggests that the outfit is totally inappropriate for the situation. You can make it a sexually suggestive statement. You can simply be stating a fact with no emotion. You can suggest that you are impatient with having to comment on the outfit. By using exactly the same words every time and just changing how you say the words you can totally change the message you are giving. That is tonality—your tone of voice when you say the words.

The words you use convey only 7% of the message.[4] All that your words do is to prove whether you are a liar or not. How often have you had someone tell you to do something, and you are thinking to yourself, "Yeah, but you do not do it!" Our words only prove whether or not we *Walk our Talk*. Have you ever had someone come on to you as though they want to be your best friend and you were thinking to yourself, "Not in a million years, buddy!" Why would you think that? Because you read from their body language that their words were not matching their actions. You knew that they were trying to manipulate you, or get something from you, and after they got it they probably would not have the time of day for you.

If all you do after reading this book is to change the words you are using to try and calm down that other person, or even calm yourself down, it won't work. Your words are a miniscule part of the message you are giving. Body language is the biggest part of the message. Become conscious of your body language and deliberately give the message you need to give. Use all of your tools for communication, words, tonality, and body language, instead of just being aware of your words. Ensure that the message you are giving is consistent between your words, tonality, and body language.

Part III: Body language to use so you do not get attacked

If you are the person who gets attacked, here is some body language that will start giving the message that you are not a safe person to attack any longer.

• Stand up/sit up straight. Good posture shows a strong body. Someone with a strong body is not safe to attack because they can take care of themselves physically or even inflict damage upon someone else. Also, we naturally equate good posture with confidence. Most people who exercise on a routine basis, either strenuously or gently, have confidence in their bodies. That translates into confidence in themselves. Do you slouch at your desk when you work? Slouching, in any setting, whether standing, sitting, walking, or leaning, indicates physical weakness, and potentially, low self-confidence. Someone with low self-confidence will not stand up for themselves in many situations. People with low self-confidence often will not tell others about situations where they have been attacked. Therefore, people with low self-confidence are usually safe to attack. In fact, most of the information we receive through the media on how to keep ourselves safe on the street involves appearing to be self-confident. Walk at a good pace with your head up. Look like you know where you are going. Look at people, even look them in the eye, when you walk past them. Keep your shoulders back.[2] Each of these factors either indicates physical strength or self-confidence. If the police recommend this body language on the street to keep yourself safe from attacks, it will probably work just as well in the office, or at home, with people you know.

• Keep your feet shoulder-width apart. When you stand talking to someone, do you take up as little space as possible (feet close together, arms crossed)? If you do, you are showing that you are vulnerable. Body language can be interpreted literally. If you are standing with your feet together and your arms crossed, you are closed off. If you are closed off when talking to someone, their safety brain is seeing that you see something to be scared of. The thought pattern of their safety brain, in this situation, might look something like this: "If you are closed off when talking to me, you are showing you are on the defensive. If you are on the defensive, then you are scared of something. Maybe you are scared of me. If you are scared of me, then I am stronger than you are. I can attack you and gain control and position." People who take up a bit more space when standing and walking, are comfortable and confident.

In the animal kingdom, an animal that is sprawled and taking up space is relaxed, and feeling safe. Within our human packs, someone who is willing to take up space is feeling relaxed and in control. Take up a bit more space when you are walking and talking. Take longer steps. Stand with your feet apart. Swing your arms (appropriately) when you walk. Leave your arms at your side or one hand in your pocket when standing and talking with someone, anything except having your arms crossed.

• Maintain strong eye contact. Do you meet the eyes of people you talk to? If you do not, you are telling them they are dominant. Some people say, "No, I'm not telling them they're dominant. I'm so sick of them coming and interrupting me when I'm working, that I refuse to look up when they approach. I'm ignoring them." Even this is admitting that they are stronger than you are. In refusing to look at them, you are saying that if you do look at them they gain control of your time and you will have to listen to them. So, the only way of keeping them from taking control is to ignore them. Therefore, they have more power than you, and more position, because there is something they can do that takes control. Eye contact is made by the stronger individual. Eye contact is avoided by the weaker individual. Make eye contact. Pretend that you are at least as strong as they are.

• Physical size is important in how you are treated. All other things being equal, if you are the shorter or smaller person in a group, people will see themselves as being stronger than you are. However, if you are overweight, especially women, you can be giving the message that you are not in shape and are physically weak. I say especially women because often an overweight man will have more control and more position, not less. Maybe it has something to do with the last few centuries where the person, especially the man, with the most money was the fattest, showing that he had the money the power. In Warren Farell's book, *Why Men Are The Way They Are,*[5] Mr. Farell explores stereotypes around men. His books are absolutely fascinating to read, and extremely enlightening. One stereotype he has researched and proven is that, in many corporations, the larger the man, the higher the position he holds in the company. Mr. Farell's research looks at how bigger men (whether they are overweight, taller, or simply large boned) are more affluent and are promoted into higher positions in companies and corporations. Of course, this is not true 100% of the time. However, it is true enough to be observable. Our children attended one of the more affluent schools in our area. After reading Mr. Farell's books, I was astonished to observe that my husband, at 6'0", and who, but for a knee injury, would have been a professional football player, was one of the smaller men at the school gatherings. He was not the smallest man. But in general at these casual functions, these men who held higher paying jobs in our city, were noticeably big men.

There is not a lot we can do about our physical size (except gain weight, and I'm not really recommending that!). We can, however, dress in a way to look slightly bigger. Women can use jackets and blouses with shoulder pads. Men can wear jackets with shoulder pads as well. Women can wear heels (something else I'm not necessarily recommending for men!). I wear a square 1"-1 1/2" heel. I do not want my heels so high that I am off balance or have to be careful how I walk, but I do want that extra bit of height.

• How do you dress? Dress professionally and be treated professionally. Dress otherwise and be treated otherwise. Two excellent resources on how to dress, especially in the office, are *Dress for Success* by John T. Malloy[6] (for men) and *Dress for Success for Women* also by John T. Malloy.[7]

Can you believe I am recommending a book written by a man telling women how to dress? However, Mr. Malloy's research methodology was superb. He photographed one woman using the same style—same hair, same makeup, same shoes, same jewelry, even the same suit, except the suit was a different color each time—he passed those photographs out to 300 people asking, "Which is the secretary?" "Which is the executive?" "Which is the …" based on just the color of the suit.

He took these pictures changing only one thing each time—pants, dress, skirt, suit, makeup, shoes, jewelry, hair, everything! For men, he changed the color of suit, cut of hair, tie, shoes, socks, everything! This methodology tapped into our stereotypes of how certain types of people dress. If you want to be treated professionally, dress professionally. And professional does not necessarily mean a full three-piece suit. There are levels of dress. Many people work outside, or in physically demanding environments, and wear clothing that is durable. However, you can raise the level of your dress. Instead of jeans and a T-shirt, wear slacks, a blouse, and nicer shoes. Read John T. Malloy's work. It is very specific and very enlightening.

• How do you talk in the office? Do you talk in a whispery voice because you have an open office environment and do not want to interrupt others? If your voice is coming from a high place in your throat, and is breathy, your voice is giving the message, "I'm weak." Bring your voice from further down in your throat and even further down in your chest. You can talk softly, yet still show, through your voice, that you are in control. Women, speak with a tone from the lower end of the tonal range that is comfortable for you. Remember, tonality is 38% of the message we are giving—the second most significant element in communication.

On the telephone, tonality becomes much greater. Believe it or not, body language still plays a huge part in the message communicated over the telephone.[6] Smiles are heard over the phone. If you want to have energy when making a phone call, stand up. Good telephone solicitors have mirrors beside their desks to check their facial expressions as they talk on the phone. Your body language is communicated through your voice over the phone.[8]

• The actual words you use can make a difference in how people perceive you as well. If you regularly use "uh" or "umm" or "like" or "cool" or "you know" or swear words or any verbal filler, you are sending the message that you are not well spoken and, potentially, not well educated. This could mean that you do not have intellectual strength, that you have below-average intelligence. If you do not have intellectual strength then I can potentially attack and gain position and control over you. Listen to yourself speak. Ask others if they hear you using any verbal fillers. If you are, stop using them. You do not need to use big words or have the ability to talk about complex or intellectual issues. If you put your words together well, in a grammatically correct way, without using verbal fillers, you will avoid creating the perception that you are intellectually weak.

In our daily interaction with others we learn that body language, tonality, and choice of words can lead others to believe that they are stronger than we are, and that if they attack us, they will probably win. Of course, that assumption may be wrong. The lady who swore at me when I crossed the street was wrong. She was right in assuming that I would not attack on the spot, but I had to go back across the street once I was finished my shopping, and I had no intention of hiking for 30 minutes around that big complex in order to avoid her. I was perfectly prepared to defend myself physically, emotionally, and intellectually on the way back. My first choice was to use body language to communicate the message that I was not a safe person to attack. As I walked back across the street, how could I ensure that she understood that I was not a safe person to attack? After all, I was in a nice suit and did not want to get into a physical scuffle. Besides, the training I was giving to that particular company was *Gain Cooperation, Not Confrontation*.[9] I knew that if I handled this situation well, I'd be able to use it as an example!

Returning across the street I had my head up and made strong eye contact with this lady. In fact, I stared her down. I had no smile on my face. My back was very straight. I walked slightly slower than I had when I crossed the street the first time. She backed up a number of paces, then turned and hurried away without saying a word. With my body language, I turned the tables. You can, too.

Sometimes, when people make the assumption that a person is safe to attack, they are wrong. If you are the person usually being attacked, you can change your body language, tonality and speech mannerisms to have them stop assuming that if they attack you, they will win.

Part IV: I am the angry person. What can I do?

We have been concentrating on changing our body language so that we are no longer perceived as passive. I have also had many people attend my workshops who have recognized for themselves, or have been sent by management, because they are too aggressive and are not getting the best efforts from the people with whom they work. These are problem people within the office because they have caused so many others to believe that they are unsafe people to be around. Aggressive people can use this same body of information to create the perception that they are approachable and safe.

- Sit down when talking to others. Standing is a power position. Deliberately give that other person a feeling of being more in control by sitting during the conversation.
- Talk more softly. Simply lower your voice.
- Dress more casually. Put away the black and navy blue suits for a while. Use sports jackets or do not wear a tie. Women might wear a jacket that is not part of the suit, but matches the outfit. Leave your jacket unbuttoned. Dress in softer colors, like browns, grays, and greens. Be careful with pastels.
- Smile. If you are smiling, you are a safe person to be with. (Make

it genuine!) When we see people smiling at us the message they are giving is that they are feeling safe. They may also be giving the message that they like us and are interested in us. A genuine smile is the quickest way to give the message that you are safe to be with.

Have you ever been sitting at your desk, concentrating really hard, and someone came up and said, "Having a bad day, huh?" And you weren't, until just that second. First, why did you instantly develop a bad mood? Because that person just told you that you were wrong to be sitting at your desk that way. When someone tells us we are wrong, we can easily perceive the conversation to be unsafe. We slam the gateway shut and activate our defense mechanisms. You got annoyed. Second, why were you sitting at your desk not smiling? Because you were concentrating, right? If we can walk and chew gum at the same time, we can concentrate and smile at the same time.

Sitting at your desk, not smiling, is a bad habit. You do not think to smile, so you do not. Unfortunately, the message you are giving is that you are having a bad day. This is not a good message to be giving to your customers and coworkers at the office. Their safety brains are likely to perceive that you are not a safe person to be around today. How many days have you given that message? I can easily see why morale is low in many offices if most of the people in the office are giving the message that they are not safe people most days. Not everyone is going to interpret an unsmiling person as being unsafe. But if someone has actually commented on you having a bad day when you really were not or, if you know that you are not getting the best results from others because they avoid you or are a bit scared of you or, if someone has said to you words such as "Lighten up," start practicing smiling. As you are driving to work, make sure you are smiling. Sitting at your desk, smile. People will be wondering what you were doing last night. Let them wonder!

If I am smiling at you, the message I am giving is that I like you. I am in a good mood. My defense mechanisms are turned off. I am receptive. When I smile at you, I am keeping your gateway open, because my body language says I am a safe person. This a good way for people in the office to see you. This is a good way for the teller at the bank, the clerk at the grocery store, and the ticket agent at the airline ticket counter to perceive you. It means that until we do something or say something that the other person perceives is unsafe, they are open and receptive to us. But the smile has to be genuine. We can spot a fake smile immediately.

- When talking to someone in the hallway, take up less space. Hold your arms to your sides, and bring your feet closer together.
- Ensure that you are not staring someone down. Make eye contact and count to five before looking away.
- If someone comes to your desk to talk, put aside all work and lean

back in your chair, giving the message that you are relaxed and giving them your full attention.

- Give people their physical space when talking with them. Do not crowd into their space.
- With your speech patterns, speak a bit slower. This gives the impression that what they said was valuable and you are thinking it through.
- Check the words you use. Instead of telling people what to do, how to act, and what to think, ask questions instead. Ask how they think things should be done. Ask for their ideas. Pat them on the back, verbally. Listen. Instead of jumping in with your thoughts, listen completely to theirs.

Changing any or all of these mannerisms, changing your body language, lowering your voice, and checking how you put your words together, will give the perception that you are a safe person, or, at least, safer than you were. These changes will give the perception that you are willing to listen instead of jumping in to take control. As you practice this with your children, your spouse, your coworkers, your employees, and your friends, you will see them become more relaxed around you. People may even comment on the changes they perceive in you. You have not actually changed. You still have the position within the pack that you have always had. Instead of keeping that position through keeping others afraid, you have that position by letting others perceive you as safe to approach.

Use this body language information to ensure that you are perceived as assertive but approachable. Everyone, staff and management, will get the message, and no words need to be spoken.

You can change all of these things about yourself, whether you are the passive person being attacked or the aggressive person being perceived as unsafe, without changing your beliefs, your views, your opinions, or your self-perception. By changing the things about yourself that others see, you are only changing how they will perceive you. Nothing on the inside of you needs to change.

Part V: The power of a touch

The most powerful body language in the office, and else where, is touch. Jack Canfield, author of *How to Build High Self Esteem*,[10] had his researchers put money in the change holders of the pay telephones at some of the major international airports in the United States. Many people, after they have finished a call from a pay telephone, will check those change holders to see if they received any money back. This is becoming less and less applicable today with calling cards, and pay telephones that accept credit cards; however, it was once very true. The researchers put over $1.00 in change in each of the change holders. Then, the researchers would walk up to the subjects as they left the telephone booths with the money, and ask, "Did you find any money?" Ninety-five percent of those people, with the money clutched in their hand, said, "No," and walked away. They lied.

Then the researchers changed one thing. As they asked the question, "Did you find any money?" they would very gently and appropriately touch the person on the shoulder or elbow. Ninety-three percent of these subjects responded to the question, "Yes, would you like it?" Not only would these people admit that they had the money, they would offer it to the researchers.

From a physiological standpoint, it makes sense. We are pack animals. Our primary psychological need is the need for acceptance. For safety, we must be accepted into a pack. Pack animals touch. Touching someone else gently or playfully indicates full acceptance of that person.

In the 1940s, the University of Michigan conducted a study with babies that we have all heard about.[11] (Brian Tracy, *The Psychology of Achievement*) One group of babies was diapered and fed and that was it. Another group of babies was touched as much as possible, held, sang to, etc. The study was taken too far: the first group of babies died. This is called Infant Grief Syndrome. The human animal needs touch. Children often demand to be touched. Colicky babies can often be calmed by being carried. Children touch each other by wrestling and bumping against each other. If your children drive you crazy with the amount of physical jockeying and wrestling that they engage in with each other, start making time for more cuddling and casual touching. Sit close together on the couch when watching a movie or reading a book. My children crowd in so close to me that sometimes I have to ask for space because it becomes overwhelming. But, as I have taken the time to stop them as I pass them in the house and give them a hug, or hold each on my lap and pet them or scratch their backs, their need for that overwhelming cuddling has disappeared. Adults have the same need, but they receive far less of their needed quota for touch per day. Adults can go through entire days or weeks or months without touching or hugging anyone else.

A few of the courses I have taken were devoted to personal growth,[12] and we really explored some old, longstanding patterns to try to get rid of them or change them. That kind of personal work makes us very vulnerable. You are showing parts of yourself to others that you have been hiding even from yourself in some instances. In these courses, hugging became a norm. Those that we had cried with and supported and been supported by were closer than any other friends or family, and we naturally turned to each other for touch. It is almost as though the greatest show of acceptance is touch. In situations where we have tried to be really vulnerable and show parts of ourselves that we had never shown to anyone else, we needed to be reassured that we were still acceptable. The most powerful way to show everyone that they were still acceptable, was through the body language of touch.

When we are in defense-attack, most of us do not want to be touched by the person with whom we are angry. I will actually flinch from my husband's touch when I am in defense-attack with him. I am trying to change that little habit. I do it with the kids, too. If they offer to give me a hug and I am really in defense-attack mode I will tell them, "I do not want a hug right now." In flinching or using those words, I am telling both my husband and my children, "I'm not accepting you right now, and, oh by the way, I am in attack mode and probably going for position, so look out!"

In today's world of sexual harassment, the only 100% acceptable touch we have left to us, especially in the office, is a handshake. A handshake is a very powerful form of communication. We shake hands with people we are meeting for the first time. I see my husband shaking hands with his good friends each time he gets together with them. We offer to shake hands with someone with whom we feel equal. We will also offer to shake hands with those to whom we feel superior. We want to help that person feel at ease so we extend our hand. Let's look back to the animal kingdom. The dominant animal offers a touch first, whether it is a friendly touch or a punishment. A weaker animal only touches first if it is initiating a challenge or asking for acceptance. Shaking hands is an assertive action. It is an action that says we have confidence in ourselves. It shows that we are feeling safe and in control simply because we are engaging in touch. If we are the ones who offer our hands first, we are saying that we feel equal to the other person, on some level, or even superior to that other person.

Men especially, within our society, have been trained to shake hands. It is a polite gesture of greeting. Many times the man from the lower social standing will offer his hand first. This could simply be because he was so well trained, from an early age, to shake hands. Being the first to offer his hand does not level the social standing of the men. Nor does it change their socio-economic standing or their professional status. The CEO is still the CEO and the janitor is still the janitor. And, if he wants to keep his job, the janitor will probably heed what the CEO has to say. However, shaking hands does create an equal emotional standing. In offering his hand first, the janitor has said that he has a lot of confidence in himself. The message is, "treat me with courtesy and respect or else. I'm not the safest person around here to attack regardless of my professional status within the company." A handshake is a powerful way to say that we are not safe to attack. Shaking hands is such an easy gesture that we should all push ourselves to initiate this gesture.

If you are faced with someone in the office who acts superior, have you ever shaken that person's hand? If you never have, or if you did once a long time ago, next time you see that person, stand up, move towards him or her, smile, and hold out your hand. "Hi, Beth, how was the drive in this morning?" "Hey, Ed, miserable morning with that rain, huh?" Act as though it is natural. Act as though you have been doing it every day for the past three years. Do it. With that one small gesture you will be saying, "I am your equal, and I have confidence in myself, and I am assertive."

I had two men at one of my keynotes who shared a situation they faced every day with a coworker who was an engineer. This engineer was a real problem person. He acted superior in his general attitude towards them by not listening to their opinions and would actually belittle them. I asked them if they had ever shaken this person's hand. Both of these men said that they never had, not even when first meeting the man. So, right from the beginning of the relationship this engineer was perceived, by all three parties, as being the dominant person. He got to set the rules, and everyone had to live by them. The easiest change for them to try would be to shake his hand. I do not know what the outcome of that situation was, or whether these men followed up on that advice, or not. However, I can guarantee that if they did, when each shook the engineer's hand, the engineer would have been taken off guard, and would probably have begun to reassess his superiority to the other two men.

For anyone faced with a situation where you are being harassed mentally, emotionally, or sexually, shaking the harasser's hand can sometimes be all that it will take for the harassment to stop. You may immediately see a change in the relationship when you shake that person's hand. When you do, your harasser will be processing two things on a safety brain level:

1. this person thinks he or she is my equal.
2. what will he or she do next?

If you suddenly start using assertive body language, your harasser will have to start adjusting his or her thoughts and actions towards you. If that person refuses to shake your hand and says something like, "What are you doing?" reply with, "I'm reading this book on communications and I'm supposed to practice shaking hands." If you have to use a ploy like this to get them to shake your hand, it may be less effective than without the explanation. However, it will still be effective because you have persuaded the harasser to touch you on your terms in a professional way. Whatever it takes, get that person to shake hands with you!

No solution will work for everyone in every situation. I had one woman share with me that she was being sexually harassed at the office. So she tried shaking his hand. He kept hold of her hand, and tickled her palm with a finger! She looked him in the eye and said, "You Pig," and walked away. Not every solution will work in every situation for everyone, but shaking hands could be a very simple solution to a potentially devastating situation. It is worth a try.

Men are trained in today's society to shake hands. Women should start practicing if they haven't already. I started forcing myself to shake hands with people about four years ago. It was very awkward at first. Shaking hands was something I had never been trained to do, and it did not come naturally. Sometimes I would shake hands, most times I would not. Now, after much practice, the gesture is automatic. I will stand with my hand outstretched, a smile on my face, until the other person shakes my hand.

Each of my three children has been trained to shake hands and to look the person in the eye while doing so. Our daughter is six-years-old, one son is eight-years-old, and our oldest son is 12-years-old. Think about your perception of a child as young as six years who can deliver a firm handshake, meet your eyes while doing so, and say something appropriate at the same time. It is not just good manners. It is also about teaching my children how to be perceived as assertive. Assertive children are not even approached by molesters.[13] The molester would face too great a risk of exposure. Assertive children often cannot be scared into keeping quiet.

I have seen children bullied by other children. I can always see, from their body language, why the victims were perceived as safe to attack. There are some common body language characteristics of bullied children:

- Coats zipped right up to the throat. Cool kids do not do that. In fact, cool kids will walk around with their coats completely unbuttoned.
- No eye contact with other kids. Most passive kids look at the ground.
- Slouched slightly.
- Shuffling their feet as they walked.

Imagine meeting a child who had these mannerisms. Remember the last time you met a child who behaved like this. You probably thought the child was passive and had little self-confidence. Teach your own children body language that will allow them to be perceived as strong and not safe to bully or molest. Teach your children assertive body language. Even if they are just pretending, their body language will be sending the right message.

I meet thousands of people a month, literally. Four years of meeting over 2,000 people a month, and I have only once had someone refuse to shake my hand. He said it was a religious thing. I do not know the details, and I did not take offense. It is rare to have someone refuse to shake your hand.

Having shaken hands with so many people, my advice would be, *start practicing*. Men might grip my hand too soft or too hard; but women often will bend their hands at the first set of knuckles. (Sorry, I refuse to kiss any hands.) Many will be carrying wallets, purses, and everything else in their right hands, and then be embarrassed at having someone offer to shake their hand, which they are totally unprepared to do. Some women have looked at me like I am an alien, the message being, "Women do not shake hands with each other." But many women have been practicing and have good, confident hand shakes.

Even from the words I have used here, you can tell the different impressions I receive from shaking hands with different people. How you shake hands, or even whether or not you do shake hands, gives a very distinct impression of who you are, and whether you are a dominant, assertive, or submissive person. It says whether you are open to others or closed off and defensive. It says a lot about your self-confidence and social presence in a group.

Shake hands. Even the playing field. At least give the impression that you have confidence in yourself. Before long, it will become an automatic gesture. It already is a very powerful gesture. Use it. And while you are using the handshake, start working on how you dress, how you walk, how you stand, your facial expressions, your eye contact, and your posture. All of these are part of your body language. Check your body language to ensure you are giving the message that you want to give. Remember, it is 55% of the message.

RECAP
Part I Anger is not an emotion, anger is one of our primary defense mechanisms. Once we have judged a situation to be unsafe, in order to get angry, we have to make an instantaneous decision that the best way to get safe in this situation is to attack. All of this happens in the safety brain. So, we get defensive and attack.

The three situations when we use defense-attack as our defense:
1. When backed into a corner.
2. When protecting someone.
3. When vying for position.

Part II We know we can attack, and probably win, mostly by reading the other person's body language.

Body language is vital in communicating to someone that we are not safe people to attack. To get someone to stop attacking you, you must change your body language. Changing your words alone will not work, because 55% of the message comes through the body language.

Part III There are a number of simple changes you can make in your body language such as good posture, eye contact, the way you dress, good vocal presence, and concise use of the language, avoiding conversation fillers such as "uh", "umm", "like", "cool".

Part IV If we are perceived as being unsafe people to be around, we can change that impression by sitting while talking to others, holding our arms at our side, lowering our voice, smiling (make it genuine), and using conversation techniques such as asking questions, listening completely, and giving the person talking your undivided attention. For those of us who come across as too dominant, we can use our body language to convey that we are safer and more approachable.

Part V A handshake is a tremendously powerful form of body language within the office or professional arena. A strong, confident handshake gives the impression that you are strong and confident. Practice shaking hands and use this gesture to your benefit not only in giving the impression of confidence, but also in establishing a connection that can be established no other way, except through touch.

Chapter 3
Clear out the Chemicals

As soon as our safety brain judges a situation, a comment, or a gesture to be unsafe we release adrenaline into our system. That adrenaline, along with the judgment that it is necessary or safe to attack, is our anger. A large percentage of our anger is physiological. That adrenaline flowing through our system is keeping our body in readiness to defend ourselves. Anger is our defense mode of attack. Our safety brain has taken over, and we are ready to go on the offensive. Have you ever been in a situation where, you first became just a bit irritated and then your anger escalated? Very quickly, you began feeling quite angry, and soon after that you found yourself raging. Yet, there was a little voice in the back of your head wondering why you became so angry about such a little thing? Once our body releases the defense chemicals into our system, the safety brain takes over, ensuring that we get to safety. It is the release of more and more adrenaline into our system that leads our anger to escalate. Physically, our body takes us up the scale, releasing more and more of the defense chemicals into our system to ensure that we stay safe. If anger happens mostly on a physical level, then there are physical techniques that we can use to control the release of the adrenaline and the other defense chemicals in our system, to help us to calm down or to stay calm in the first place. We can prevent the release of the adrenaline, we can manage the adrenaline once it is released, or we can hasten the clearing of the adrenaline from our system. In doing any of these we will be physically controlling the chemicals and, at the same time, controlling our anger. We will stay calm or calm ourselves down much faster.

In any given situation where our safety brain has decided that a situation is unsafe, we instantly release adrenaline into our system, giving us the added energy for running, hiding, or attacking. The adrenaline releases fat into our bloodstream. The fat in our bloodstream is there for the extra energy needed for running and hiding or fighting. We have heard news reports about excesses of energy and strength, recounting a mother's ability to lift up a car to rescue her trapped baby. Other stories involve somebody dashing heroically into a burning building to rescue a person or an animal. These feats of strength seem impossible. And they are—until our safety brain triggers the release of adrenaline, which triggers the release of fat into our bloodstream. Once that fat is in the bloodstream, it seems that almost any feat of strength is possible.

Part I: Awareness and understanding

One of the key ways to control our safety brain is through awareness and understanding. To stay calm, our first technique is to think about and internalize the fact that anger is not an emotion. Anger is a defense mechanism. If it is only a defense mechanism, then we can do something about it. If our anger is just our judgment that a situation is unsafe, then we can control what we judge to be safe or unsafe. However, we will be working against the safety brain, and the safety brain usually wins when it comes to a head-to-head conflict with the thinking brain. Access to the thinking brain is possible, even when our safety brain has decided the situation is unsafe. Police do it. Military can do it. Lawyers do it. Executives do it. And we can do it. All it takes is practice. Practice once a day for at least 21 days straight, thinking about the fact that most of the situations in our lives are safe. Even the ones that we usually judge as being unsafe are probably safe. Pay attention to that little voice that is saying, "It is no big deal. Let's think about it instead of becoming angry." Many times, just understanding that we think this is a dangerous situation (with a coworker, a spouse, a friend, or a child) is enough for us to stay calm. It is not a dangerous situation. It is just a conversation. How could a conversation with a two-year-old be dangerous? Even a conversation with our teenagers or our spouses is not dangerous and we do not need to defend ourselves and attack them. We need to talk, listen, and find a solution.

Knowing that my safety brain is trying to trick me into doing conversations in the same, old, safe, yucky way is enough for me to fight against the pattern of attacking and, instead, keep my thinking brain in control. I am leading my horse to the meadow and trying to get it to step off that deeply worn path into the grass. It takes practice. For me, that practice was not a simple 21 days. For me, that has been a four-year process, and I am still working on it. Anger is one of my most deeply grooved paths. Just yesterday, I asked my husband to step into the kitchen because he had put something in the wrong place. As I started to talk about it, he jumped in with why he had put it there. Then, he walked out of the kitchen so I could not even say what I wanted to say. Phooomph! It was like throwing gasoline onto a camp fire. I was instantly raging! I yelled at him. I am embarrassed to say that I swore at him. My oldest son said later that the only reason the movie *Matrix*[1] was rated R was for obscene language and that he had heard worse from me. In my defense I can only say, "I am working on it!"

In the past, in this kind of situation, I would not have walked away. I would have allowed my anger to escalate. In fact, even yesterday, after four years of working on it, I momentarily thought that I should sleep on the couch that night to show him how unacceptable I found his behavior. (I'd make him sleep on the couch, but he'll never cooperate with me to that extent!)

However, after a very short burst of rage, I went upstairs. At the top of the stairs I found myself smiling and ready to laugh at the whole situation. But, it was not over yet. Downstairs again, I fell into an old pattern. As soon

I made eye contact with my husband, I looked away, showing him that he was still unacceptable to me. I went into the kitchen to make a snack and found myself thinking that this was a perfect situation to show the kids a new way of handling anger. Yes, they had heard me yelling and swearing, but I could show them a new, better way, by letting it go and offering to make my husband his usual share of the snack. After a short argument between my thinking brain and my safety brain, I asked him, in a perfectly normal, non-sarcastic tone (I was really proud of myself for keeping the sarcasm out) if he wanted me to make him some. I then sat in the living room near him, while I read with our eight-year-old, and made regular everyday comments to my husband in a regular everyday tone of voice.

I am able to pay attention to that little voice in the back of my head more and more, realizing that little voice is my thinking brain trying to help me do life in the new way. Listening to that little voice simply takes practice. The first time you actually follow the thinking brain's suggestion while you are angry, you will have made a faint path through the grass. The next time will make that path a bit more visible. It does not matter whether the next time is the next day or the next week or the next month, the new pathway has been started and your horse will be able to find it. Of course, your horse is going to want to take you down the safest path each time, and the safest path is the one that is grooved the deepest. It is going to try to get you back to reacting in anger. Eventually, with enough trips down the new pathway, it becomes as deeply grooved as the old one. The old path begins to grow over through disuse, and the new way of responding becomes the easier way. You will have created a new habit. It just takes time. The practice starts with the thought, "Anger is not an emotion, anger is simply a defense mechanism."

Your thinking brain will only win some of the time, especially as you begin using this information. Of those times when you hear your thinking brain trying to take control, your safety brain will win most of the time, and you will get angry. That is OK. Just keep trying. It gets easier as you practice. You will make the new way of handling conversations into the safe way, and the old way of going to anger, unsafe. It just takes time. It takes practice. And, especially, it takes not giving up. So, you did not manage to listen to your thinking brain this time. Maybe you will be more objective and better able to do it next time.

I have been working with this information for over four years. I have internalized it. I truly understand and teach it. I still get angry. Anger is natural, it just isn't necessary. If it is natural, it is OK to experience it. I do not get as furiously angry as I used to. And I do not get angry for as long as I used to. I had a fight with my husband a few weeks ago. It lasted about 10 minutes. Then I was able to joke about it, and let it go. That kind of argument in the past would have gone on for up to four days, and there would have been absolutely no joking, unless he wanted his eyes scratched out! I've made progress!

Part II: Deal with the chemicals

The second way to handle our defense mechanisms is to deal with the chemicals. If we can clear the chemicals that create the defense out of our system, we won't be defensive. We can be calm, loving, and able to deal with the situation, instead of defending ourselves.

The adrenaline has been released into our system to give us the extra energy for the fight or flight. If we do not use it for fight or flight, what do we use it for? If we do not run and hide and we do not stand and fight, then we feed the adrenaline back into our defenses and get more and more irate. Recall the last time you got angry with one of the kids. Or, if you do not have kids, recall a situation that sounds similar to this with a partner, a friend, a sibling, or a coworker. "Put your shoes away. How many times do I have to tell you to put them away? You are so irresponsible. You never put your shoes away. And you never bring your homework home, either. You're going to fail if you don't become more responsible. And look at your room. You never pick your clothes up around the house. You are so irresponsible! If you do not start taking responsibility for yourself you're going to end up in jail!"

Sound familiar? As you talked, did you get angrier and angrier until you were in a rage? The words you were using with that child, or person, kept escalating and escalating. Why did we get from, "Put your shoes away," to "You're going to end up in jail?" A better question is, "How did we get from mildly irritated to raging?" That is the role of the adrenaline. We escalate the situation, often to an absurd degree, because the adrenaline in our system keeps pumping us further and further into defense mode, and attack. The exact neurobiological processes that cause this to happen are unknown. To say that we have judged the situation to be unsafe and released adrenaline into our system is basic. Our safety brain made the decision to attack. From there, if we released more adrenaline into our system, we became angrier, until we were raging. The intricacies of what is happening on a neurobiological level are simply too complex for our purposes. If we can understand, at this basic level, that the adrenaline, along with the judgment to attack, is our anger, then we have enough understanding to start working with our anger on a physical level, controlling it and even clearing it out of our system.

Many people have told me that they escalate the situation with friends, acquaintances, and coworkers to the point where, by the end of the raging, they have ended the relationship. If you think back to the original problem, objectively, this small problem was nothing to end a relationship over. Yet, because we keep feeding the adrenaline back to the defenses, the need to get to safety becomes stronger and stronger, and we use stronger and stronger words and actions until we have done or said something that is really offensive and hard, or impossible, to repair.

Once you have released the adrenaline into your system, and the fat into your bloodstream, if you do nothing to flush it out, it takes 20 minutes after you calm down for the adrenaline to fully leave the system.[2] If there is even a bit of adrenaline in your system, it acts like the hole in the dike. If a big wave hits a hole in a dike, the dike can explode, letting all of the water rush through. The smallest amount of adrenaline combined with the least irritation can lead to a flood of raging.

Remember the last time you had a really bad day at the office. You were pretty calm by the time you got home, but when your spouse or one of the kids provided the slightest irritation (such as breathing), you jumped all over them. You started raging at them, and really, for no good reason.

Or, you had a really rough time getting out of the house in the morning. Everything that could go wrong, did. But you had yourself under control by the time you sat down at your desk. Then you looked up and saw that person walking towards you, and you just wanted to scream at her or him—or maybe you did! That is the work of the adrenaline in your system, the hole in the dike waiting for the big wave. Once you are calm, there is a 20-minute window of which you need to be aware.

You can, however, actively flush the adrenaline out of your system, and calm down faster. If you use any one of the following techniques, you can shorten the time needed to calm down and become rational in a much shorter time. Ordinarily, if we just let the adrenaline run its course, we calm down, then it takes another 20 minutes to reach the safe zone. Any of the following techniques can shorten the time needed to just a few minutes.

A. Exercise

A natural way to clear the fat released by adrenaline out of our bloodstream is to exercise. If you are in a position to walk out the door and get some exercise as soon as you feel yourself going to defense-attack, then you have managed your anger on a physical level. Going for that 10- to 20-minute walk will clear the adrenaline out of your system and the fat out of the bloodstream. Use your walk to pay attention to that little voice from the thinking brain. If you listen to that little voice, you will be opening the synapses to the cortex and reactivating your thinking brain. As you return to the house or office, you will be calm and able to handle the situation rationally and objectively. If you spend the entire walk ranting and raving to yourself you will need another 10- to 20-minute walk!

Exercise releases endorphins into the system. Dr. Cary Foster, neurobiologist and professor at the University of North Carolina,[3] says that the endorphins actually stop the release of the adrenaline and activate some of the pleasure centers in the brain as well as triggering the release of some of the "feel good" chemicals in our body like oxytocin. Oxytocin is the chemical that is released during some of the activities that make us feel good, like eating chocolate and having sex. What happens to the adrenaline that is already in our system, and why it loses its power over us, has not been clearly explained. A very basic understanding would be that the endorphins flush the adrenaline out of our system in some way, allowing us to fully access our thinking brain once more. When we send messages to the different parts of our brain, it is as though there is a bridge from the safety brain to the thinking brain. We already know that there are many neurological paths and many biological paths, but, as a metaphor, imagine that there is a bridge between the thinking brain and the safety brain. When the safety brain takes over, releasing the adrenaline and judging that we should attack, it is as though a gateway slams shut, closing off the bridge between the thinking brain and the safety brain. We no longer have access to our thinking brains, and we react solely the way our safety brain dictates. However, there is also the back gate to the thinking brain. If we are able to go for that walk when we start getting angry, and we pay attention to that little voice of reason in the back of our head, we are going through that back gate to the thinking brain, calming down, and releasing endorphins into our system. As we calm down completely, we are raising the front gate on the bridge again. This metaphor is very basic, but it works. We will continue to use it as we explore some of the other physical techniques we can use to release endorphins into our system, clear out the adrenaline, calm down, and start thinking rationally.

Exercise is one of the key ways of getting that gate to lift back up and give us access to our thinking brain again. Exercise works very fast because we are using our bodies in the way they were meant to be used when facing a dangerous situation. Once we, as the human animal, had put enough distance between ourselves and the danger, then we no longer needed to be on the defensive and could get back to the business of survival. The adrenaline would flush out, and we would be calm again. Any kind of exercise allows this same process to happen. So, exercise can work very quickly.

The fact that adrenaline releases fat into the bloodstream is an important factor in our health. Have you heard of Type A behavior? Type A behavior is seen in people who are busy all the time. They are very concerned with getting tasks done so they can get on with the next task. They hate wasting time and become irritated if anyone slows them down, gets in their way, or does not do a job to their high standards. They are often critical and criticizing—of themselves and others. They often do not exercise because they are so busy.[4]

Some studies indicate that people who engage in Type A behavior have a higher degree of stress than others. These studies also indicate that people who engage in Type A behavior have up to 65% greater probability of having heart attacks. However, it is not just being stressed and engaging in Type A behavior that gives the greater incidence of heart attack. The common element between the Type A people who had heart attacks was anger. Dr. Friedman led research at Stanford University on the link between anger and heart attacks. Of the men and women in the study who had heart attacks, those who were counseled on how to control their Type A behavior (described as hurried, controlling, aggressive, and hostile behavior) were able to reduce the number of recurrent heart attacks by half.[5]

People who often get angry are releasing the adrenaline into their systems. The adrenaline releases fat into the bloodstream each time. If they do not get any exercise, where does the fat go? No, it does not come spitting out of their mouths as angry words. Those are just nasty words. No, it does not go to their finger. That is just a nasty gesture. Where does the fat go? Nowhere. It sits in the arteries. And the next time they get angry, a bit more fat is released to sit in the arteries. Along with the heart beating faster, rising blood pressure, and narrowing coronary arteries, the blood becomes more gelatinous. People who are often angry have a much greater chance of having heart attacks. A 1995 study published in the October first issue of the American Heart Association Journal, *Circulation*, showed that the overall risk of suffering a heart attack increased by 2.3 times in the immediate two hours following an episode of anger, compared to conditions where there was no episode of anger.[6] A study involving approximately 1,300 older men over a seven-year period found that those men with the highest levels of anger were three times more likely to develop heart disease than men with the lowest levels of anger.[7]

Exercise is good for our health. Strenuous exercise keeps angry people alive longer because the exercise uses the fat in the blood stream so that it does not block off the arteries and lead to a heart attack. People who exercise on a routine basis are calmer people. Norepinephrine, one of the adrenaline chemicals, is one of the chemicals that can keep our body in a state of defense for days once it is released.[8] If we exercise strenuously after the norepinephrine has been released, we can flush it out and calm down. If our skin is the largest organ of our body, and people who sweat regularly stay calmer than other people, then the skin must be partially responsible for helping us to stay calm. It is a supposition on my part that some of the adrenaline and stress chemicals that are released into the body when we get angry accumulate in the skin. If we are flushing the skin on a regular basis with sweat, then those chemicals have no chance to accumulate. Much of the adrenaline and other stress chemicals are flushed out in other ways, but some get stored in the skin. As the blood flows through the skin it picks up some of the adrenaline and stress hormones and keeps them flowing through our systems.

Have you gone through periods where you find yourself being angry a lot of the time, for little or no reason? I am sure there are all kinds of reasons for this. I have absolutely no research to back up the hypothesis that the accumulation of adrenaline and stress chemicals in the skin feeds into our being angry a lot of the time. What I do know, and what has been proven, is that people who have a regular exercise regime are calmer.[9] If you are one of those people who exercises regularly, have you ever missed a week or two for some reason? You were probably not a very nice person to be with during that time. Perhaps you were quite irritable and had a tendency to get annoyed, frustrated, or outright angry a lot.

In 1997, when I became a professional speaker, I gave up my daily walks and bike rides. Until that time, I had been very active, preferring to ride my bike or walk, even when I was doing my grocery shopping. Once I started travelling internationally, I found I did not have the time or the inclination to go walking in strange cities and strange countries.

For three years I did not get any really regular exercise. Twice over that three year period, for over four months each time, I ended up with a facial skin rash, something like eczema—really red and really ugly, with a number of patches very obviously all over my face. I went to the doctor many times and tried all kinds of different creams and salves to clear it up. Nothing worked. The first time the rash went away was when I started carrying my rollerblades with me, and "blading" three to six times per week, even while I was travelling. I found it quite easy to pull on my rollerblades at the end of the day and spend 30 to 60 minutes blading. I also figured that just carrying the rollerblades was added exercise. However, I could not blade when it was raining. And I did not blade when I was really tired. Then I gave it up, because it was winter, and because … of all kinds of excuses my safety brain provided. My skin rash had completely cleared up within three weeks of beginning that exercise regime—and came back a few months after I stopped blading regularly.

In 2000, I began Hap Ki-do at the Hyun Soo Park Korean Martial Arts School in Calgary. When I joined I had five very red, distinct patches of skin rash on my face. Every session of Hap Ki-do had me dripping with sweat. It took only seven days of Hap Ki-do to clear up my skin rash. I have continued doing Hap Ki-do between three to six times per week. I am a lot fitter and immensely calmer with no skin rash. I think that the chemicals were regularly being stored in my skin and accumulating, because I was still quite stressed and angry a lot of the time. I started sweating profusely three to six times a week, and the skin rash went away. I have no real proof, but it makes sense to me given that the body and mind are so intimately connected, biologically and neurologically.

You'll notice that I didn't stick with the first exercise I tried. I tried walking. I tried jogging. (I really hate jogging.) I tried rollerblading. I tried getting back into badminton (the sport of my youth). I tried volleyball. I promised myself that I would work out in the fitness rooms at the various hotels. (I did not even make it into one fitness room.) Some of those I stuck with for two days. Some for two weeks. Hap Ki-do works for me. At home and on the road, I am committed to my one and a half hour Hap Ki-do workout. Try every sport that has ever interested you until you find the one to which you can really commit.

To stay healthy, and to stay calm, get some exercise. Even 10 minutes a day will help you to manage your health, and be a calmer person. Can you take a 10-minute walk during one of your coffee breaks or lunch breaks at work? When you feel yourself start to get upset, can you grab a stack of photocopying and go down the stairs, to the offices two floors below, to use theirs? When those people are talking to you in the office, and they go to defense-attack, hand them the photocopying and send them down two flights of stairs to get the photocopying done. Suggest, or force, that other person to get some exercise. Exercise releases endorphins into the system. Endorphins clear out the adrenaline quickly. Get some sort of exercise, even 10 minutes, every day. Stay calm.

B. LAUGHTER

Laughter also releases endorphins into the system.[10] When things get tense, either in the office or at home, a joke gets everyone laughing, relaxed, and able to get on with solving problems. Unless that person who never laughs is in the room, then, cracking a joke is always a mistake! Bring laughter into the office and into your family.

The number one thing that changed our family dynamics (and I am positive saved my husband and me from divorce) was bringing laughter into the house. Initially, parenting was a very serious job in our house. We were serious parents. Every mistake, especially someone else's, was a crime of the highest magnitude. When we realized that laughter was missing in our household, we started to deliberately tell jokes, have fun, and laugh. Laughter allows all of us to clean out the adrenaline, and our parenting has improved immensely. (Our kids are forever grateful.)

My husband and I have a problem with each other's driving. "Backseat driver" does not begin to describe it. We came across a cartoon one day of a man and wife on a camel in the middle of the desert. The camel was running quite fast. The man was in front, driving. There was nothing in this desert except a cactus, and it was far, far away from the couple on the running camel. The caption on the cartoon, voiced by the wife, was, "Look out for that cactus."

That cartoon struck both of us as funny. We clipped it out and stuck it on the dashboard of the car. "Look out for that cactus," became our driver's comment, when the passenger was getting out of hand with his or her backseat driving. We had created a standard joke that we both found funny to make a point in a way that did not activate the other person's defense system. It got laughter. The endorphins were flowing. And the passenger realized he or she had gone too far, and backed off with the comments.

This can be an extremely effective way to deal with recurring irritants in a long-term relationship, be it with a coworker, boss, spouse, or child. You can create or find a funny comment that speaks to both of you about that situation, and then give each other permission to use it. A standard comment, that is a pat on the back for my children, when they do something really well, that's quite out of character for that child is, "I love you and want to keep you, but who are you and what have you done with my real child?" Standard, funny comments that both of you find funny are great ways to diffuse potential defense-attack situations.

C. TEARS

Tears work to calm us down and keep us from going to defense-attack. Some people almost never show their anger. Their primary need in life is for people to get along. These people never attack. Instead, they go directly to the fear that is triggering their defense systems, and they cry. Sometimes these people will experience the anger momentarily, then start crying. Instead of the rest of us getting uncomfortable with these people, we should be admiring them. They have hit on an easy and quick way to clear the adrenaline out of their systems. They are dealing with the fear, instead of attacking.

For those of you who do go to tears instead of attacking, relax—it is a good thing. I have often had women come to me during workshops, crying. Each woman explained, while tears poured down her face, that she cried at everything. She cried when she was happy. She cried when she was angry. She cried when she was confused. She cried when she was sad. Her basic question was, "What's wrong with me?" Nothing. Everything is right. Tears show that you are dealing with the fear instead of going on the attack. If you need to, excuse yourself to the washroom and finish crying. Then wash up and go back to the discussion. You could even explain to the people you work with that you are a crier.

Why do the tears work? Again, there is little research to explain it. My thought is that they work like sweat might work—as a chemical flush. The tears flush the adrenaline and other stress chemicals out, and because the person is dealing directly with the fear, instead of having gone on the attack and escalated the situation, psychologically and neurobiologically, the tears work faster than anything else we could do. Most of us have had the experience of having a good cry. After a good cry I always feel like a dishrag—drained of all emotion.

For those of us who have to deal with a crier, understand that they have a great way to open up the gateway to their thinking brain, faster than the rest of us. We should be congratulating these people that they can deal with whatever their fear was, without attacking. So let your criers finish crying and then calmly go back to the discussion. Relax with your criers and you might even congratulate them *unless* your crier is using tears as a negotiation tool. When a person uses tears to manipulate you, hand that person a tissue and go on with the conversation. People manipulate with tears because it works. We feel guilty when we make someone cry, and then we give in. Handle these manipulators in a calm, objective way. Sympathy is not necessary in this case. Re-engaging that person in the discussion is necessary. You could say something like, "I can see that this affects you quite deeply. Do you need a tissue? Now, as I was saying…" Do not let them leave the room. Your actions will communicate that you will no longer be manipulated in this way.

One senior executive, Bill, tried something exactly like this. When the manipulator began to cry, he acknowledged the tears and went on with the discussion. Bill said that he had never before seen tears actually sucked back up into the tear ducts but he was pretty sure that is exactly what happened when he tried this technique.

D. BREATHING

There is a specific kind of breathing that you can use to stay calm or calm down very quickly. The adrenal glands are located in the kidneys. The kidneys are located in the lower back. If you can clench all of the muscles of your abdomen, which will include your lower back muscles, you can hold the adrenal glands closed. The adrenaline cannot be released. You will not activate your defense mechanisms. You will stay calm.

The easiest way to clench all of the muscles of the abdomen is to blow out all of the air in your lungs. All of the air. Hold that position for as long as possible and concentrate on holding all of the muscles in your abdomen really tight, as though you were expecting someone to hit you in the stomach. When you need to take a breath, take a really deep breath and release it slowly. This is called *abdominal breathing*. Try it right now. Blow out all of your air. Hold. Big breath in. Release. When you hold the position with no air in your lungs, you should feel all of the muscles in your abdomen tightening. You are holding the adrenal glands closed. Then take in a deep breath, filling your body with oxygen.

The first time I used this breathing, I was in California, trying to find the building where I was giving a full-day seminar. I left my hotel at 6:15 a.m. I should have gotten to the building and the room where I was holding the seminar by 7:00 a.m. But with road construction, detours, and a strange city, I finally found the building at 8:50 a.m. I was to start the seminar at 9:00 a.m. Normally, by 7:05 a.m. I would have been furious and frantic; however, not wanting to turn off my thinking brain in the middle of rush hour traffic near Los Angeles, I used this abdominal breathing exercise many times during my two hours of being lost. It was very effective. I stayed calm. I asked directions. I got to the seminar room and had a great day. The day could have ended very differently, if I had gotten really upset and engaged in road rage.

Singing naturally uses the abdominal breathing technique. You use up all your air as you are singing the words, when you need a breath you take a big, deep one. Singing in the car has always calmed me down. The only time I get upset when I am singing is if the kids try to interrupt me; "Leave me alone, I'm singing!"

E. WRITING

Writing uses our thinking brain. Many of us have had the experience of being furiously angry with someone, sitting down to write him or her a letter, and feeling calmer midway through writing it. We stopped telling them all the things that were wrong with them and started addressing our feelings. Perhaps we even started telling them what we needed and what our solution was. By midway through the letter we had complete access to our thinking brain.

It is not natural for us to sit down and write a letter when we are angry. In fact, when we are angry we usually feel the need for action. We are jumpy and antsy and feeling the need for physical activity. Often when I am angry, I will clean the house. Usually, as I clean the house I get angrier, because now I am starting to think about how the house is a pigsty and how, "they treat me like their slave." The other reason it is very hard to sit still when we are angry is that we are prepared to attack, verbally and physically. However, if we sit down and write a letter when we feel the need to defend-attack, we are using the safety brain against itself. We are tricking the safety brain into clearing out the adrenaline and lifting the gateway to the thinking brain. The pathway of being calm and happy when we are writing someone a letter is pretty deeply grooved. It is a well-engrained habit. So, if you are angry and you pick up a pen and start writing, you are tricking your horse into stepping onto a different path, the calm path where you feel a connection to someone.

You did not send that letter, did you? Do not ever send those letters! The beginning of those letters are filtered through our defense mechanisms. They can be nasty words that break trust and can never be unspoken. And, remember that it is far too easy to hit "Send" after writing an e-mail. E-mails can destroy trust just as easily, and once trust is destroyed, it is a long, very difficult process to rebuild it. If you are angry in the office, write a letter, venting, and then destroy it. Or, if you do not want to vent, maybe you have a work-related memo or letter that needs writing. Work on it. Force yourself to jot down a few words. Very quickly, you will find you are able to think about what needs to be said. The memo or letter gets written and you calm down.

Here's another tip for the office: If you become involved in an angry discussion with someone, adjourn the meeting, saying, "We both need time to think about this. Why don't you jot down your thoughts and a solution. I'll do the same and we'll talk further at 2:00 p.m. this afternoon to compare notes." They will probably start writing because everything will be fresh in their mind. You will have prodded them to calm down quickly and effectively.

Many parents who have sat down to color with the kids really relax when they do so. I love coloring with the kids and I am very calm and relaxed until my daughter looks at my picture and says, "Mommy, your picture is beautiful. Can I help you?" My response is, "No! Get away! This is mine!" (I still have a few things to work on.)

F. LOGIC PUZZLES

On the way back from working in England in June 1998, I picked up a book of Logic Problems[11] from an airport store. One of the problems in the book was: there were four men running a national race. None of them finished the race. From the clues given, figure out the name of the man in each lane; which county each was from; and why each man did not finish the race. (Do you remember these kinds of puzzles from Grade 5? Do you still hate them?!) The way logic problems are set up in these books allows us to actually solve them, within 15 to 20 minutes.

Every time I get on a plane, I promise myself I will get my paperwork done. After working in the United Kingdom for three weeks, I had a stack of paperwork. Of course, I never actually get my paperwork done on any plane. "Of course I'll have a cup of coffee. Yes, I'll have dinner. Oh, I've only seen that movie eight times. I had better watch it again." Along with all of my excuses, I had this little voice from my logical brain saying, "Get to work. Get your paperwork done. Come on, you said you would." (It is a very tiny voice that easily gets drowned out by the louder excuses.) I ran out of things to do and thought that I should pull out that book of logic problems. After all, I had spent money on it. I pulled out the book and did the first puzzle in about 20 minutes. Then I pulled out my paperwork and worked on it until it was done.

This was unheard of! I never do paperwork on the plane! About 30 minutes after completing all my paperwork, I was looking at myself, and asking, "What just happened here? Why was I actually able to do my paperwork?" I realized that procrastination was us getting defensive because of thoughts we have about the job we don't want to do. "Oh, I hate paperwork. There's so much of it, I'll never get it all done. It is so boring." Those negative thoughts activate our defense mechanisms. Negative thoughts are not anger, but, because the book of logic problems works for procrastination as well as staying calm or calming down after we have readied ourselves for attack, we will briefly explore that benefit as well.

When we are procrastinating, the negative thoughts we have are actually persuading our safety brain that that activity is unsafe. We have actually released adrenaline into our system and our safety brain will protect us from the danger of doing whatever job it is we are trying to avoid. We are protecting ourselves because of those negative thoughts we are having about that job. We need to open up the gateway again and get on with whatever we are trying to avoid.

The logic problems do four things: First, we have picked up a pen. Since we are using a tool, we have activated our thinking brain. Second, we are fully employing our thinking brain because the logic problems need our full thinking brain in order to see the full problems and the solutions. We have to really look and think to get all the clues, logically. Third, endorphins are released when we accomplish something. That release of endorphins ensures that the gateway at the bridge between our safety brain and thinking brain is fully open. Fourth, we are tricking the safety brain, just like we did with writing.

Bookstores have racks of different kinds of puzzles and logic problems. Buy one with a variety of puzzles to discover the kind of puzzles that you like to do, whether they are word search problems, cross words puzzles, mazes, logic problems, or lateral thinking problems. Then keep them handy. You can use these in the office and at home. When you start to feel irritated or frustrated, or you find yourself putting off a task that needs doing, pull out the book and do the next problem. You will find yourself calming down or getting at that task with little effort.

At work, put out a page with one logic problem, or 10 small word games, in the coffee room or lunchroom. Put up a sign that says you will provide the solutions the next day. And get ready to track some great results.

Many people engage in gossip and negativity when they get together with others from the office in the lunchroom and at coffee breaks. By the time people go back to work they feel worse than when the coffee break started.

Often, people return to their desks feeling angry at the negaholic (people who are 100% committed to pointing out what is wrong with everybody and everything) or at the people the negaholic was talking about. In pointing out everything that is wrong, through being negative and complaining, our negaholics are showing us that our work site and our coworkers are unsafe. Everyone slams down their gateways and activates all defenses. Negative thoughts, gossip, and complaining are all factors that our safety brain will take into consideration when judging a situation to be unsafe. We hear these things and go to defense-attack. This is one of the reasons we begin to dislike going for coffee or lunch with those negaholics. If all we hear is how wrong everything is, it is easy for our safety brain to decide we need to go into defense mode. This does not happen every time and it does not happen with all people. But it does happen enough that we need to look for solutions. If we do crash our gateways down because of that negativity during coffee or lunch, we won't have access to our thinking brains when we get back to our desks. So much for getting any work done after a coffee or lunch break.

An easy solution is to give people something else to do during coffee or lunch. Leave these puzzles in the lunchroom. Watch production and morale in your office go up. Instead of releasing adrenaline into their systems and shutting off their thinking brains during coffee and lunch breaks, people will be activating their thinking brains. They will be completely deactivating their defense systems, and remotivating themselves. Most people love to try these, especially in a group.

Here is one puzzle. This is a common phrase. See if you can solve it. The best way to try to solve these problems is out loud. Mutter out loud, especially if you are trying to solve it in a group. Someone else's words will trigger your thoughts and the solutions come a lot faster.

B.A.
M.A.
PH.D.

0

(Answer: three degrees above zero. I didn't say it was a good one.)

Here is a way to use the puzzles idea around the office to keep people motivated, happier, and not gossiping. In one of my jobs, I started putting a sheet of 10 of these types of puzzles on all of the tables in the lunchroom. I put up a note that said I would provide the solutions the following day. I changed the sheet of puzzles every two to three days. Everyone enjoyed trying to solve the puzzles. People were happier, more productive, and moral went up. Give it a try. It is a perfect way to stop the gossiping. You have given everybody something else to do, something that could lead to more work getting done and better attitudes in the office. It is a great way to keep people positive instead of allowing them to wallow in the negatives until they go to defense-attack.

When I am procrastinating, when I am irritated or frustrated with something in the office or at home, I will pull out a book of logic problems and do one. But only one. We can always waste the good effect by then going on to do more of the logic problems, instead of getting back to work. Use these. If you can pull out a book of puzzles, and spend 15 to 20 minutes solving one, you will find yourself calming down and regaining full access to your thinking brain.

G. SMILE

Your body language and your emotions have been linked together since birth. You have known since birth that if you are happy, you smile. Because you have linked feeling happy with smiling and have reinforced that learning a few billion times since you were born, they are now inextricably linked. And this is now a two-way street. If you are in a rotten mood and you smile, you will be able to change your mood. If you are angry and ready to attack, and you put a smile on your face (of course, at first it will look like a grimace), and you keep the smile on your face for 15 seconds, as it starts to become real you will start to feel better. You will let the anger go, calm down, start thinking rationally, and maybe even see the humor in the situation. Smiling is linked to feeling good, and that is a deeply grooved path. You can walk both ways down that path. When we feel good, we smile. If we smile, within 15 seconds we will start to feel better. What we are doing is tricking the safety brain into changing our feelings, based on our body language. Habitually, when we have a smile on our face, we have no adrenaline or stress hormones racing through our systems. So, we are tricking the safety brain into clearing out the adrenaline and into helping us feel calm and relaxed, even happy, rather than defensive and ready to attack, by putting a smile on our face and keeping it there long enough that our horse steps onto the happy pathway and clears out the adrenaline.

In 1997, while I was in the United Kingdom, working, I lost my wallet. I jumped on a train, going from King's Crossing in the middle of London to a city outside of London. It was about a two and one half hour trip. The train got underway and, as I was getting settled, I noticed a pocket on my backpack was open. That would be the pocket with my wallet in it. The first thing I did was close the pocket. (I really didn't want to know.) Then I slowly opened up the pocket. The wallet was gone. I closed the pocket and, after thinking really positive thoughts, I opened it again. Nope. The wallet was still gone. I searched my entire backpack. No wallet. Every penny I had, gone. My passport, gone. Every credit card, gone. And, most important, all of my expense receipts for the entire three-week trip, gone.

In this type of situation most of us activate our defense systems immediately, and either get angry or cry. Given my background as a Customs Officer, my first instinct was to stop the train and strip search everyone on it. (Of course, I was a bit out of my jurisdiction.) Instead, I looked out the window and smiled. How many of you are thinking, "Oh, come onnnnnnnnnn!"

What were my choices? I could waste the next two and a half hours of my life crying and brooding over a situation that I could do nothing about, or I could enjoy the train ride and deal with the problem where, and when, I could actually have some effect.

I spent about the first minute with a very wobbly smile on my face. I was darned close to crying. The next three minutes were used to make a plan: what to do when we reached my destination. Bottom line: how much time would you waste—do you waste—brooding over things that you can do nothing about? Put a smile on your face. Keep the gateway up between your safety brain and thinking brain. Watch how much more productive you are and how much better life can be if you smile through stressful situations where, in the past, you would have activated your defense systems and attacked the closest person.

Use your body language to control your mood. Before you discipline your kids, put a smile on your face. It will look like a grimace for the first 15 seconds. When you feel the happier feelings take hold, then you are in a position to open your mouth. If we discipline while we need to attack, we often regret what we have said and done while the safety brain had control and the defense mechanisms were fully activated.

RECAP

Simply understanding that our anger is a defense mechanism can help us to stay calm. Realizing that our safety brain is trying to trick us into staying safe in the same, old, unacceptable way leads us to really commit to having conversations in a different way.

We can also manage our anger physiologically.
1. Exercise every day to stay calm and healthy. Ten minutes a day will do, but an exercise regime that gets us sweating is even better.
2. Laughter releases endorphins into the system. Endorphins clear out the adrenaline and give us full access to our thinking brains.

Three other statistics on laughter:

a. People are 300% more creative after a good belly laugh. If you have an old problem that you need to solve, get everyone laughing, then do your brainstorming. You will get new solutions to that old problem.[12]

b. People are 50% more productive after a good belly laugh. Get people laughing. They will get more done.[13]

c. Ten good belly laughs is the same as ten minutes of sit-ups. Perfect. I hate sit ups.[14]

Create standard jokes to ongoing irritants. If you can laugh at it, the joke can be used to make the same point every time, without activating anyone's defenses.

3. Crying—If you are a crier, crying is a fast, practical way to flush your system and get back to work. So, relax with this natural chemical flush. If you deal with a crier, do not be uncomfortable: they have a great release mechanism—unless they are using the crying as a negotiation tool.

4. Use abdominal breathing. Blow all of your breath out. Hold it. Then take a really deep breath in. This squeezes the adrenal glands closed, and you stay calm because the adrenaline cannot be released to activate your defenses.

5. Writing (the ability to write comes from our logical brain. When we are angry, do any kind of writing exercise: venting (do not ever send those letters), a memo, a letter, coloring (a coloring book at the office might be interesting!)

6. Logic puzzles are extremely effective. You activate the logical brain with the writing hand. Finishing the puzzle gives you the added endorphins from the sense of accomplishment.

7. Smile—body language and emotions are a two-way street. When your emotions change, your body language changes. Therefore, if you change your body language, your emotions will change. Smile—within 15 seconds the anger will lessen, and you will be calmer.

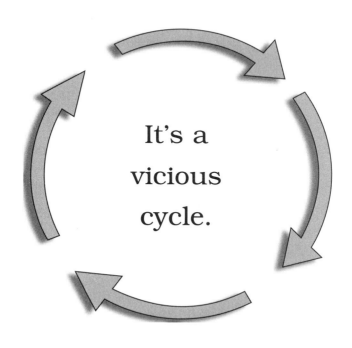

It's a
vicious
cycle.

LEVEL II

The Negative
Thought Cycle

Introduction

The Negative Thought Cycle

Level I dealt with how we activate our defense mechanisms. Anger is one of our primary defense mechanisms. We judge a situation as unsafe, and we attack. Level I also explored what happens in our bodies, physically, when we activate our defense mechanisms and what then happens when our safety brain decides that attack is the safest way to handle a situation, whether it is a conversation with a child or a situation with an adult. In Chapter Three we learned that there are a number of physical techniques we can use to shut down our defense systems, and reactivate calm, rational thought.

In Level II, we explore some of the thoughts that lead our safety brains to decide that different situations are dangerous. Level II will explore the Negative Thought Cycle. Ninety-five percent of our thoughts are negative, which means that 95% of the time we are looking at what makes situations and conversations dangerous. A large portion of our anger comes from continuously pointing out dangerous factors in situations, instead of the safe factors. We will explore how concentrating our attention on the negative leads to defense-attack. Then we will take a look at what we can do to start focusing on positives to change our patterns of anger and enjoy life a lot more.

Chapter 4
Focus 95% on the Negative

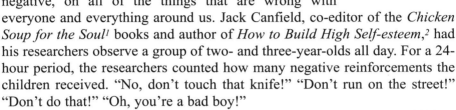

Part I: We focus 95% of our attention on the negative 95% to 5% Negative

In our society, we have been trained from birth to focus a tremendous amount of our attention on the negative, on all of the things that are wrong with everyone and everything around us. Jack Canfield, co-editor of the *Chicken Soup for the Soul*[1] books and author of *How to Build High Self-esteem*,[2] had his researchers observe a group of two- and three-year-olds all day. For a 24-hour period, the researchers counted how many negative reinforcements the children received. "No, don't touch that knife!" "Don't run on the street!" "Don't do that!" "Oh, you're a bad boy!"

Come on you parents, how many negative reinforcements do children two- and three-years-old receive in one day? On average, the researchers counted 432. That is an astounding number of negative reinforcements in a 24-hour period. When I think of my children at that age, they were sleeping 12 hours a night and having an afternoon nap. Four hundred and thirty-two negative reinforcements per day is more than one in every two waking minutes. One of the children they followed around thought his name was "No no." If you don't think you were that negative with your children when they were that age, think back. For most children, one of the first words they learned to say was, "No." If that was one of your children's first words, they must have heard it more than they heard almost any other word.

How many positive reinforcements did the children in the study receive in that same 24-hour period? "Go for it!" "I love you!" "You can do anything you want!" On average, in a 24-hour period, the children received 32 positive reinforcements. Four hundred and thirty-two negatives in a 24-hour period, 32 positives in the same period. The percentage of negatives to positives is very close to 95% negatives, 5% positives.

What does this say about you and me? What does it say about our children? Our grandchildren? Our parents? Our grandparents? Our nieces and nephews? Our best friends? Everyone else in our society? It says that we all received the same training. From birth we have been trained to focus 95% of our attention on the negative and focus only 5% of our attention on the positive. We all received this training and continue to re-enforce it. Most of us have heard that we should, "Pat them on the back, focus on the positive, tell people what they are doing right, not what they are doing wrong." We have heard that we should do this with our children to gain better cooperation and help to build their self-esteem. We have heard that we should do these things with the people in the office to gain their cooperation and get more work done. Yet, for those of us who have tried it, how easy is it? About 5% easy. And if you think you are really good at being positive, start monitoring yourself. I wonder if people who think they are really good at being positive are positive more than 10% of the time, which is not a great deal better than the original training.

Other research that confirms Jack Canfield's study was done by Dennis Waitley, cited in *The Psychology of Winning*.[3] Dennis Waitley had his researchers count how many negative news clips we were exposed to on television in a week. How many? Six thousand. How many positive news clips in the same week? Three hundred. And the percentage is 95% negative and 5% positive. Some complain that there aren't enough positive programs and news stories on television, but television executives say that they program negative news and negative TV shows because that is what people watch. We are all in our comfort zones. We are all on that pathway that has been grooved very deeply from birth. The people who make TV shows and the news, and the people who watch them (us), all received the same training. You might think you would watch positive TV if they showed it. Have you seen the PAX channel? It has wonderfully positive TV shows. Were you even aware it exists? And if you are, how often do you watch it? I wonder if it is much more than 5% of the time.

If we were to focus 95% of our attention on the positive, we would be so much more at ease. People would be much calmer. Road rage probably would not exist. Some of us become irritated or angry if we see a driver changing lanes without using his signal light. If he changed lanes safely; no need to get angry. But, because we focus on the negatives of the situation, we activate defense-attack thinking about what might have happened instead of what really did.

This happens often in situations involving young children. Many parents have temporarily lost contact with their younger children in a busy store or a mall. I become calm and totally rational when this happens. I figure out exactly where they might be and I find them. Once I have found them, I give them a hug and then I blast them. "What were you doing wandering away like that? You could have been stolen. I was so worried." The situation is over and done with and the children are safe, why the defense-attack? The defense-attack comes from that focus of 95% of our attention on the negative. We think of all the things that could have happened to them and go into attack mode.

Focusing 95% of our attention on the negative has even greater repercussions, though, in terms of how we live life and how often we go into attack mode.

Part II: Our minds think in pictures

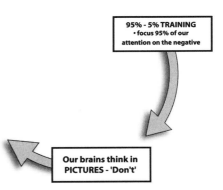

The part of our mind that thinks in pictures is the safety brain. In fact it is the parahippocampal area which forms images of indoor and outdoor spaces, and the fusiform face area, which forms images of faces, that think in pictures.[4] Before we had words, we still existed. We were still able to find safety. We were able to picture what was around us and run and hide if necessary. It is the safety brain that thinks in pictures. It forms pictures of everything it takes in, processes the information, and judges whether the situation is safe or not. Remember that all information goes into our safety brain first. So, everything we taste, touch, feel, see, smell, hear, and think goes to the safety brain first. The safety brain forms a picture of it. Then the safety brain judges whether it is safe or not. And all of this takes place in less than a split second.

Think about a banana. What color is the banana? Yellow. Green. Brown. Black. Freckled (yellow with black spots). Do you see the banana? Some people see the banana very clearly. Some people do not believe that they see it. So, let me give you another example.

Don't think about your shoes.

What are you thinking about? Why are you thinking about your shoes? Most people would say they thought about their shoes because I told them not to. It is like a defiance. Someone says "Don't" do something, and that is exactly why we do it. That is what kids do, right? We tell them not to do something and, just to be perverse, they do it. I will tell my kids, "Don't leave your shoes at the front door." Every day they leave their shoes right there at the front door. And they are doing it just to get me, right?

We encounter this same problem at work with irritating people who cannot seem to take direction. They seem to be incapable of performing the simplest tasks in the way we have requested, "Don't do it this way again." We have said it to them a million times and they are still doing it the wrong way. Even the very simple, "Please, don't interrupt me when I am on the phone." How many times per day do you have to say that one?

What do these three examples have in common? In the original example—Don't think about your shoes—what part of that statement can you make a picture of? Your shoes. All information goes into the safety brain first, and the safety brain thinks in pictures. You immediately made a picture of— thought about—your shoes. How long did it take for you to think, "Ooops, she said, 'Don't'?" It took just a split second for most of us. Why? Because there is no picture of, "Don't." Actually, there is a very recent picture of "Don't," but none of us mentally draw a bright red circle around our shoes, and put a big, red slash across them. That symbol is only a few years old, while our safety brain is a few 100 million years old. Because the word "Don't" cannot be processed by the picture side of the brain it has to filter over to the thinking side of the brain in order to be processed. The word "Don't" has to get across that bridge from the safety brain to the thinking brain in order to be processed. The thinking brain processes words. You thought of your shoes. Then the "Don't" got over to the side of the brain that processes it, and you thought, "Don't". But it was too late.

Dr. Lester Weiskranz proved this point through his research. In his research he has shown that once we form a picture of something we have that click of comprehension. Images of words or phrases are components of mental models, and reasoning with them entails nonverbal structures. [5]

The problem with the way we process "Don't" is that if we are told "Don't do something," the implied message is that we did it wrong the first time. We are being criticized. If someone implies that we did something wrong, if someone criticizes us we can very quickly and easily judge the conversation to be unsafe, release adrenaline into our system, and shut off access to our thinking brains. When someone tells us "Don't," our safety brain can see this as a dangerous conversation and activate our defense systems, slamming shut the gateway to the thinking brain. Unfortunately, the word "Don't" did not have enough time to get through the gateway over to the thinking brain. It is stuck on the wrong side of the gateway. It is stuck in the safety brain, which cannot process words. So, if the "Don't" does not get over to the thinking brain, where does it go? Nowhere. It disappears. It is gone. And what picture have we been left with. Someone says, "Don't do it this way again." The safety brain slams the gateway shut. The "Don't" cannot be processed so it disappears. What picture is left to act on? "Do it this way again."

This does not happen every time. And it does not happen in every situation. Look at that huge billboard that we see beside roads around North America that says, "Don't Drink and Drive." We understand that the message is drinking and driving is unsafe and against the law. We have seen that sign so often that our thinking brain is able to process the message the sign is intended to give. But, in personal conversations, we do run the danger of activating the other person's defense systems when we tell them "Don't." Again, it will not happen every time, and it will not happen in every situation; however, it can happen often enough that we find ourselves irritated, frustrated, and angry with that person because they won't do what we have asked them to do.

I tell the kids, "Don't leave your shoes at the front door." Slam goes their gateway. The word "Don't" disappears, and what picture have I left with the kids? Leave your shoes at the front door. (And it may well be that teenagers just walk around with their gateways down all the time.) Our next statement is usually, "How many times do I have to tell you 'Don't leave your shoes at the front door'?" Well, how many times will we have to tell them? Forever. Or until they leave home (whichever comes first.) And, in fact, whose fault is it? Ours, because we keep drawing the wrong picture. When we use the word "Don't" the picture that follows will always be exactly the opposite of what we want them to do. They have no choice. They are not doing it deliberately. It is just that there is nothing else there, from your words, except for the picture of the wrong thing.

Then we start resenting the kids and going to defense-attack with them. We resent them, and we go to defense-attack because we think they are doing it to us on purpose. They heard what we had to say. They understood. Yet, they chose to defy us. When people, even children, deliberately choose to do exactly the opposite of what we have asked them to do, that would make the relationship unsafe. They are defying us. We go to defense-attack in order to regain or maintain our position within that pack. We need to show them who is the boss.

We have this same type of problem in the office. We tell someone, "Don't do it this way again." Slam goes the gateway. "Don't" disappears, and what picture have we left with that person? "Do it this way again." We go to defense-attack with these people around the office. They can be the most difficult people with whom we have to work. We start wasting our time resenting them, maybe even gossiping with others in the office about their careless and irresponsible behavior. We start to think that these people are out to get us. They are defying us deliberately. From here, we can create a really negative and even nasty work situation that is based only on our miscommunication. They are not out to get us. They are not stupid. They are not careless and irresponsible. In fact, they have done exactly what you drew them a picture to do—Do it this way again.

Hopefully, as you read this, you are seeing other situations where you use the word "Don't" and are beginning to see how we create a lot of our own problems in communicating with people. We continually draw the wrong picture for others to follow, and then we go to defense-attack with them, because they do exactly what we have told them to do. The simple solution is to draw a picture, with your words, of exactly what you do want them to do. With the kids, instead of saying, "Don't leave your shoes at the front door," draw a better picture: "Put your shoes away," or "put your shoes in the closet." With our coworkers, instead of saying, "Don't do it this way again," we could say, "do it this way," or "let's try this." Instead of saying, "Please, don't interrupt me when I am on the phone," a better picture would be, "please talk to me after I've hung up." In other words, use positive statements of what you want people to do, rather than negative statements of what you do not want them to do.

A client, and a good friend, shared with me the first time she really started trying to draw positive pictures with her daughter. The daughter was three years old at the time. Invariably, right before dinner, the three-year-old would come into the kitchen and ask for two cookies. Most of us would respond, "No. It's just about dinnertime," at which point a three-year-old starts negotiating. Who are the best negotiators in the entire world? Three-year-olds. They will stop at nothing to get their own way.

The first time Belinda used the positive picture, it was priceless. Right on schedule her daughter walked into the kitchen and asked for two cookies. Belinda's reply was, "Yes you can have two cookies, right after dinner." Her daughter actually left the kitchen, then stopped and looked back—trying to figure out what had just happened!

We need to answer, "Yes" to every question posed by our kids, our spouses, our friends, our coworkers, our clients, our customers, our bosses, our siblings, and our parents. It is the picture we draw after the "Yes" that will be challenging. "Yes, you can have that, when you're 18 years old." "Yes, if we still produced that piece of equipment, we would have it on your desk tomorrow," "Yes, I'll buy you a car, with your inheritance, after I die!" Sometimes, those pictures that you draw will look a bit ridiculous. But saying "Yes" and keeping the other person's gateway up, regardless of the picture to follow, is going to make for a far easier conversation than saying "No" and having them activate their defense systems.

Our communication with others is so vital in our lives. Yet, when we ask others to do something, we draw negative pictures with our words 95% of the time. Instead, if we draw positive pictures we will get better results from people, we will communicate more clearly, and we will erase a lot of anger from our lives. However, because we have been trained to focus only 5% of our attention on the positives, it will be difficult to make this change. Our safety brain is committed to keeping us thinking negatively. Our safety brain is committed to keeping us frustrated and going to defense-attack when we continually get the exact opposite response to the one we wanted, from those we talk to. It is definitely worth the focus and practice it takes to change our communication to positive pictures. If we talk in positives, and draw pictures of what we want from others instead of what we "don't" want, there is a much greater likelihood of gaining cooperation and getting what we want.

Part III: Casual comments cause defense-attack

Not only do we need to be careful in how we communicate directly with others, we also need to be aware of the casual statements we make. Here are just some of the stereotypical comments we engage in around the office:

Watch out, she's at it again.

They don't pay me enough.

Same old, same old.

Is it Friday, yet?

Oh no, it's Monday again.

They'll never hire enough people.

They expect way too much.

I hate this place.

I'll never get through all this work.

Nose to the grindstone.

That's not my job.

Uhhggg, I have to go to work today.

This place makes me sick!

Have you heard what Fred's up to this time?

He sits in his office all day, doing nothing.

I do all the work and what thanks do I get?

Do any of these sound familiar? When we make these casual statements we are making the office an unsafe place to be. People might not be quitting, but morale is low. People are not happy. People are on the defensive because we are focusing 95% of our attention on the negatives around the office, engaging in the stereotypical negative talk, activating defense systems, and getting irritated, frustrated, resentful, and angry. It drains us when we focus so fully on the negatives. When we hear enough of them—and that could mean when we hear the first one—our safety brain activates our defense systems. Our systems go on full alert. Our heart rate goes up, our blood pressure goes up, and, physically, we are on full alert all day every day. No wonder we are so tired when we get home at the end of the day. No wonder we are often resentful and irritated and frustrated in the office. It is a constant battle trying to stay positive. And we are constantly battle-ready because of the casual comments our coworkers make. In fact, it is almost impossible to stay positive around people who focus 100% of their attention on the negative and constantly point out to us how unsafe we are. Sooner or later, our safety brain will judge one of their comments as unsafe and away we go. Or, maybe we recognize the negative person as unsafe to be around, and our safety brain activates our defense systems as soon as that person walks up and starts talking.

Many of us avoid negaholics—people who are focused almost 100% on the negatives. We find them tiring and draining because we are in defense mode around them. We feel better when we have little to no contact with them simply because we are more relaxed. When someone comes to work in a bad mood, within minutes, or even seconds, everyone is in a bad mood. Why? Remember, we are members of a pack, and the pack becomes defensive when it is alerted to danger by one of its members. It is that simple. If one of the pack indicates danger, through anger or other negative behavior, then the rest of the pack becomes defensive, too. Many of us do this at home, as well. Do you go to defense-attack every time your spouse or one of the kids attacks? It is a natural reaction when a member of our pack shows us there is something dangerous close by.

Now that you know your negative mood is simply a physiological reaction to someone else's behavior, you can use this knowledge to stay calm. "Harry obviously felt threatened by something he experienced this morning. The company isn't in trouble. Nobody is being fired. I don't have to feel threatened. I can go on calmly and happily with my day." It can be this simple, but it is not easy because it requires practice and constant awareness to override our defense mechanisms. The safety brain is powerful and quick. Staying calm when others in our pack are indicating danger is difficult.

The casual, stereotypical comments we make at work are very powerful, and often very negative. With my first contract as a professional speaker I found my niche. I love everything about this career. For the first six months, though, I could not actually voice the words, "I love my job." In many companies, it is not acceptable to say that we enjoy our work. We have to hate our jobs, or at least complain about them. Those of us who do enjoy our jobs fear that we will not be accepted by our packs if we do not complain as everyone else does. It took me six months for me to let go of that old societal training and begin admitting that I love my job. You can break the negative thought cycle, too.

We need to be more careful of the casual comments we make, not just at work, but with our friends, as well. Think about the last time you were together with a few other parents, and you all started talking about the kids. Was it positive or negative? Did you make negative comments such as the following:

> They are so irresponsible.
> Little Jonny is so lazy.
> They never do what they're told.
> They're at it again.
> You are so lucky you had boys.
> Boys are so aggressive.

Wait until yours are teenagers.

Kids these days have no respect.

If we engage in this type of conversation with other parents, our mood when we are with the kids is not going to be very positive, either. If you just agreed with the statement, "Kids are so irresponsible these days," then your kids jumped into the car, it is natural to for the picture of irresponsible kids to color your conversation with the kids. "Did you bring your homework. You forgot your coat, again. You are so irresponsible." Negative comments perpetuate negative thinking which perpetuate defense-attack. There is nothing wrong with a conversation about how wonderful kids these days are, and how smart and helpful they are, except that it is so rare, it even sounds weird here, as we read this. Switch to the positive. Concentrate your energy within your work and your family on the positives and life will seem better, simply because you see the positives. You will activate your defense-attack less because life is good, not horrid.

Part IV: Television trains us to communicate negatively

Popular television shows focus almost 100% on the negative: *Beevis and Butthead, The Simpsons, The Jerry Springer Show. Even M*A*S*H* and *Three's Company*, shows that I was brought up on, tame compared to current programs, entertain by putting people down. Sarcasm is negative and that is where most of the laughs are based on, in sitcoms. It took me years to realize television does not accurately portray reality. Few people will laugh and remain your friend when you are sarcastic with them. Unfortunately, we learn much of our communication within the family from television shows. Television offers numerous family models that teach us to speak negatively to our families and about our families. Some of our training comes from what we heard our parents and our friends say, but more of that training comes from what we hear and see on television, depending upon how much television you watch.

Sandra Blakeslee, author of *Seeing and Imagining: Clues to the Workings of the Mind's Eye*,[6] showed that our safety brain does not distinguish between fiction and reality. Because the safety brain sees pictures, it is not possible for us to rationalize the violence or other negativity on television and perceive it as untrue. We react defensively and learn negative behavior from television in spite of our better knowledge that we are watching fiction. Some shows, docu-dramas, are based on real life. Because we believe the docu-drama is true or based on truth, these shows especially re-enforce our negative training. William A. Belson proved that children do become more violent after watching violent cartoons and shows on television. [7]

Aside from the sarcasm and negativity, television re-enforces other messages that, when we really think about them, are ludicrous and harmful. Television, along with rest of our society, stereotypes blondes and ridicules men. Men are typically the butts of jokes on television. This is frightening because the more we ridicule men on television, the more acceptable it will become to consider men ridiculous. The continual message cuts a deep groove in our safety brains telling us reflexively that those statements are acceptable and true. The "dumb blonde" message is so culturally accepted that people are said to "be acting blonde," or "having a blonde moment," when they make a mistake. Our safety brain could be, and probably is, making untrue and irrelevant judgments based on hair color. One rational moment of thought right now should be enough for us to realize that hair color has absolutely nothing to do with intellect. Yet these comments have become such an acceptable part of our society that my eight-year-old started telling dumb blonde jokes at the dinner table. (Those jokes were immediately banned from our household.) What atrocious training for our children. What a potentially devastating way to portray any segment of our population.

Warren Farrell gives a remarkable example in his book, *Why Men Are the Way They Are*,[8] of harmful, stereotypical training. In our culture, if a 12-year-old girl accuses a male teacher of sexually molesting her and eventually admits that she was lying, the teacher will recover neither his job nor his reputation. As a group, we believe that men in positions of authority molest girls and are not to be trusted, even men who are decent, hardworking, compassionate, caring, and innocent of any wrongdoing. Mr. Farrell's series of books are remarkable for revealing some of the bizarre fallacies and stereotypes that our societal pack has decided are true. Many of the stereotypes he reveals are so deeply held that we do not even recognize them as such, until they are pointed out to us objectively and scientifically. We rarely stop to think about the origins of our beliefs, but if we would examine what is false in them, we would rid ourselves of some of the cultural negativity that makes us irrationally defensive.

Dr. Karl Menninger, in his book, *The Human Mind*, proved that we think at between 80,000 to 120,000 words per minute.[9] J. McLaughlin and A.E. West in a study in 1978 say we think at well over 60,000 words per minute.[10] Dr. Richard Welsh says that we can take in over 2,000,000 words per minute.[11] How many of those 80,000 words per minute rule our lives? How many of those thoughts are negative? How many of those thoughts make us defensive? We have been trained from birth to focus 95% of our attention on the negative, and some of that training and re-enforcement comes from television. This training is constantly re-enforced in conversations we have with others and through how we choose to spend our leisure time (watching television, reading the newspapers). We are stressed, negative, and angry often because we focus on what is wrong. Change it to what is right. Focus on the positives and see your life instantly become better, not because you are living differently, but because you are thinking differently.

Part V: 95% negative affects how we live

Our conversations with others and the shows we choose to watch are 95% negative. So are 95% of the comments we make to and about ourselves.

> That was a stupid thing to do.
> I knew better than that.
> I should have taken more time with it.
> I knew better than to do it that way.
> I am in a lousy mood today.
> I always get headaches in the afternoon.
> I'll never get all this off my desk.
> I am fat.
> It was a stupid idea.
> It'll never work, so I won't even mention it.
> I never remember names.
> I couldn't save a penny if my life depended on it.
> I am so stupid sometimes.
> I look awful today.
> I just keep getting fatter and fatter.
> I am always broke.
> This is not a good day for me.
> They just drive me crazy.
> I never know what to say.
> There's just not enough time.
> I am getting older and I have nothing to show for it.
> I never have been very talented.
> I am just not a creative person.
> I'll never learn.
> I am hopeless.
> We all lose our memory as we get older.
> Why do these things always happen to me?
> I just had a senior moment.
> I should've done so much more with my life.
> I'm having a bad hair day.

Every thought in your conscious, thinking brain is a message that your safety brain tries to make come true in your life. Every picture you draw for your safety brain is a command that it tries to make happen. For example, think about the last argument you had. Some time later the right words popped into your mind and you said to yourself, "That's what I should have said." During the argument, you thought that you would really like to think of the right words. Your safety brain got to work on it. Two days later the words popped into your thinking brain, "That's what I should have said." It feels like the words came out of nowhere.

What kinds of pictures are we constantly drawing for ourselves? The pictures you feed your safety brain are reflected in your life. These are what you think you deserve. This is how relationships are supposed to be, because you learned it somewhere and re-enforced those pictures often, and now your safety brain helps you to make those pictures happen.

Where did most of these thoughts start? How much money did your parents earn while you lived at home? How should children be treated? How do you treat a spouse? How does an adult act? What kind of marriage do you have? Or are you married? Do you want to be married? How much money do you make? Enough? As much as you want? Do you own your own home? Do you want to? Do you own the car of your dreams? Do you have the vacations that you want? Do you have your dream job? Do you have wonderful relationships with every person in your life—friends, family, and coworkers? Where did you learn these lessons and have them re-enforced a million times? In the family within which you grew up. Most of our emotional patterns are set by the time we are 4 years old.[12] Some of the studies say that our emotional patterns and deepest lessons in life are learned by the time we are three years old. We live what we tell ourselves that we want and deserve. "I want to lose weight." Why is that such a hard goal to accomplish if our safety brain is trying to make it happen? Because of the other thoughts that follow. "I can never lose weight." "Mothers are overweight." "I've tried before and I just can't make it happen." "I'll have to buy a whole new wardrobe if I do." "I'll have to starve myself." The picture of losing weight is very powerful and the safety brain wants to make it happen. But the other pictures overwhelm it.

In 1997, I had been working as a Customs Officer for six years. I was miserably unhappy. Theode and I were talking about divorce. I hated my job. I was making my three children's lives miserable. John Randolph Price, author of *The Abundance Book*,[13] introduced the idea to me that I could have anything I wanted in life. All I had to do was want it and get rid of the thoughts that told me I did not deserve it. So I thought a lot about: What made me happy in life? What did I want in life? How did I want my relationships with my husband and my children and my friends and my family to be? How much money did I want to earn? What kind of job did I really want?

At this time my husband and I were fighting most of the time. I knew I still loved my husband. I knew I did not want to get a divorce. My very first goal was, "I have a forever after loving relationship with my husband." That seemed to be a really good, specific picture to get my safety brain working on. It certainly was a picture that I had never before drawn for my safety brain. In fact, I was living the marriage that my parents had while I was growing up. How many times as a child had it been re-enforced for me that parents yell and scream and get angry and attack their spouses? I even saw the parents of a close high school friend fight just the way my parents did. That must have meant that this really is the way marriages are. So, that is how I was living my marriage and hating it. I was angry all the time. It felt like I was stuck in a rut with no way out. I was talking about divorce even though I still loved my husband and could not imagine life without him. But I could think of nothing else to do. Whenever I tried to treat him differently and not get angry, I could not make that change. It felt pretty hopeless.

After reading *The Abundance Book* it seemed far more likely that I could make a change. So I followed the 40-day plan in *The Abundance Book*. I wrote down my goals every morning as well as doing the meditation Mr. Price gives for each day. I started with the goal, "I have a forever after loving relationship with my husband." After writing this goal down for about a week, I realized that there was one word missing. His name. You have to be really, really specific with the pictures that you draw for your safety brain to work on. With the statement the way it was, I could have found myself divorcing my husband and being in a forever after loving relationship with someone else! So, that first goal then read: "I have a forever after loving relationship with my husband, Theode."

It is remarkable to note the opportunities that my safety brain started finding to make that new picture happen. I would find myself in the middle of a fight with Theode, and my safety brain would point out an opportunity. I would hear this little voice in the back of my head during the fight: "Hello, are you creating a forever after loving relationship here, or are you creating a divorce?" Some of these opportunities you will follow through on, and some you won't. About half the time when I heard that little voice I would think, "Oh, yeah!" I would apologize to my husband, and then I would try to find new words to continue the discussion. But the other half of the time when that little voice piped up, I would ignore it and keep fighting!

In August 2000, Theode and I had been working on our relationship for four years. He told me about a study that he had read in the National Post in September 2000.[14] The study said that men fall in love again when they are between 40 and 50 years old. Theode said to me, "I am one of the lucky ones. I fell in love with my wife, again." That is how loving our relationship is today. I did not know marriages could be this loving. How could I? This kind of a marriage was totally outside my realm of experience. I did not see this growing up. You can have anything you want, as well. All you have to do is draw a really clear picture in your imagination for your safety brain to work with.

My second goal was monetary, "I now earn $10,000 a month." Let's get real. At that time I was working for the Federal Government as a Customs Officer. I was earning about $28,000 per year, and here I was saying to myself that I now earn a third of that every month! The first time I wrote that down, I started laughing so hard I fell out of bed and hurt myself! Five and a half months later I was earning $10,000 per month.

Are you worth $10,000 a month? Are you worth that? Let's look at it from a different angle. Do you earn $10,000 per month? If you do not, then you are not telling yourself you are worth it. It is that simple. If you have never said to yourself that you are worth $5,000 or $10,000 or $25,000 a month, then you have never seen all of the opportunities around you. And the opportunities do surround you. If you can look at someone else's life and think that you would like to have what he or she has, then you know that someone else has it. If someone else has it, then it is possible. Even if someone else does not have it, it is probably still possible. The question is: "Why don't you have it in your life?" Because you are telling yourself that you are not worth it, or you do not deserve it, or real people don't live that way. Whatever thought is preventing you from having what you want in life, you can replace with the picture of what you want, instead.

I did not have to go back to school. I did not have to get more work experience, or more education. My safety brain took all of my previous experience and learning and presented me with exactly the right opportunity. The safety brain does not recognize lies. All it sees is the picture that is drawn for it. The safety brain does not recognize fiction, or pretense. It sees the picture and works towards making those pictures happen.

When we live our lives based on old patterns we often become bitter, frustrated with life, resentful of what we have and do not have, and we are angry, often. It can feel like life is pretty hopeless. This training—focusing 95% of our attention on the negative—can lead our safety brains to judge most situations, even with ourselves, to be unsafe. Once we admit what we want in life, and lead our safety brains in that direction by drawing really clear pictures of those goals, we can find ourselves living a life that we enjoy. If we enjoy it, we can focus more clearly on the positives. When we focus on the positives we have no reason to activate our defense systems. We are calm, happy, and productive most of the time, instead of defensive, feeling stuck in a rut, and attacking the innocent people around us.

Chapter 5
Loyalty = Safety = Bad Decisions = Anger

Part I: We are loyal because we are safe

That the human animal is most comfortable in a pack has been established. We belong to all kinds of packs. Our family is a pack. The people we work with are a pack. Your church is a pack. The friends you spend time with are a pack. Your neighborhood is a pack. You

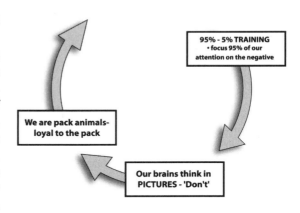

95% - 5% TRAINING
· focus 95% of our attention on the negative

We are pack animals- loyal to the pack

Our brains think in PICTURES - 'Don't'

might not know everyone in the neighborhood (or even your next door neighbors!), but you have found safety in this neighborhood and it is a pack. Men belong to half the human race, the male pack. Women belong to the female pack. If you go to the same grocery store all the time, it is a pack. You went there the first time, found your way around, discovered that it was safe, and now you go back to the same store again and again. You recognize some of the tellers, and may have even established a more personal relationship with one or two of them, because you see them so much.

What happens with people who are loners, who don't belong to any packs? We hear of horrible incidents in the news where an adult or a child has deliberately picked up a gun and started shooting everyone in a restaurant or a high school. What do the neighbors always say about these people? What comments do we hear from other kids? "He was a loner," or "He kept to himself," or "Nice guy, but I didn't know a lot about him."

The human animal belongs to packs for safety. If we do not feel safe because we do not belong to a pack, then we have no loyalty to any pack, maybe not even the "human" pack—mankind. There is nothing to keep us from attacking anybody, anywhere. It would seem that any human who does not belong to a pack would have a greater likelihood of becoming antisocial to the point of violence. In your dealings with people who are antisocial, or who bully others, do not ostracize them from the pack. Find a way to deal with them that keeps them included. If your children are being bullied on the playground, teach them how to deal with the bully and still be friends. Never teach your children to ostracize that child. If you have someone in the office or neighborhood who is being ostracized by the rest of the pack, stop it! Find some way to include that person into your pack. We could be contributing to our larger social problems if we teach these people that there is no safe place for them.

We belong to many packs and we want to ensure that others feel that they belong to our packs. Think about the last time you knew someone—maybe you or a good friend—who was thinking about leaving a pack. Maybe this person was thinking about finding a new job or leaving a relationship or moving to a new area. As this person was trying to make the decision, how was he or she talking about the old situation? Negatively. Really, really negatively. The old job sounds like the worst place in the world to work. It is unbelievable that he or she has not ended the relationship already. The house sounds like it should have fallen down two years ago! When I talk with people who are thinking about leaving a pack, whatever that pack is, I always wonder why they are still there. From the way they talk about it there is absolutely nothing good in the old situation.

We talk so negatively about the old situation because, if there is even a shred of safety left in the old situation, we will stay in it. We will not leave it to try something new. We literally have to talk ourselves out of the old situation. We have to make that old pack so horrid, so bad, that it is now completely unsafe to stay there. It is dangerous. Then we can leave.

There is a problem with this need to make an old situation unsafe before we can leave. We have been trained from birth to focus 95% of our attention on the negative. We are constantly, minute by minute, drawing negative pictures about everything around us. Now we begin to understand that in order to leave an old situation and move on to something more to our liking, we focus completely on the negatives of the old situation until it is unsafe to stay. Then our safety brain kicks in and helps us to find something that is less dangerous, or even safe, to move to. This would be one circumstance in which our safety brain encourages change.

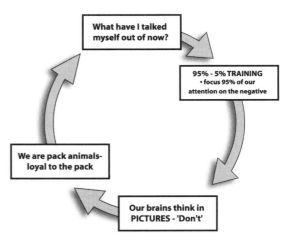

Part II: We talk ourselves out of things we like

The last part of the negative thought cycle is, "What have you talked yourselves out of, recently?" Sometimes we leave a situation and within a very short time we wonder why we ever left. We left because of a very bad habit—focusing 95% of our attention on the negative.

We focused so totally on the negatives that we forgot there were any positives in the first place. We talked ourselves out of staying in a situation that was just fine. Sometimes we talk ourselves out of achieving new goals. We focus on all the negative aspects of the changes demanded of us in order to reach those new goals. Many of us decide to lose weight, to exercise every day, to spend more time with the kids or our spouses or partners, to take a class. These are common goals that many of us set, many times. How long do those goals last? A couple of minutes, two hours, two days. Then the Negative Thought Cycle swings into action and we talk ourselves out of achieving these goals. Just as often, we talk ourselves out of enjoying our current circumstances, because we fall into the Negative Thought Cycle and focus on all the things that are wrong, instead of all the things that are right.

How many of us have talked ourselves out of enjoying our jobs?

How disillusioned and bitter and resentful are we towards our jobs?

How many of us have talked ourselves out of enjoying our coworkers?

How resentful and angry and frustrated are we with one or many of our coworkers?

How many of us have talked ourselves out of enjoying our spouse or partner?

How angry are we, all the time, with our spouse or partner? How resentful? How critical?

How many of us have talked ourselves out of enjoying our children?

How angry do we get with our children, every day, over little or nothing?

How many of us have talked ourselves out of enjoying … life?

How many of us feel stuck in a rut, and wonder, "Is this all there is?"

Why? Because of a very, very bad habit, because of very poor training; the training we received from birth to focus 95% of our attention on the negative.

I would suggest that many of the problems that we have in life, well over half, are not even problems. They are creations of our Negative Thought Cycle. I wonder how many friendships I have talked myself out of because I got caught in the Negative Thought Cycle? Too many. They were good friends, but I got stuck thinking negatively about those people until I had made them unsafe people and then simply stopped contacting them or said I was busy when they contacted me. Stop. Think with your thinking brain.

Real problems can be easily fixed. The Negative Thought Cycle builds small problems into huge problems. It can create big problems where there was no problem at all. The problems can become overwhelming when we focus the energy of the Negative Thought Cycle on them. We often feel that we cannot do anything about problems that are overwhelming because we do not even know where to start with problems that big. Nothing we could do would have any effect. What we can do is turn the Negative Thought Cycle into a Positive Thought Cycle. If we can focus on the positives in situations, instead of the negatives, we will see everything that is good and right with life, instead of everything that is wrong and dangerous.

Here is one small technique to get into a Positive Thought Cycle, and get on with our lives in the way we want. Think of the person who is the biggest problem in your life—maybe from work or maybe in your personal life. Get that person fixed firmly in your mind. Now, right here, right now, write down three positive things about that person. Go!

1.

2.

3.

If you cannot think of three positive things to say about the person who most bothers you, then you are simply stuck in your safety brain. Our safety brain knows that it is very dangerous to think of three positive things about our problem people. If we start thinking in positives, this person might not be a problem anymore. Then our lives will have to change in some way. "What could happen in my life with just this one little change? Who knows? Don't write down three positive things because that means you are trying to change. Change is dangerous. Don't do it!" If you are unable to think of even one, much less three, positives about your problem person you are definitely stuck in the Negative Thought Cycle. Force yourselves to do this simple little exercise. This is a real person, a human being with strengths and weaknesses. There are hundreds of great things about him or her. Three is a very small number!

Once you finish writing down three positives things about this problem person, you will feel better about him or her. You will start to see that there are solutions to the problems you have with this person. We are separating the person from the problems. The person is OK, and the problems become manageable. If your problem person is still horrible after writing down three positives, then increase the number and write down five positive things!

The first time I used this exercise, I was in Texas doing a number of seminars. This was in 1998, and Theode and I had been working on our marriage for two years. Life was really good. We had made remarkable progress in creating a forever-after-loving relationship. However, on the way to the airport we had had a fight. Now I was on the road, and I had all kinds of nasty thoughts about him. "Why can't he be more supportive? Why can't he just understand what I am going through?" until I arrived at the thought, "I am leaving. I want a divorce." When I hear myself thinking that I want a divorce, I know that I have fallen back into the Negative Thought Cycle. Why is it so easy, even after two years of working really hard to create something positive, to go back to the negatives? Because that Negative Thought Cycle started getting re-enforced at birth. It is deep and it is strong, and unless we guard against it constantly, we will go back to it. Today it is far easier to focus on the positives than it was four years ago, but I will still find myself walking that more deeply engrained habit of focusing on the negatives.

I arrived at the hotel and the first thing I did was pull out my journal. I wrote down Theode's name and I made a list of everything positive I could think about him. What were some of the positives about him today? What had attracted me to him originally? Everything. Then, for good measure, I wrote down each of the kids' names, and wrote out a list of what was so great about each of them. It took me about 45 minutes to complete those four lists. Then I phoned home and read each person's list to that person. What a great pat on the back for Theode and each of the kids. And what a great way to drag myself and my safety brain kicking and screaming out of the Negative Thought Cycle into a more positive frame of mind. If I had stayed stuck in the Negative Thought Cycle, thinking of my husband as such a horrible, nasty person, how quickly could I talk myself into a separation and divorce?

Too many couples do this. Instead of stopping their negative thoughts, and focusing on the reality of their relationship, couples focus on the negatives. If we focus on the negatives day after day for months or years, we can easily talk ourselves into a separation and divorce. If you can make a list of positives about your spouse, you are stepping out of the Negative Thought Cycle and back into reality.

To this day in the morning, along with my three goals, I write down what I call my List of Gratitudes. "I am so very Grateful for Theode because he is supportive and loving and a great father and believes in me." "I am so very Grateful for Brett because he is funny and smart and handsome and makes me think about things." "I am so very Grateful for Rhys because he is loving and kind and a cuddlebug and smart and he tries so hard at everything he does." "I am so very Grateful for Gia because she is independent and creative and smart and loving." "I am so very Grateful for my career because…" Sometimes I spend two minutes listing my Gratitudes, sometimes I take 45 minutes. It depends on how awake I am and what comes to mind. I write down each of my current three goals and my list of Gratitudes first thing in the morning, before I get out of bed. When I finally get out of bed in the morning, I feel great. I have so much in my life to enjoy. That positive attitude permeates my day.

What do you say to yourself as you are getting out of bed? "Oh no. I have to go to work again." "I hate that place." "I'm so tired." "I just want to stay in bed all day." I can guess what attitude permeates your day. I do not even have to guess how easy it is to go to defense-attack if something goes wrong in the day and you had already pointed out a number of unsafe elements in the people and situations around you. If you already had a list going of the negatives, it's really easy to get to the last one and go to defense-attack. When we are listing the positives instead, it takes a long time to get to defense-attack because when something goes wrong, it is the first thing on the list, not the "last straw."

Staying in the Positives takes work. I find, to this day, I will slide back into the Negative Thought Cycle and have to work to get out of it. The best way I know to get myself back into the positives is to grab one of my audio cassette learning programs. Someone talking about goal-setting or self-esteem or abundance is pointing out all of the things I know I want in my life. Because I have fallen back into focusing on the negatives, my safety brain has been persuading me to ignore those goals and maybe even persuading me that I will never achieve them so I might as well forget all about them. I have found that most of the people who have created audio cassette learning programs are talking positively. It only takes about five minutes of listening to one of these programs for me to start feeling better about life. I am able to easily pull myself from the Negative Thought Cycle with the help of someone who is focused on the positives and focused on all the great things I can do in my life to get what I want.

Who else can we turn to? I love my husband dearly, but he focuses about 95% of his attention on the negative. I love my best friend dearly but she focuses 95% of her attention on the negative. There are few people in our day-to-day lives who have not received the same training we received. However, most people who are trying to teach us something new are focused on the positive. When we are learning, we have our thinking brain fully turned on. If your thinking brain has been overpowered by your safety brain while you are learning, you will have thoughts like, "This is a waste of my time," or "I've heard all this before," or "I know all this already," or "I don't have time for this." Your safety brain will throw excuses in the path of the learning so that you are not tempted to try anything new in life.

In fact, it is easy to learn and implement new ideas listening to an audio learning program. We have been trained since we were five or six years old that when we are sitting and listening to someone, we need to turn on our thinking brain. When we listen to new ideas, we hear them with our thinking brain, and we implement them faster and easier. Repetition is the key. Our teachers knew this. They would have us focus on a concept over and over, through reading and exercises and studying. Advertisers in the media know this. They show us the same product over and over and over until we have see it so often that it becomes the safe product to own. Listen to an audio cassette program over and over. Eventually, your safety brain will think that the way the trainer says to do it on the audio cassette program is the right way, because you have heard it often enough. This makes it really easy to make changes in your life. You are leading your safety brain in a new direction. You have created a new path, almost without the safety brain realizing what has happened, so it does not fight the change.

Start creating a Positive Thought Pattern. Focus on all of the things in your life that are great, instead of all of the negatives. Force yourself to spend two minutes or 15 minutes first thing in the morning writing down all of the things that you have in your life for which you are grateful. You will see your attitude shift. Instead of getting defensive and angry, you will be calm and happy.

Before you decide to leave any situation, sit down and make a long, long list of the positives about that situation. Before you write someone off, in either your personal or your professional life, make a long, long list of everything that that person has going for him or her. You will be amazed at how you feel after you make that list. Before you have a conversation with a difficult person, make a list of everything that is great about him or her. The entire conversation will go differently than if you go into it thinking, "I hate her. She's going to make this difficult," or "he's the worst person in the world to try to have a conversation with." If you are thinking to yourself, "I can't stand this person," or "This is going to be difficult," your body language will be telling them how you feel. If you do not like someone, your body language gives you away. By making a list of all this difficult person's positives you will be in a more positive frame of mind during the conversation. Your body language will tell them that you are relaxed and that you have changed your mind about him or her. You will be calm and less apt to get defensive and attack. The conversation will go totally differently than if you go into the conversation with those other, negative thoughts.

If our decisions to leave one of our packs are based on the Negative Thought Cycle, then we are talking ourselves out of many situations that, realistically, we actually do not want to leave. In order to ensure you are making a reasonable decision, instead of a decision based on the Negative Thought Cycle, there is a very short, easy conversation you need to have with someone whom you can trust about this particular situation. Tell this person to listen for whether or not you have a reasonable list of positives about the situation or if you are focusing the majority of your attention on the negatives. Please do not try this alone, talking to yourself. Your safety brain is far too good at tricking you into making decisions that it wants you to make, instead of reasonable, rational decisions.

In teaching just this point in a five-session Peaceful Parenting class, I had one mom who said that there are some toxic people out there who are so negative that there is nothing nice to say about those people and we should end those relationships. My Negative Thought Cycle antennae went up. It sounded like she was describing a personal situation, so I asked Carol to tell us a bit about it. I did not hear Carol say one nice thing about this person in the five minutes that she took to describe her. Had Carol been able to describe this person in glowing terms and then say that there was one aspect of the relationship that bothered her, I would have said that she was being realistic and logical about the relationship, instead of having fallen into the Negative Thought Cycle. Heads up. Her husband agreed with her. If you are going to try to pinpoint whether you are in the Negative Thought Cycle or not, you may want to find an objective friend to discuss it with, instead of someone who is already agreeing with your assessment of the situation.

Be careful about falling into the Negative Thought Cycle. The Negative Thought Cycle is one of our key thought patterns that keeps us in defense-attack. If we spend 95% of our day looking for what's not safe, then most of life is not safe, and we will get angry often, to defend ourselves. Try starting out your day with your list of Gratitudes. Life will start to look so much better. If you have this much in your life to be grateful for, it must be a pretty good life. Once we start setting those positives pictures of the things we want, and paying attention to the opportunities our safety brains find to make those pictures happen, our lives will get even better. We can make the changes we want, and be happy, calm, and productive by focusing on the positives. We can pull ourselves out of defense-attack simply by enjoying life and living the life we want.

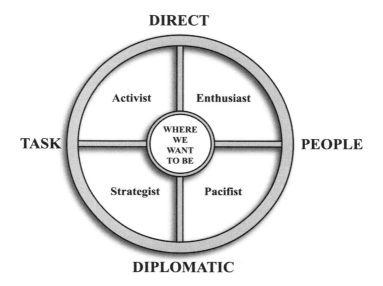

DIRECT

Activist   Enthusiast

TASK   WHERE WE WANT TO BE   PEOPLE

Strategist   Pacifist

DIPLOMATIC

LEVEL III

The Golden Rule
Causes Conflict

Introduction

The Golden Rule Causes Conflict

We try to teach our children the Golden Rule—Do unto others as you would have them do unto you. The Golden Rule is a wonderful way to begin training our children to give consideration to others. However, there is a step after the Golden Rule that many of us were never taught. The Golden Rule assumes that we are all the same and that we all want the same things. Of course it is simply not true that we are all exactly the same and we want exactly the same things. Have you ever received a Christmas or birthday gift that you had absolutely no use for, or even hated? Most of us have. For whom do the givers really buy the gifts? Themselves. They saw something they liked and naturally assumed (naturally, because the training of treat others the way you wish to be treated is so deeply engrained) that we would like it, too. But we all like different things, we all need different things in our lives for us to be happy, and we all need to be treated differently from each other. We need to be treated the way we want to be treated, not the way they want to be treated. I have heard so many women tell me that they received a power tool on Mother's Day from the father of their children. He bought it because he saw it and liked it so much. He assumed that his wife would like it, too. Some women receive kitchen or cleaning appliances as gifts because their husband likes tools. Knowing that his wife would not want a power tool, the concept gets translated into giving any tool as a gift. So, he gives her a vacuum cleaner, an electric knife, or some other kitchen appliance for Mother's Day instead of what she really wanted. We buy for others what we like. Have you ever bought a gift that you absolutely hated for someone else? (And not out of spite, either!) It is very difficult to actually spend money on something that you dislike. If you hate it so much how could anyone like it? The assumption that others want the same things we want is exactly the mistake we are making with the Golden Rule. Not only do different people like different things, they communicate in different ways.

There are four communication styles in human beings. Every person in the world has a dominant communication style based on this model. If we continue to give people information the way we want it, which is what most of us do, then we are communicating in the wrong way with up to 75% of the people we meet.

The four Communication Styles:

     1. Enthusiast
     2. Activist
     3. Strategist
     4. Pacifist

A detailed look at the four Communication Styles will clarify many of the problems we have with other people. We will see our bosses, each of our coworkers, our spouses, our friends, our parents, our siblings, and all of our children, even that one child that we know came from our bodies, but are sure belongs to a different family.

We will look at the general characteristics of each of the four Communication Styles. We will see their strengths and weaknesses. We will realize that people from each of the four Communication Styles show anger in different ways. We will find out the hardest thing to teach each of the four Communication Styles. We will learn there are no personality conflicts, if only we will make the effort to recognize from which dominant quadrant each person communicates. Then we need only make the effort to communicate with them in the way they need their information, instead of the way we need to give it. We will examine real-life situations that show how the differences between the four Communication Styles cause conflict and the easy way to resolve these conflicts. And we will show real-life ways of dealing with each of the Communication Styles to gain cooperation instead of conflict.

The Communication Styles, based on research by Carl Jung, in the late 19th-century,[1] Tony Alessandra, *Relationship Strategies*;[2] and Daniel Goleman, *Emotional Intelligence*,[3] are not about good and bad, or right and wrong. What we will see are strengths and weaknesses. Throughout Level III we will see that one quadrant will have a weakness in exactly the same area that is another quadrant's strength. In order to create a strong team we would need people from all four quadrants on our team, whether this is the person you married, or a team at work. If someone else is strong in an area that I am weak in, together, we make a strong team. However, a team made from all four quadrants is also the hardest team to work with, because the members of the team are approaching every issue from a different angle. With this information you will be able to work with anybody, anywhere, calmly and productively, without getting angry, without thinking, "They are out to get me." Instead, we will be able to gain full cooperation and greater productivity. We are exploring some inherent characteristics in different people.

We all have a dominant quadrant. We have a second-strongest quadrant that will take over quite often. We have a third-strongest quadrant from which we will deal with some situations. Our fourth quadrant will be where many of our weaknesses lie. We have all four quadrants in us. It is as though, when it comes to styles of communicating, the brain is divided into four quadrants. One of those quadrants developed more strongly from birth. Which means that from birth we have a preferred way of communicating. Many of us will slip into different ways of communicating depending upon the situation.

This is not brand new information. We have been using this information, unconsciously. We know that there are some people we can joke around with and others with whom we would never dare. We recognize their communication style and adjust ourselves accordingly. With the conscious understanding we will gain from Level III, we will be able to adjust ourselves more consciously, in more situations, with greater effect. However, in any kind of a stressful situation, a crisis, or an emergency, we invariably communicate from our dominant quadrant. The dominant quadrant is the one that our safety brain has found most effective in most situations. With practice we can learn to deal with even a crisis in the way that will garner the most cooperation from the others involved, by dealing with them in the way they need information, instead of from our preferred communicate style.

Each person is a unique combination of the characteristics from the different quadrants, which means we are unique. However, our dominant quadrants shine through. We walk, talk, dress, shake hands, have hobbies, and communicate who we are, mostly from our dominant quadrant. Having worked with and taught this information for many years, I can identify the dominant quadrant of anyone I meet, almost immediately. You will be able to do this as well, with practice. I am getting quite good at identifying people's secondary quadrants, as well.

When I was first introduced to this information, it was brand new to me. Yet, it made such immediate sense that I made the commitment to work with it until it became a habit to identify people's dominant quadrants and try to deal with them in the way that worked for them. In crisis situations or when I am stressed, I still have that inclination to deal with the situation with the characteristics from my dominant quadrant, but I am getting better and better at keeping my thinking brain turned on during those situations, and using my knowledge of the Communication Styles to gain cooperation, instead of conflict. You will, too.

Chapter 6
The Enthusiast

Driving need: To get attention

The primary, unconscious driving need of the Enthusiast is to get attention. This need drives all of their thoughts, all of their actions. These people are always talking. At the dinner table they take over and you can't get a word in edgewise. These are the children who take over all conversations in the car, at the dinner table, in front of the TV, everywhere. We need to realize that Enthusiasts don't want to be talking all the time. They need to be talking all the time. There is the huge difference. The Enthusiast thinks out loud. Their brains go into motion when their mouths are in motion. They use all of that air space surrounding them. Every single one of their ideas gets voiced.

Enthusiasts love public attention. The more people paying attention, the better. This is your child who speaks loudly, all the time. The words "use your inside voice" have absolutely no meaning. These children (and adults) have only one volume—loud!

Enthusiasts are the people at your work site who are always away from their work station, talking to someone else. Many of us have been interrupted so often by these people that we can hardly bear to see them coming towards us anymore. "If only they would go away and leave us alone." Many of us have actually said to these people something like, "I have a lot of work to do today," and we expected them to go away, because the message that we were conveying so diplomatically was, "Go away and leave me alone!" What did your Enthusiast do? He or she stood there talking some more! "Oh, I have a lot of work to do today, too. I have to do this. And then I have to do this. And then maybe I should take care of this." Your Enthusiast stood there for another 30 minutes listing all the things he or she needed to get done, instead of going and doing them!

I thought we just told those people to, "Go away. I'm busy." That was certainly the message we were trying to convey. But we did not actually convey that message. If we phrased the message diplomatically, we come from the indirect, people-oriented quadrant. We like to be diplomatic. Unfortunately, the only way to get the Enthusiast to go away and leave us alone is to look him or her directly in the eye, and say in a loud, firm voice, "Go away. I'm busy!" Then, finally, the Enthusiast will go away and let us get back to work. But many of us would never say that out loud to someone because if someone said it to us, we would find it so rude. We would be so offended. This is exactly the problem. We treat others the way we wish to be treated. We assume, at a safety brain level, that everyone is just like us and wants exactly what we want. This is what causes many of our relationship problems.

The Enthusiasts are from the direct, people-oriented quadrant. They need to hear the action we want them to take, or they will not hear the message. That means that when we said, "I have a lot of work to do today," we did not tell them the action that we wanted taken. Because we did not voice an action, the message we gave was that we were willing to bring up all kinds of topics for chatting. The Enthusiast is at our desk to chat, and we fed into that need.

We go to defense-attack when we think we have given a message and they deliberately ignored the "Leave me alone" message. If they are deliberately ignoring us our safety brain activates our defenses. We started resenting them. Then we got angry because they were doing it to us, again. Doing it to us, deliberately. If someone is out to get us, they are very unsafe people to be with. Slam goes the gateway, and we get angry to protect ourselves.

The real problem is the assumption that we are all alike. If we are all alike then I would know that standing at your desk talking to you will drive you crazy. Yet, I do it day after day after day. Then I'm doing it just to get you, right? Wrong! I have no idea it is driving you crazy, because I have not heard the message that you are giving day after day. You have used words that work for you. Not once have you stated this message in words that work for me. I have completely not heard your message.

These are your children who learned to talk the earliest. One child I know put his first two words together when he was 13 months, and they were totally understandable. These children and adults talk quite fast, will interrupt while you're talking, and run away with the conversation if you let them— and sometimes even if you don't!

Both child and adult Enthusiasts are very good with words. They can talk their way into and out of anything, and often the other quadrants get talked into things they never meant to agree to, because the Enthusiast is so good with words. They can turn other people's words around and give them a meaning that was never intended. In fact, sometimes the other quadrants will find themselves apologizing to the Enthusiast for something the Enthusiast did, because the Enthusiast has turned the situation completely around, and so quickly that we do not even know quite what has happened.

These are the adults and children who argue incessantly to get out of doing something or to get what they want. You say "No," and you've just bought into a 30-minute monologue from your Enthusiast. Often, if we aren't very careful, we get sucked into their arguments—either changing our minds or following along their new tangents. Their arguments can sound very logical and very reasonable until later when you get a chance to think about it. These are the children who will talk their siblings into following them into trouble, or talk them into giving up their possessions.

They will get their basic driving need for attention fulfilled, with positive or negative attention. This is not a conscious need. The safety brain drives their behavior. The safest thing for the Enthusiast is to be the center of attention.

Do you have one child who is constantly picking on his or her siblings? Is this also the child who constantly interrupts while others are talking? With homework, this is the child (my oldest) who bounces out of the computer room (where he is working on an assignment) every 5 minutes to say, "Hey, Mom, I just got this and this and this done," or "Mom, do you want to come and see how far I am now?" It has only been five minutes! Or, he will simply interrupt a conversation I was having with his younger brother, because he needs a fix of attention. What is the Enthusiast's favorite topic of conversation? Themselves!

Secondary driving need: To be liked

More than any other people, the Enthusiast needs to feel liked. They need to feel that you are a friend. They are friendly folks, themselves, and are interested in what you do outside of work, what your hobbies are, whether you have a family. Mostly, they are interested in what you do to see if the two of you have common interests, because friends share common interests.

In order to ensure that Enthusiasts will cooperate fully, smile when you talk with them. Talk about their favorite topic of conversation, themselves. If you do these two things, you will find that the Enthusiast will do almost anything for you. Because of their need to be liked, they rarely say "No" to someone they consider to be a friend. Of course, they expect you to rarely say "No" to them, as well.

General characteristics

Enthusiasts have a lot of energy. The other quadrants often find that the Enthusiast has too much energy. They can be tiring to be around. They can be almost frenetic at times, trying to fit in all of the things they want to get done. Enthusiasts need to have fun, adventure, challenge, and excitement in their lives. They love to find new ways of doing things. The same old thing, day after day, drives them crazy.

Enthusiast children may get this need met by rearranging things around the house: the kitchen cupboards, the furniture in their bedrooms, the furniture in the main rooms in the house! Enthusiast adults are much the same. They like to replace the old with the new or change things around to make them look new and different.

Enthusiasts love recognition, even third-party recognition. They love to tell you what famous people they have met, or which famous places they have gone. Advertising that links products with famous people is aimed at the Enthusiast. Enthusiasts will buy because they'll be more like that famous person if they own the product.

Enthusiasts love doing things a new, original way. Enthusiasts like to own all the newest toys and gadgets. They don't necessarily plan on using them. They just want to own them! They have all the latest sports equipment, the latest models of car, the newest computer equipment. Enthusiasts have probably created all the newest fads, and buy into the newest fads easily.

Enthusiasts are very informal. Upon first meeting you, they will treat you like a long-time friend. They like to dress casually. They use less formal language. They are friendly people to be around, and are the first to break the ice with newcomers.

They love to have fun and adventure. They love to tell jokes. They usually have a smile on their face. These children become the class clowns in school, which fulfills two of their basic, primary needs—the need for attention and the need to have fun. These children can also be the family clown, playing practical jokes and bringing humor into the house. Of course, it's the same at work. The Enthusiast will be the person who tries to lighten the atmosphere with jokes and laughter.

These people are our social butterflies. They naturally have the skills to make lots of friends. They read people easily and respond to other people's body language and smallest signals. They make friends with people who will share fun and adventure with them. They do not necessarily spend a lot of time discussing feelings and showing their vulnerabilities with their friends so their friendships may be rather superficial, but they know, and spend time with, a lot of people. They get really down if they have to spend any amount of time at home alone. They are constantly phoning friends (personal phone calls at work) and inviting or being invited to join these friends.

The Enthusiasts do not actually go to work to work; they go to work because it's one more place for them to socialize! The Enthusiast's favorite meeting place is the bar! They do their best work in a fun, relaxed environment. At work, if you want to get some good work out of your Enthusiasts, create a relaxed, friendly, work environment. Many offices these days have done just that. Dress codes have been relaxed, for example. This works very well for the Enthusiast.

These are our naturally extroverted people. They actually gain energy from socializing. At the end of the day, if these people are down, and have a chance to visit with friends, you will see them re-energize. An Enthusiast person who is home with the kids all day, will drive her spouse crazy by talking nonstop when he gets home from work.

Enthusiasts love excitement and challenge. Enthusiasts probably created X-treme sports: snowboarding, bungy jumping, mountain biking, etc. They love the excitement of pitting their physical and mental skills against something. They love risk. They love that adrenaline hit that comes from defying death. In the office, that can be risking time, money, reputation. Enthusiasts are not fiercely competitive. They love to win because of recognition, but they are gracious winners and losers, because they need people to like them. Enthusiasts love the game, the process, not necessarily the winning or losing. These are your people at work who love incentives and reward programs that look like games. Any time you can turn work, or a chore with the kids, into a game, they love it and will put extra energy into that chore.

Enthusiasts are idea people. They come up with new ways and new ideas, almost a new idea per minute sometimes. These people are starters. And they are great motivators. They speak with passion and conviction. They are able to put words together in a way that really gets other people to buy into their ideas. They love the energy created at the start of a new project.

The Enthusiast is very good at reading body language. They have such a strong need to be liked that they watch people. They are the most sensitive to whether people are being genuine, or not. The Enthusiast's strongest sense would be that of sight. They watch what is going on around them, and the people around them, to ensure they are getting their attention, and that people like them.

We can judge these general characteristics as positive or negative depending upon what experience we have had with Enthusiasts. For example, if you have an Enthusiast in marketing or advertising, he or she can probably talk a client into buying anything. However, if you have come into conflict with your Enthusiast, he or she probably talked circles around you, and nothing got resolved. Their agility with words can be seen as positive or negative. However, there are some very specific challenges that our Enthusiasts face, because of their basic needs.

Challenges

Non-Compliance These people are not compliant. Their motto in life: *It is easier to ask forgiveness than permission.* They don't like to comply with the way "things have always been done." They aren't particularly interested in complying with laws—which means the adults have no problem ignoring traffic laws (like the speed limit; or 'No U-turn' signs). Larger laws they might obey, simply to stay out of trouble, but lesser laws mean nothing to them. The children in this quadrant will disobey house rules and school rules, whenever it serves their purpose. They will do what they want and ask for forgiveness later. They are not doing it because they are "out to get us" or "to show us" that they can. They do it because they, more than any other quadrant, need instant gratification. They also like to make up new ways of doing everything. Our adult Enthusiasts will make up their own rules at work. They might try to persuade everyone else to go along with their rules, or they might just do it their way. If they get caught then they try to talk their way around it.

Details Our Enthusiasts find details absolutely boring. Besides, if it has a lot of detail, that might mean there is an old, 'tried-and-true,' boring way of doing whatever it is. They won't write things down, because then they might have to do it that same, old, boring way. Instead, if they don't write it down, or don't read written instructions, then they can make up their own new, original way to do things. Of course, this might mean they do it all wrong. In the office, this means that the Enthusiast will not read the policies and procedures manuals. They might not even read those e-mails and memos that go out explaining how certain things need to be done. You might find that they don't read anything that you've given them (especially instructions for schoolwork). If you need to give them instructions, do it verbally. They need human interaction.

The Enthusiast will not sit through a detailed explanation or a lecture. They like the big picture, the end result. In a discussion, start off by telling them why they want to sit and listen to you—what's the end result. If you start off with the detail, you've lost them. They will not be willing to work with you, or even listen to you.

Completion Enthusiasts have a hard time finishing what they start. They'll have great ideas on how to do the project, and huge visions about how the end project will look. These huge visions often appear unrealistic to the other Communication Styles. Remember, the Enthusiast is simply thinking out loud, not committing to anything, just thinking. Give it 10 minutes and they'll have a whole new idea. But they will get into the middle of a project, or even just get started, and then walk away with a better idea. It's not that they have a short attention span, it's that they have a short excitement span. As soon as something isn't exciting anymore, the Enthusiast walks away looking for something else that's fun and exciting to do. So, the Enthusiast will often leave a trail of incomplete projects behind them.

Disorganization The fourth major challenge for the Enthusiast is that if asked, "How's that project going?" he will assure you that he has it all under control. Never believe him. It's not that this person is lying to you. He does have it fully under control in a way that works for him. And the way that always works for the Enthusiast is to leave everything to the last minute because that way he gets his basic needs for excitement, adventure, challenge, and fun met by trying to get it done on time. The Enthusiast simply doesn't understand any other way of organizing, because she is fulfilling so many of her primary needs in leaving everything to the last minute.

Hardest thing to teach our Enthusiasts

The hardest thing to teach our Enthusiasts is strong morals and values. Because the Enthusiast needs instant gratification, is primarily concerned with her own wants and needs, and likes to think up new ways of doing things, the Enthusiast has a hard time understanding the concept of morals and values and personal integrity. They do not see any reason for following societal laws. They are only polite and courteous to others because other people seem to like that, not because they have any real understanding of what it means to respect others.

Personal space

What does an Enthusiast's personal space look like—whether desk space in the office, or a child Enthusiast's room? It is an absolute mess. If you ask your Enthusiast coworker for something, he or she will be pushing things all over and even off the desk trying to find it.

What do the Enthusiasts have up on their walls? Pictures of themselves, a mirror, pictures of them with the famous people they have met. Kids have music or movie stars on their walls (adults might, as well!)

Employment

What kinds of careers would our Enthusiasts be attracted to, at which they would excel? Marketing and advertising, information lines, reception with interaction over the phone or with people walking in the office, human resources (especially the interviewing part), sales, acting, motivational speaking, all the performing arts and politics. Politicians aren't necessarily deliberately lying to us. Rather, they are fulfilling their basic needs. They will say what needs to be said in the moment to ensure that the electorate likes them. It might not be true. It might not even be a possibility, but it will be said, because of the need to be liked. Our 18 year old Enthusiasts with no job skills will be attracted to telemarketing, waiting tables, retail, and lifeguarding.

How does an Enthusiast get angry

The Enthusiast gets angry loudly. Even, or maybe especially, when our Enthusiasts are in a bad mood, they want their attention. When they get angry, they talk. These people can't let something go until it is worked out. So they talk, talk, talk, and often prod the other person into exploding!

Negative Enthusiasts are sarcastic and are our back stabbers. Sarcasm is double-edged. If you try to catch an Enthusiast on something that was said sarcastically, they will reply, "Just kidding." To your face Enthusiasts will be nice because they need to be liked, but behind your back, watch out; especially if the Enthusiast thinks you don't like him.

Working with the Enthusiast

1. Begin every conversation with a smile on your face. Enthusiasts need to know that you like them. If you also begin every conversation talking about their favorite topic of conversation, them, these people will do anything you want. Once you fulfill their primary needs—the need for attention and the need to be liked—they will literally do anything for you.

2. Let them talk. At the dinner table let them be the first ones to talk about what was great in their day and what wasn't. When it's someone else's turn to talk, gently remind your Enthusiast child that she'll get another turn.

At our dinner table, each person gets a chance to answer these two questions without interruption, "What was the best part of your day?" "What was the worst part of your day?" We started this ritual when our oldest child was three years old, mainly because I was a stay-at-home mom at that time, and when my husband got home from work, I wanted to monopolize his time. The ritual of allowing everyone to have their speaking time without interruption:

      A). ensures that everyone in the family feels important enough
          to be heard,
      B). allows our Enthusiasts to get their attention in a very
          acceptable way, and
      C). teaches our Enthusiasts to listen to others without interrupting.

3. Enthusiasts need help in developing strong morals and values. Start working with your Enthusiast children now, teaching them what is right, what is wrong, and to always choose right. Our six-year-old daughter is our Enthusiast. If we walk away after asking her to put something in her room she puts it in the nearest plant or behind the nearest chair. She's not malicious or disobedient but if something isn't fun, or if something fun is happening somewhere else "hide it and run," is her rule. She is also our liar. We simply work calmly with her catching every lie we can and ensuring that she then tells us the truth as often as possible.

If you are faced with an Enthusiast adult who you know is lying to you, point it out. The Enthusiast will invariably deny it, but if you catch them a couple times, you will have made it unsafe for them to lie again, because they might get caught again. You might stop liking them if you keep catching them lying, and since the Enthusiast's basic need is to be liked, they stop lying.

4. Enthusiasts don't work well alone. If they are isolated, whether it's a work space in the building that is far away from everyone else, or a one-man office, they won't work. The Enthusiast needs company. Our Enthusiast daughter does a very poor job if she is expected to clean her room by herself. Invariably, we find everything stuffed under the bed, under the covers, and behind the door. When someone is in the room with her, maybe not even helping, but just keeping her company, she works really well. With a bit of direction about doing a good job, and someone to chat with, she is remarkably competent. Even walking down to the basement by herself to get the cat food used to be almost impossible. She would insist that she was afraid of spiders, just so she could have her brother's company. Now that she's six years old, going down to the basement by herself isn't a problem anymore. She knows that because it is such a short trip she will be back with company in no time. These children are the most resistant to bedtime. They want to stay with the company. They don't want to miss anything.

5. You can get your Enthusiasts to work hard at their work stations. Tell your Enthusiasts that if they come to your desk you won't talk to them, but you will stop by their desk three times a day to chat. All day they will be watching for you to come to their desk. When you go to their desk glance over their shoulder and ask them what they are working on. Your Enthusiasts will spend about two minutes talking about the problems they are having. Then they'll start seeing solutions. And within five minutes you'll hear these words: "Go away, I'm busy!" Their brains go into motion when their mouths go into motion. If you get them talking about their work, they will be brainstorming. They'll get remotivated, and they'll get back to work.

6. Another way to get your Enthusiast to leave you alone so that you can get your work done is to make your watch the bad guy. When the Enthusiast approaches your desk, smile at him. Make eye contact, and say, "George, I always like talking to you. I have about five minutes then I have to get back to my work. What's up?" Enjoy George's five-minute conversation, and keep a discreet eye on your watch. When the five minutes is up say something like, "You always brighten my day, George. My five minutes are up and I have to get back to work. Talk to you later." This a direct yet courteous way to deal with your Enthusiast. And you are not the bad guy, your watch is.

7. Organize the Enthusiast with leading questions: "What's the first thing you could do with that?" "What can you get done first?" "What is the first step you could take?" They will be talking about the work, and organizing it as they talk. Ensure that they set tight deadlines, because they

love playing games. You have helped them turn their work into a game. They will be committed and working hard.

8. When you talk with Enthusiasts, use the words that I have used to describe them: fun, adventure, challenge, excitement, risk, informal, let's talk about it, play, games, attention, you, ideas, brainstorm. If you use these words with your Enthusiasts you will be speaking their language. They'll really hear you and do anything you ask them to do.

9. Be enthusiastic. If I am in Enthusiast mode, and someone from another quadrant shares an idea with me, but does not appear to be enthusiastic about it, I simply assume that it is not important and I forget all about it. When my husband starts talking about our investments, if he sounds passionate and excited, then I can listen to him talk about them for hours. I will even become excited about them, too. If he comes into the discussion being calm, rational, and low key, I go to sleep (literally). Also, show enthusiasm for ideas that your Enthusiasts share with you. Even if you do not agree with the idea, or if you can see that it is a "pie-in-the-sky" idea, if you say, "That will never work because ..." you can watch your Enthusiasts crash their gateway down on you, and get defensive. Keep the Enthusiast's gateway up by showing some enthusiasm and let them get over the initial excitement of the idea, before you start discussing the idea rationally.

Common situations
Situation:

A strong Enthusiast will have a really hard time with a home office. Working by themselves all day, trying to get anything accomplished, will be nearly impossible. Knowing that they are strong Enthusiasts, and knowing that the lack of human bodies in their 'office' will, in itself, lead to non-productivity, Enthusiasts can structure their days, and structure their time, to ensure that they have human interaction—phone meetings, face-to-face meetings, all help. I faced exactly this problem when I was first starting out with my own company. I had a home office, and could not get anything accomplished. At one point, I rented office space from my realtor just so I could have hustle and bustle around me. I did not need a lot of 'talk time' with the other people in that office. Having people around me, plus and little bits of conversation with those people, was enough to keep me energized.

Situation:

A common complaint I hear about Enthusiasts is that they do not follow through. Some of this complaint is based on the Enthusiast's predilection to thinking out loud. One client complained that his wife was constantly making plans to do things with the family, then never followed through. On

Monday, Erica would say something like, "We should take the kids to the zoo on Saturday." Steve would agree that that was a good idea. All week, Steve would be waiting for Erica to finalize the plans to go to the zoo. They never went to the zoo. In fact, Erica did not follow through on 99% of these plans.

Do you see the miscommunication? Erica is an Enthusiast who thinks out loud. On Monday, she thought of the zoo. That was at about 7:45 a.m. By noon, she had probably had 15 other thoughts about what would be fun to do on the weekend. Steve, being a Strategist, thought that Erica had committed to a plan. But by Saturday, Erica had had 3,000 other thoughts about what would be fun to do on the weekend. She ended up going out with friends and left the rest of the family to fend for themselves!

First, the rest of us need to understand that most of what an Enthusiast says is just thinking out loud. Don't take too much of it seriously until the Enthusiast actually plans to take action on something. When the Enthusiast gets to the point of taking action, you will know they have committed. Second, if your Enthusiast comes up with a plan that excites you, you need to tell them that you are excited about it. Then, either you push them to take action on the plan, or take action yourself to make it happen.

Have I described you? Have I described someone you know? Is this the person with whom you get the angriest? Hopefully, you are starting to understand that they are not out to get you. They do life based on their two basic driving needs. If you can communicate with them in a way that taps into these needs, you will gain full cooperation, and have an enthusiastic, energetic, hardworking coworker.

Remember, this is a dominant communication style. If you have seen some of these characteristics in you, you will also have characteristics from the other three. But in any kind of a crisis situation, or stressful situation, you will communicate and take action with characteristics from your dominant quadrant. Any time someone has gone to defense-attack they are stressed. If you can communicate with them with words and gestures that they use, they will feel a kinship with you. Recognizing you as a safe person, they will calm down faster than if you continue trying to communicate with them with words and gestures that they find awkward, unacceptable, or confusing.

Chapter 7
The Activist

Driving need: To get it done

      Activists focus on getting something done every moment of every day. On vacation, in their personal lives, at work, these people are result oriented. They want to see what they are accomplishing. They want to see everyone around them getting things done. This is the manager or supervisor who expects you to look busy. They are impatient and abrupt. They never waste time. They walk fast and talk fast and dress fast and eat fast and drive fast. They do everything fast so they can get it done and get on to the next task. They spend every weekend, at home, accomplishing. They respond to the question, "How was your weekend?" with a litany of the projects that they completed. We often feel inferior to Activists because they get so much done, while we spend our weekends sleeping and relaxing. Alternatively, asking them about their weekend might earn you a stare and the question, "Why do you want to know?" At work they want to concentrate on work, and feel that the office is no place to talk about personal lives. They are simply living their lives according to their driving needs. You can spend your weekends in the same way as they do theirs, only if you are also an Activist. Otherwise, you live according to your needs.

      Activists hate wasting time. They consider social chit-chat in the office a waste of time. They do not waste time on extra actions. They look for the quickest and most efficient way to do things. They do not waste time on extra words either, words like, "Please." "Thank you." "Good morning." You are more likely to hear them say, "I need that Hamilton report on my desk, now," as they walk into the office Monday morning.

Secondary driving need: Take action

      The Activist's secondary driving need is the need to take action. In a meeting they only want to hear what decisions have been made, and what action needs to be taken. Then, they want to walk out of the boardroom and take that action. If an Activist feels that you are wasting his time he will tap a pen on the desk, or a foot on the floor, or sit back and cross his or her arms and say, "What's the bottom line?" or "Could we get on with it, here." or "And the point is?" or "What exactly did you want?" This Activist has just crashed down the gateway in his brain. You have lost his cooperation. He becomes impatient, feels unsafe. It is definitely time to end the conversation.

General characteristics

Activists need to take action. Activists love to take control. They love to make decisions. Their motto in life is, *If I want it done right, I'll do it myself.* They feel that their way of doing things is the best way, so if you'll just do it their way, life will be good. These people will try to gain control of the office or at least some aspect of it. When these people become overcontrolling we use the terms "control freak" and "power struggle" to describe their behavior.

These people are our most efficient workers. They multitask. They will have eight or 10 or 15 tasks on their plate, and keep track of all of them, and do a good job on all of them. They are aggressive. They are direct and they do not take other people into consideration, because they are completely focused on getting the job done and on to the next task. They simply tell you what they want and when they want it.

My dominant quadrant is Activist. In fact, I would call myself an Enthusiastic Activist. Activist is my dominant quadrant, and Enthusiast is my secondary quadrant. A telephone conversation with my best friend used to be straight to the point without any social pleasantries, "Hi. This is what I need. Can I have it by Friday? Thanks. Bye." It didn't occur to me to ask how she was or how her husband and children were—that would have been a waste of time. It was a major realization to learn that other people needed that kind of polite, caring conversation before getting down to business. To this day, I'm never the first one in a telephone conversation to send my regards to family or a mutual friend. In fact, as an Activist, I do not keep in constant contact with friends. I think of people when I'm working on a task that reminds me of them, or when I need something from them (sad, but true.) This is simply who I am. I am learning, and so can you. As you discover that these various characteristics are part of your dominant Communication Style, you can start relaxing with yourself. OK, so I am not naturally inclined to make small talk on the telephone. Now that I realize other people need that, I can give it to them. All it means is that I am meeting some of their basic communication needs. If I do not naturally keep in constant contact with friends, I can still contact them when I think of them. It might only be once every six months. I have to assume that they love hearing from me when I do call, and get over feeling guilty!

I recently had to explain this natural trait of mine to my youngest brother. He immigrated to Australia from Canada about a year ago. He e-mailed me within the first four months. It took me about six weeks to respond. When I did finally respond by e-mail, it was 15 pages long, describing everything in my life since I had last seen him. As an Activist, I see this as the most efficient use of my time. My brother e-mailed me right back asking a few questions. He got the response to those questions about eight weeks later. In the mean time, he talked with both my mom and my oldest brother telling them to "tell Jeanette to e-mail him." I had not forgotten about him. It simply was not the most efficient use of my time to send an immediate response. That he might have needed an immediate response never occurred to me.

Activists love to make decisions and, as my husband assures me, Activists can make decisions with no information. He's close to being absolutely right! When asked a question, Activists will look at only the essential facts and make a decision without wanting all of the details. If you try to give them all of the details, you are wasting their time, and they will let you know it.

In the office, for example, an Activist might approve a request for $35,000 from the budget for a project you are working on without more information than the request itself. They have given proper consideration to all of the facts they need. They know there is enough money in the budget for this. They quickly weigh how important this project is. They look at you and know whether they can trust you to use the money well and do a good job. Within three seconds of making the request you get a, "Yes." Then they get back to their work. If they look up, and you are still standing there, they are confused. "Didn't we just finish this conversation. Is there something else?"

Children who are Activists, engage in constant power struggles. They, more than any of the other quadrants, need to feel that they have control over their lives and their surroundings. These children will ask you for a decision, then argue with you until you are ready to tape their mouths shut! They will point out all of the reasons why you need to give them what they want. They are completely focused on their wants, their needs, themselves. Enthusiasts will argue for the sake of hearing themselves talk, and playing the game. They argue to see if they can get you to change your mind. The Activist argues because she wants to gain control of the situation. She has seen the way this task should be done, and will argue forever, trying to get you to let them do it their way. The Activists are the adults and children who take offense when you point out that the way they did something was not the best way, because the Activist believes that his way is always the best way.

When you ask an Activist to do something, just give him the bottom line. Ask him if he understands. The answer will probably be a scornful, "Of course I understand." Then get out of the way and let him do it his way. If you stand there trying to tell Activists how to do something, they will become very impatient and irritated with you.

Activists often appear to be very intelligent people because they think quickly, reach conclusions quickly, and are ready for action before others. Of course, this can lead to sloppier work. Their work won't be the neatest, but it will be done first. With children, poor handwriting can be indicative of an Activist. They rush to get their schoolwork done, not neatly, but done.

Activists are extremely competitive. They want to be first. They want to get the trophy or award. They are not motivated by fun; they are motivated by winning. Who's the best? Who can get the results? Who can get it done quickest?

Activists hate to revisit decisions. If the decision was made a week ago, and agreement was reached, the subject is closed for the Activist. This is true in personal relationships, as well. One workshop participant told me that his wife is an Activist. Susan suggested that they go out for dinner. Ed asked her where she would like to go. She told him it did not matter, that he could decide. So he did. He pulled into a parking lot at a restaurant they had enjoyed before, got out of the car, went around and opened her door. She looked at him and said, "I don't want to eat here."

If your Activist has suggested doing something, i.e. going shopping, going out for a meal, going to a movie, he has already made up his mind. He might not have thought it through completely, or he might be trying to be diplomatic. However, in this situation, if your Activist tells you to go ahead and decide, don't do it! Unless you are really in tune with your Activist's moods, you will probably guess wrong, and your Activist is going to get upset! If you really want to avoid a confrontation, ask some leading questions. "What are you in the mood for?" "Did you have something in mind?" If he really insists that you make the decision get his agreement that whatever you decide, he will accept it graciously!

One of the reasons my husband and I cannot stand each other's driving is because we come from opposite Communication Styles. For the Activist, driving is a race. She who gets ahead of everyone, wins. I explained that to my husband one day, but he is a Strategist and just doesn't understand. It drives me crazy that he is not interested in winning the driving race.

The Activist's strongest sense is the sense of smell. I think this is based on their need to win. As the human animal, they were the most likely to challenge another of their pack. They needed to smell the fear from their competitor. The Activist is the best at realizing whether others will back down, if attacked. Because they want to be the leader and have control, they are sensitive to the slightest fear in the people around them.

Challenges

Details You have probably already realized, from the general characteristics, that Activists do not like details. They get impatient with other people's need to give all the details. Get to the bottom line and get on with it, is the Activist's basic need in any conversation.

Listening Activists don't know what the word *listen* means. Activists give advice. They take control. They take charge. They tell people how to do things, and expect them to follow through, independently. They don't listen.

Are Rude and Abrupt Activists come across as rude and abrupt. They have a strong opinions about everything. They don't listen. They are direct and tell people exactly what's on their mind. They never stop to consider other people's feelings. They say and do things in a way that offends other people. They do not do this deliberately. It simply has never occurred to our Activists to take people's feelings into consideration. Their basic philosophy is, "We have a job to do. Let's get it done. Where do feelings come into it? Get the job done!"

If you have ever had the opportunity to pull an Activist aside and tell him that his behavior hurt your feelings, or that you would feel better if he just said things like, "Good morning," "Please," "Thank you," the first reaction you will get from the Activist is surprise. We Activists have no idea that you are taking offense to these things. The second reaction will probably be a willingness to make the effort to do things in a more diplomatic or courteous way.

Be prepared. If you ask your Activists to just say, "Please," when they hand you a job, and they agree, next time they hand you a job, they'll put it in your hands and tell you what they need from you and then walk away. Then they'll remember the agreement, stop, pivot to face you, and with a frown on their face, bark, "Please," and continue walking away! They have done what you asked. If you need them to do it with a smile on their faces, you'll have to specify that, too.

Shut Down Activists can be doing 10 or 15 tasks, all at the same time, and doing them all very well. But, if task #16 makes them feel overwhelmed, they do not just stop doing #16, #15 and #14. They shut down. They stop doing everything. They crash and burn. The problem with Activists shutting down is that they get their feelings of self-worth from accomplishing. If they shut down, they have no idea what has happened, why it happened, or how to get themselves going again. Activists, more than the other Communication Styles, have the hardest time figuring out their emotions. They do not think about emotions—not theirs, and not other people's. So, they struggle trying to figure out why they have shut down. Sometimes, they never figure out what has happened. Sometimes they instinctively know how to deal with the shut down, but many Activists need help when they shut down.

Paula is a strong Activist. She and her family moved to Alberta from Saskatchewan (two provinces in Canada) when Paula's youngest child was 15 years old. During the packing process, Paula said that she wasn't getting involved in any of the committees in the town to which they were moving. Between wrapping up her part in those committees and the details of the move, she felt overwhelmed. So, after they moved, she did not get involved in anything. She stayed at home, did not get involved in any of the town activities and did not make many friends, for 18 years. She was a negative, unhappy person over those 18 years, and nobody understood what had happened.

Yet, in retrospect, with this body of information, it's so clear. When Activists shut down it can go on for a long time. If you have Activists in your personal or professional life who have shut down, help them set a goal based on something you know they have enjoyed doing in the past, and then help them achieve that goal in any way you can. Once the Activist has one achievement under his belt, he will get up and running again. A few years ago Paula got involved in the Senior's Bridge club and the Senior's Choir. Her whole attitude changed. She is much happier. She's busy and she's active.

I have seen Activist children shut down when faced with a large school project that is really large. One child, when faced with the assignment of designing a house out of a shoe box, decorating and furnishing the house, and then doing a full, working alarm system in that house, sat for over an hour, stripping the plastic wrap off the wires. Not really understanding where to start, and what the first steps were, he felt overwhelmed yet he still needed to take action. This was one thing he thought needed to be done. So, he stripped wires, and did nothing else.

Hardest thing to teach an Activist

Activists have no respect for other people for the following reasons:
1. They think and do things faster than everyone else, and, therefore, think that they are superior.
2. Activists never take other people's feelings into consideration, so if your feelings can be hurt, you are weaker, and therefore not worthy of respect.
3. Other people usually give in to the Activists, because life is easier if they do. That makes those other people weaker in an Activist's eyes.

Personal Space

An Activists' desk space, or personal space is cluttered, but organized. They will have stacks of paper for each project they are working on, but they know exactly where everything is and can hand it to you in an instant. Never clean up an activist's personal space!

Activists decorate their walls with awards, degrees, diplomas, and trophies. They show off their achievements.

Employment

Activists work in management and supervisory positions. Even our 18-year-olds feel they are perfectly equipped to run a company! They are attracted to fast-paced, action-oriented jobs such as stock broker and racecar driver. Enforcement jobs are attractive to someone who likes to take control: Customs officer, police officer, security guard, bylaw officers. What kind of jobs would our 18-year-old Activists be attracted to, that they could get with no job skills? Fast-food restaurant. One of our Activists' top motivators is money. These are our children who were entrepreneurs, early. They had paper routes and shoveled walks. Our oldest son and his best friend started a landscaping business when they were 12 years old. They bought the lawnmower and weed whip with their own money. They spent a lot of time that summer knocking on doors to get business. One day they made almost $70 (that's at $15 a job), and spent all the money by the end of the day!

How Activists get angry

When Activists go to defense-attack, they get more forceful. They want their way, and they will push you until you give into them. They get louder, more arrogant, and ruder. Activists do not mind confrontation. Because they never take people's feelings into consideration they push until they get their way and then they get over it. It doesn't occur to them that you will feel hurt for a long time. Bullies are definitely Activists.

Working with the Activist

1. Get to the bottom line. Tell the Activist exactly what you need, and then ask them what facts they need. That way, you are not wasting their time with what they consider to be needless details.

2. Use words like, results, achievements, timeline, deadline, save time, fast, your way, bottom line, let's not waste time, action. You will be speaking their language and they will clearly hear you.

3. Give your employee and children Activists control over something; otherwise, you will find yourself in power struggles over everything.

4. Set boundaries. Strong, obvious, boundaries that never move—not when your Activists argue about it, and not when you are having a weak moment.

5. When my 12-year-old Activist starts to argue, I will look him in the eye and say, "Do you think there is anything you can say that will make me change my mind?" (The answer here is "No.") Faced with that boundary, he will usually stop arguing.

6. Be strong. If you stand your ground, just once, the Activists will begin to respect you.

7. Tell them what you find offensive, and be very direct and specific in what you ask them to do instead.

8. Let them work alone. Activists are not people-oriented, and do not need people around them to get things done.

9. Share this information with your Activists. This information

helped me realize that other people weren't stupid, they just had a different way of taking in information. I started to respect other people. Thinking that other people are stupid is a characteristic of Activists. Learning this information will change that.

Common situations

Situation:

As an Enthusiastic Activist, I usually have a list of things to do a mile long. I have a lot of energy. I am usually talking. I will bop around the house seeing all the things that need doing, and as I see those things, will mention them. I do everything fast. I'm goal-oriented. I like to win (even board games with the kids), I even talk fast.

And..........my...........husband.........talks.............at............ about.........this..........speed.

It hurts me to even type like that! By the time he's finished his first sentence, I've finished his next 30! We have been married for almost 10 years. By our second year of marriage I can guarantee that he knew that talking slowly drove me crazy. He still does it, though. That must mean that he's doing it on purpose! How many of us think exactly this way? Those other people are doing what they are doing deliberately to drive us crazy. However, when I learned that Theode has a different innate Communication Style it totally changed our marriage. The first thing I did was to set the goal of having a forever-after-loving relationship with him. Then I started paying attention to my safety brain when it gave me the opportunities to make that goal happen. This block of information was one of the key opportunities. Theode is not out to get me when he talks slowly, and neither are any of the other people in your life. They simply acquire their information differently and have different priorities. Then, they treat you as if you want information in the way they do.

So, why does my Strategist husband talk so slowly? A conversation with him will go like this: I ask a question, and I give him his usual two seconds to answer. When he does not answer after two seconds, I ask a second question, give him his two seconds to answer, then ask him a third question. By the fourth question I'm thinking, "What, are you stupid? Just answer the question!" and he's thinking, "Would you shut up and let me think!" Of course, he's far too polite and diplomatic to actually say that, because he comes from the Strategist quadrant.

What's happening in this conversation? When would an Enthusiastic Activist not immediately start answering a question? As an Enthusiast, I think out loud. Even if I do not know the answer to the question, I'll start answering. Eventually, I'll hit on the right answer. As an Activist, when asked for an opinion,

I have eight! The only time an Enthusiastic Activist would not immediately start answering a question is when he or she did not understand the question.

So, treating my husband the way I want to be treated, I ask him a question. If he does not immediately start answering the question, I assume that he did not understand the question. So, I reword the question and ask it again. He does not immediately start answering this question, so I assume he did not understand it, again. I reword the question and ask it again. He does not immediately start answering the question. By the fourth time I have to ask the question, I assume he's slllllllllllllllow (As in, he's stupid.) Given the way an Enthusiastic Activist communicates, that is a reasonable thought. I have heard many, many people who are Enthusiastic Activists, or Active Enthusiasts, echo this thought. Why is my husband not immediately responding to the question? Because he's out to get me, right? Wrong! He's a Strategist.

Chapter 8
The Strategist

Driving need: To get it right

The Strategist's basic driving need in life is to get the job done right. These are our perfectionists. Their motto in life is, *It'll get done when it gets done, but it will be done right.* These people are our compliers because they want to get everything right. They want to read all the rules and regulations and ensure that they fully understand them, so that they can follow them to the letter and do everything right.

These people comply with every law ever written. They actually drive the speed limit, or slower than the speed limit just to make sure that they are doing it right! I think my husband, whose dominant quadrant is Strategist, actually follows laws that were written 300 years ago. As long as it's still on the books, it must be the right way to do it.

Strategists are so focused on getting it right that when they look at the work others have done, they focus on how it can be improved. More than any of the other quadrants, Strategists have a hard time telling others what they have done right. I asked my Strategist husband to proofread the first chapter of this book for me—of course, he is very good with detail. After reading the first chapter, he pointed out all of the things that were wrong with it. I was pretty demoralized. It sounded like it was absolute junk and I should throw out the whole idea. I needed a bit of praise. I even said that to him, "Tell me something I did well." He focused some more on all of the things that were wrong. This was an argument that went on for 30 minutes, my trying to get him to say one thing that was right, and his totally focusing on every word, comma, and sentence that was wrong. I finally realized that any Strategist who is asked to look for details that are inaccurate, will literally not see what is right. They will only see what needs to be corrected.

Secondary driving need: Understand the details

You can see that the need for all of the details is tied very closely to the Strategist's primary need, to get it right. Our Strategists want to know all of the details, before they can take any action. All of the details. And, the Strategist wants those details in writing, so that they can look back on them a thousand times to ensure that they are getting it right.

General characteristics

Strategists are detail-oriented. They read non-fiction, to get all of the detail. I have seen my husband read history textbooks, for fun! This means that our Strategists have a lot of detail stored in their heads. And they never forget a fact. Or, if they think they might not remember it exactly, they will remember where they read it and look it up just to ensure that they are getting it right.

Strategists love the process. They love to analyze and plan and look up every detail. They are organized and thorough. If they tell you they will do something, they will. If they tell you they will get back to you on something, they will. They take care of the little details: things like balancing a cheque book. They will take as much time as is necessary to ensure that they do a good job the first time. Strategists know that any job should only need to be done once. It might take six months, but it will have been done right the first time. You will constantly hear words from them like, "Let's take our time and do it right." "We need to look at it one more time, to ensure that we get it right."

Strategists love to work alone for three reasons. First, they have such high standards that only they can get it right. Second, they are introverts and re-energize by being alone. Third, our Strategists do not multitask. They want to do one job from start to finish without interruption. Other people talking, are interrupting, and Strategists have a hard time with that. From this last point, you can see where Strategists would have a hard time working in an office or classroom environment that is wide open and, rather noisy. A Strategist would use the word chaotic to describe this kind of environment.

The Strategist believes that there is a place for everything and everything in its place. They are neat. They are quite formal. They will dress in a more formal manner, and very neat, and they will not be the first one to make small talk. They are loners. They are focused on the task, and have no need to talk with other people. Strategists are quiet people. They only talk when something is a priority, or when they have made a decision, or when something is really important to them. Also, they are quiet because they are listening and collecting details from what others have to say. One older gentleman who I know is a very strong Strategist. He can sit through a three-day family gathering of 25 people and not say a word to anyone. But, when someone happens to mention a topic that he has a fair amount of knowledge about, and real belief in, he will hold a one and a half hour moratorium on that topic. When I first met this man, I was intimidated. He did not talk to me so I thought he did not like me. Then, when he did talk about something, he was so passionate and so adamant that there was no room for discussion. Being a Strategist, he had all of his facts and details lined up to prove that he was right. It's hard to have an Enthusiast's debate with this type of person.

Strategists only say something once. They expected you to pay attention to them when they said it, because they pay attention when you say things (treating you as a Strategist wants to be treated). One common situation that was brought to my attention was a wife who was going through marriage counseling with her husband. One of her key needs that she had actually told her husband, was that she needed him to tell her he loved her, regularly. He had not told her once in their 20 years together that he loved her. His response to her request was, "I married you." That was the end of the discussion as far as he was concerned. Some of us can see the problem—hmmmm? The wife, an Enthusiast needs the words because words are the most powerful, for her. Yet, for that Strategist husband, it was so clear that in marrying her he had shown her that he loved her, why should he need to ever say the words?

Our Strategists do not have a lot of body language. They do not smile much. Their hands and arms are at their sides when they talk. I have actually encountered people who work in offices where they have been told to not use their hands when they talk, because it supposedly demonstrates that they are unorganized, have a poor vocabulary, and are unsure of what you are trying to say. Unbelievable! I have encountered this in different places in North America. Which quadrant will use their hands when they talk? Enthusiasts. Which quadrant made up the office rule to not use your hands when you talk? Strategists— because they do not use their hands when they talk and, therefore, see no reason why anyone should. When would Strategists use their hands when they are talking? We've just heard. When "they are unorganized, have a poor vocabulary, and are unsure of what they are trying to say." This is another example where treating others the way we want to be treated causes problems.

Our Strategists come from the indirect and task-oriented quadrant. Our Strategists are not people-oriented. These are our adults and children who do not seem to understand what is appropriate, socially. They do not study people. They do not understand other people. They understand rules and regulations that are written down. These children and adults stand a much stronger chance than the rest of the quadrants, of being ostracized.

I have seen many inappropriate Strategist children in social settings. They do not understand other people's body language, and so do not understand when the people around them have had enough. One seven-year-old child had heard some sexually-based jokes from an older sibling. Of course, the older child had gotten a good laugh from her friends when she told the joke. The seven-year-old took the joke to his friends, and told it again and again and again, until everyone was sick of hearing it. But the seven-year-old did not pick up on the social cues from the other children that they had had enough. The seven-year-old had learned that sexually-based jokes would get a laugh. So, he started doing things like dropping his pants and showing his buttocks to the other children, "mooning" them. He did not understand where appropriateness ended, and inappropriateness began.

Other Strategist children have learned that teasing gets a laugh from people. They will start teasing a friend, and not stop, taking it way too far until their friend is yelling and crying because what the Strategist child was doing and saying was so inappropriate. Sharon shared with me that, of her two sons, her oldest, Kevin, is her Enthusiast. Her second son, Andrew, is a Strategist. The boys go to the same school. Kevin has told Sharon that Andrew does not know when to stop at school. He has actually pushed things so far with some of the older kids that Kevin had to step in to keep Andrew from being beaten up. Some of those older boys were Kevin's friends and knew Andrew. Yet, Andrew, because he does not know what is and is not appropriate, pushes things too far.

So, with your Strategist child, begin teaching them what cues to look for in other people. Have those discussions using language like, "What is right? What is wrong?" Strategists pay attention to this language because they have an intrinsic need to do things right.

Strategists are our packrats. They save everything because they might need it, later. My husband used to have the tax information from 20 years ago.

The Strategist's are most sensitive to sounds. They are constantly listening to ensure that they are getting all of the details from the conversations and situations around them. Our middle son is a strong Strategist. When he was younger he would react to the fire alarm in the house or at school by screaming and crying for a long, long time. Open classroom and office settings are very difficult for our Strategists. They are trying to take in all of the details of all of the conversations and situations around them, and feel overwhelmed. They need quiet, isolated spaces to work, in order to be productive and do a good job.

Challenges

Analysis Paralysis If a Strategist does not get enough information, or feels that he is not getting all of the details, he will simply stop trying to make a decision. If you have ever been in a conversation that was going just fine, until the other person sat back, crosses his or her arms and said, "You go ahead and make the decision," you experienced a Strategist who had just realized that he or she was not getting all of the details.

No Deadlines Strategists do not pay attention to time. They pay attention to doing a perfect job, which, of course, can takes weeks. Remember their motto: It'll get done when it gets done…. I distinctly remember learning this about my Strategist husband.

We are up early on Saturdays because I always have a long list of things to get done on the weekend. At 8:00 a.m. we were planning our chores for the day, and I asked Theode, "Do you want to do the shopping, or do you want me to do it?" He wanted to do it. That was fine. I looked at my watch and said, "Well, if you get on the road right now, you could have all the running around done and be back by 10:30 a.m." At 10:30 a.m. he had not gone out to do the shopping. "Honey," I said, "do you want me to go do the shopping?" No, he was going to do it. Noon came and went. "Honey," I said, "You probably want to get out there before everyone else hits the road to do their Saturday shopping." Yup, he agreed with me, but he still did not head out to do the shopping. At 3:30 p.m. on a Saturday afternoon, he was ready to head out and do the shopping. On a Saturday afternoon every one of the 800,000 people in Calgary is out on the roads shopping. He left the house at 3:30 p.m. He got home at 7:30 p.m. It took him four hours to go to three shops. If he had gone out at 8:30 a.m. he would have been home in less than two hours.

I remember thinking, "What is the matter with him? Why can't he plan his time better than this?" At which point I had an epiphany! He had planned his time perfectly, for him. He did not mind puttering behind 800,000 drivers on the road. He does not mind standing in line in stores. He has no problem with taking four hours to do a shopping trip that would take me less than two hours. He planned his time perfectly, for him! Of course my next thought was, "Why didn't he just do it my way, which happens to be the right way!" (a thought straight from the Activist quadrant!)

A client described this same trait in a coworker, Barbara. She was heading across the city to drop off some paper work. She was going to leave her office at 9:30 a.m. and planned on being back in her office in time for her 10:00 a.m. appointment. Simply driving to that other office would take her 30 minutes. Driving back would take another 30 minutes. She would not be back in the office until 10:30 a.m. or later. She did not really think the time factor through. I have heard of this particular trait about many Strategists—they do not understand how much time something will take because they have never taken time into consideration.

No Multitasking Strategists do not multitask. They do one thing from start to finish. If they are interrupted, the Strategists might get flustered, or stop what they are doing to start whatever it is they have been asked to do. It then takes them quite some time to get back to what they were working on, if they ever do go back to it.

Dislike People Strategists give the impression that they do not like other people. This is based on three of their characteristics. Strategists like to work alone. They are quiet, and only talk when something is really important to them. They have very little body language (like smiling). The rest of us think that Strategists do not like us. Now that we know how Strategists communicate, we know better than to take this behavior personally. Strategists should make the effort to connect with others around you. Try smiling. In my workshops, when I challenge the Strategists to smile, they barely flex the corners of their mouths.

One client said that his staff came to him and told him that for the past three years they had been trying to make him smile, with little to no success. They were at the point where they wanted to quit, because he obviously did not like them. We worked with the staff, and this one piece of information about Strategists made all the difference in their relationships. He was able to tell them that he really valued them all and enjoyed all of them. I know that Strategists like other people, they simply do not show it in an overt manner. Now the rest of you know it too!

Hardest thing to teach a Strategist

The hardest thing to teach a Strategist is to pat people on the backs for what they have done right. They point out everything that has been done wrong, so that it can be fixed. They see the part that was done right briefly, then they ignore it. The parts that have been done wrong are often treated as punishable crimes. In the office and at home, this Strategist characteristic can be very demoralizing for the rest of us.

These people are our nay-sayers. If you have a negaholic in the office or in the family, you have a person who is stuck in Strategist mode. With coworkers, with spouses, with kids, our Strategists will focus so completely on what has been done wrong, that the other person will walk away thinking, "Why do I even bother. I can never get it right." Everyone has a hard time with a Strategist pointing out everything that is wrong but I think it is hardest on children.

Personal space

A Strategist's personal space looks like nobody works or lives there. *A place for everything and everything in it's place.* If they are busy, what they are working on will be the only thing on their desk. And when it is done, or at the end of the day, everything gets put away. I love this characteristic in my husband. It means that when we get home from a camping trip he is perfectly willing to unload the car and put everything away. As an Enthusiast, I have absolutely no inclination to help. The camping trip is over, cleaning up is a detail I prefer to avoid. I feel guilty about not helping, but I get over the guilt quickly.

What will our Strategists have up on their wall space? Charts and graphs. Facts and figures. Details. And they will have used the tape measure to ensure that everything is straight and symmetrical.

I know one Strategist woman, who has Spring and Fall cleaning. Her house is spotless. She has a schedule; Monday is for laundry. Tuesday she does the ironing. (Isn't there a nursery rhyme like this?) Her mother comments that she's uncomfortable going for a visit because it feels like she gets in the way of the schedule. Of course, the Strategist would never alter her schedule for something like a visit from family.

At one workshop we all sat back, astounded, as a Strategist described how he kept the filing in the office: his system color coded all of his bosses—not only color-coding the files with their work, but also color-coding their schedules in his calendar. For example, all of Bob's meetings and appointments were recorded in green. All of Edith's meetings and appointments were in blue, etc. Now, that's pretty reasonable, and actually a good idea, it's just that that was only the first step. He kept a schedule of which files had been removed from the cabinets, and by whom. Everything was also alphabetized, time-lined, and dead-lined. By the time this man had finished describing how he kept organized, we could all see that most of his time went into keeping himself organized, rather than getting any work done.

Employment

What kind of careers will attract Strategists at which they would excel? Engineer, architect, researcher, scientist, anything to do with computers, lawyer—the research and paperwork side of that career. What kind of job would our 18-year-old Strategists be attracted to, that they could get with no job skills? They will have thoroughly researched what they want to do. Then, they will get any job they can in a company in the field of their choice and plan to work their way up ladder. Our Strategist children will have saved their money so they are ready to implement their plans when they leave high school. Strategist children have a tendency to save their money. They plan what they will spend it on. They are rarely impulse spenders. Many Strategist children are naturally attracted to post secondary education, because it offers them more details and information.

How Strategists get angry

It takes a long time for Strategists to get angry—they have to think about it. When they finally do go to defense-attack (and it probably is a logical, conscious decision), they explode. These people are our volcanoes. Their resentment builds and builds until finally they explode. When your Strategists explode in anger, pay attention! They only talk about things that are important to them, so if they are angry, they are sharing with you what they consider to be unsafe. Really pay attention and work through it.

Strategists who have gone to the extreme will shut down. They will have nothing to say. I have seen this decimate an office. One person, who was in a management position, used the "silent treatment" very effectively, to gain control. Her immediate supervisor, and executive manager, tried many different techniques to get the Strategist to open up and talk but nothing worked. The Strategist controlled the office with a very powerful tool, silence. If the Strategist won't even tell you what the issues are, how can you resolve anything? And Strategists can stay silent for a long time, because they happen to like silence!

Working with a Strategist

1. Thank the Strategists for all of their attention to detail and their hard work. Strategists usually have their efforts discounted with comments like, "You don't need to go to all that trouble, let's just finish up." "I don't need all the detail, just give me the bottom line." "This is good enough, I don't need any more." They have never been thanked for all the detail and hard work they put into everything they do.

2. Strategists are 100% committed to their work and their relationships. They came to the relationship or the job after a lot of thought. My Strategist husband considered many factors before he decided to have a committed relationship with me: I was educated, and would therefore continue to work after we were married. I enjoyed intellectual discussions on a variety of topics. I had a lot of energy. I enjoyed a variety of situations; from going to elegant restaurants to following him across a river into the backcountry in the Rocky Mountains. He thought about my socio-economic status and even my province of birth and how we grew up in similar situations. He listed my athletic abilities. He took into consideration the time that he threw a set of keys to me in a parking lot, and I caught them. In his words, "I thought about thousands of things. I thought about everything," before asking me to marry him. I asked Theode one October if he wanted to go out with me. He thought about it until December.

As an Enthusiastic Activist, when he asked me to marry him my thought process took two and a half seconds, not three months. I thought, "He's tall, dark, and handsome. And I love him." I said, "Yes."

3. Strategists need time to think it through. If this is the first time you have discussed a problem or project with a Strategist, he or she will not be able to give you an immediate answer. Give them time to think it through and get back to you.

4. Give your Strategists their information in writing. They want to look back on it a thousand times to ensure they are doing it right. Strategists are our people who will describe what needs to be done, once; and then they repeat the instructions again and again and again, because they do not think that we are getting it. Next time your Strategists come to you and give instructions on how to do something, grab a pad of paper and write down the key points as they are talking. When they start to repeat say, "I was writing down all the key points. Did I get them all?" and hand the Strategists your list. They will look at it and either accept it as is or make a couple of additions in writing, and walk away. You will have shortened a 30-minute conversation to

five minutes. If you are the Strategist who keeps repeating yourself, describe the details for them once, face-to-face, then hand them the written instructions. They will have all the detail in their hands to look back on.

5. If you ask them a question, shut up and let them think it through. When we ask Strategists a question they start a thought process. Inside their head they gather together all of the details he knows about that particular topic, silently. Because Strategists collect information, and have good memories, this process of searching their memories for all of the details they have collected about a particular topic can take quite some time. Then, still without talking, Strategists put those details into a logical, sequential order, in their heads. Next, they analyze the information, still without talking. They are looking at what's right and what's wrong and what's good and what's bad. Then, after completely analyzing the information, the Strategist will make a decision, still without talking! And then on a good day, if we are really, really lucky, our Strategists will share their decision with us. The Strategist's decision-making process can be quite lengthy.

In the conversation that I described at the end of Chapter 7, between an Enthusiastic Activist and a Strategist, an Activist will ask a question, wait two seconds, ask a second question, ask a third question two seconds after that, and then ask a fourth question. By the fourth question the Activist was thinking, "He's stupid." This kind of conversation drives the Enthusiastic Activist crazy. It drives the Strategist crazy, as well. What's happening with the Strategist in these conversations?

We ask a Strategist a question and he or she starts a thought process. If we ask a second question two seconds later, the Strategist has to stop the first thought process and start a second thought process. Then we interrupt that thought process with a third question, and he or she has to stops the second thought process and start a third thought process. By the fourth question, the Strategist is thinking one of two things: either, "Shut up and let me think," or "Just go ahead and make a decision because I'm so confused I can't think anymore!"

6. Give your Strategists all of their details, up front. Otherwise, you will get a multitude of questions asking for the details. We see this in the office when documents coming back to us covered in red questions in the margins, asking for more detail.

7. Let your Strategists set the deadlines when you have that leeway. If you set a deadline for them, they probably won't meet it because they will not feel that they have done a good enough job. This is the person in the office who you know you don't have to check up on because they always do a good job, they just haven't met the deadline.

8. The more air space you give your Strategists, without filling up that air space with your own chatter, the more of an invitation you will have

given to your Strategists to talk. As I have learned to be quiet and let my husband talk, the more he does talk. I learn more about him and his thoughts and feelings, and we communicate better. Use this strategy with your Strategists who are extremely quiet.

Common situations

Situation:

One family described this situation to me. They were out for some exercise as a family. Dad and oldest son were on bikes. Mom and younger son were on rollerblades. The oldest son dashed ahead on his bike. They were on a pathway to Heritage Park, in Calgary, Canada. The entrance to Heritage Park is marked by a 30-foot wooden 'H.' The oldest son had wanted to climb that wooden 'H' since the family moved into the area. So, the oldest son raced for the wooden 'H' with his dad, leaving mom and the younger son well behind on their rollerblades. 20 minutes later the oldest son came back to mom crying, "Dad won't let me climb the wooden 'H'."

Mom asked, "Why not?" Son sobbed, "I don't know!" Mom responded, "Well, let me talk to dad about it." Dad rejoined the family a few minutes later and mom asked, "Why didn't you let Chris climb the 'H.' He's wanted to since we moved into the area." Dad's response was, "There are no signs."

Dad is a Strategist. He needs to do things right. If there are no signs saying you can climb the wooden 'H,' he won't. Mom is an Enthusiast. Her reaction was, "If there are no signs saying you can't climb the wooden 'H,' then it's OK." Enthusiasts find it easier to beg for forgiveness than to ask permission. Mom and dad were both looking for signs for exactly the opposite reasons, based on their communication styles. They did resolve the issue. Mom asked, "Do you mind if I take Chris back and let him climb the wooden 'H'." Dad's response was, "No, I don't mind, but I'm not coming with you!" Perfect resolution for the situation.

Situation:

A few years ago, with our three-year-old daughter in the back seat in the car, I picked Theode up from work on a Friday afternoon. His first comment, as he was getting into the car was, "Can we stop and pick up that piece for the dishwasher on the way home?" The dishwasher had been out of commission for about three weeks. I had been running around all day and my response was, "No, I'm tired. Let's just go home." He didn't mind and got into the passenger seat. As we drove, I was thinking of solutions for picking up that piece for the dishwasher. I asked, "Can we pick up the piece tomorrow, Saturday." "No, remember all those things we have planned. We won't have time." "Is the shop open on Sunday?" "No, I checked." (Of course he did, being a Strategist. As an Activist, I would have checked on Sunday at about 10:00 a.m., found out it wasn't open, and planned on doing something else.) Then I thought, maybe we should stop and pick it up, but I hadn't completely decided. So I asked Theode, "Do you want to stop and pick up the piece for the dishwasher or not?" We were actually driving almost right by the shop on the way home. It was only a block off our route. When an Activist indicates indecision it means she has already changed her mind. Someone at a workshop called it mind games. But it isn't really playing mind games. All of this is happening unconsciously, for the Activist. So I asked my husband if he wanted to stop for the piece for the dishwasher or not. We had a mile or two before we got to the turnoff for the shop.

He said, "Well, I've had the dishwasher apart for three weeks. Remember when I tried making a new filter. But that didn't work. And then I tried to clean the (whatever) and that didn't work either."

We were getting closer to the turnoff.

"Honey," I interrupted, "did you want to stop for the piece for the dishwasher, or not?"

"Well," he responded, "we can't go tomorrow because we have to go shopping. And then we have to clean the house. And our friends are coming over for dinner tomorrow with their kids. So we won't have time to go tomorrow. And we can't go Sunday because the shop isn't open."

By now we were only two blocks away from the turnoff.

"Honey," I said in a loud, frustrated voice that indicated I was trying to not get angry, "did you want to stop for the piece for the dishwasher or not?"

"Well, the kitchen is a mess right now. I have the door of the dishwasher off. I know that you're upset about the mess. I just don't know what else I can do. I guess I could try…"

We had now passed the turnoff for the shop, but I was not going to let this go!

"HONEY!" I am really angry at this point, gripping the steering wheel, and shouting, "DO YOU WANT TO STOP FOR THE PIECE FOR THE DISHWASHER, OR NOT?"

And a little voice pipes up from the back seat, "Daddy. Just say 'Yes.'" (A girl after my own heart!)

What was going on in this conversation? I was in Activist mode. I had already changed my mind, but wanted confirmation from him that we should stop. His answer should have been, "Yes," but as a Strategist, before he can even give a 'Yes' or 'No' answer, he has to go through all of his details, and analyze them.

Does this conversation sound familiar? Many of us have conversations exactly like this, almost daily, and they end in anger or tears.

Yet, as you keep this information in your mind, and work with the different people in your life, you will find yourself making adjustments to the way you talk with people from different quadrants.

Situation:

When we moved into our beautiful house in the southwest of Calgary, in 1998, I was determined not to do things the way I had in the old house. How does an Enthusiast usually pack and move? Everything is done at the last minute. As the packers are walking out the door with the boxes, I'm shouting, "Wait! I have one more thing for that box!" And when you get to the new house, then what? Then you live out of boxes for seven years. Doesn't everybody?

Determined to keep the new house organized, beautiful, and clutter-free, I decided to hire a someone to organize the new house for us. We hired Tricia, a Pacifying Strategist. Her home is immaculate. I was over at her house one day to pick something up, and she was ironing the family's t-shirts. You Strategists are asking, "What's wrong with that?"—the rest of us know the answer!

Tricia was delighted with the prospect of being paid for something that she took pleasure in. The first thing she had us do is go over to the new house with tape measures. We had to measure everything. Do you know that there are eight ways to measure a cupboard? Front to back, diagonally, depth from the wall, width, height, etc. Then she took the measurements home and drew our house, to scale. When she phoned me and told me what she had done, I could hear the satisfaction in her voice. She was quite proud that it had only taken 10 hours to do it.

Ten hours! We were paying her by the hour! I could not believe it. She was gouging us! (A thought straight from the Activist part of me which is most concerned with money). Was she gouging us? No. Not deliberately. She was doing exactly what I was paying her to do, a good job. For a Strategist, this was part of doing a good job. That's the main reason I said nothing to her. I had picked Tricia very specifically because she was so detail-oriented and would do a great job. Her process drove me crazy. My husband heard many times over the next few weeks, "Do you know what she's doing now?"

After drawing up the house, to scale, the next thing she did was number all of the cupboards, closets, etc. Then she made a list of everything that would go into each cupboard and closet. Next she came to me and told me that when I was packing everything, I should put everything for cupboard #1, into box #1. You number boxes when you're moving? My blank stare must have communicated a message by this time.

Her process was unbelievable, to me. The end result was incredible. I got exactly what I had hired her for—a beautifully organized home. Everything is still exactly the way she planned it. There is a place for everything and everything in its place. Everything was well planned and logical. Years later Tricia still has those lists, should I ever need them again.

I deliberately hired someone who had strengths where I had weaknesses. I could have organized my own house, but it would have taken me hours of research to figure what would really work, because I don't come by those skills naturally. Or, I could hire someone who naturally had those skills, hold my tongue, and keep out of her way so she could do the job I was paying her to do.

Understanding the Communication Styles allows me to identify my own strengths and weaknesses. Instead of beating myself for weeks on end because I'm procrastinating and not getting anything accomplished, I can look at the tasks, at my strengths and weaknesses and decide whether it's time to develop my weaknesses into strengths or if my time is better used accepting what will be difficult for me and figure out another way to get the job done.

Situation:

A couple was telling me about getting each other gifts. Cindy gave 44-year-old Todd a surprise birthday party at a laser tag game. We've done this with the kids. They chase each other around for 20 minutes, trying to see how many people they can shoot with laser guns, trying not to be hit themselves. A computer counts the number of hits from the special vests they wear. Todd had expressed interest in participating at one of the kid's laser tag parties they had previously attended. Cindy thought it was a great idea for him. So, she sent out the secret invitations to all of his males friends to meet at the laser tag building. To get him there, she told him that they were going to one of their son's soccer games. But she kept making the wrong turns. Cindy is an Activist, yet, in the car, as she's trying to get them to laser tag, she kept saying (in an airhead tone), "I just don't know what I'm thinking. How could I take another wrong turn." (Activists would never use that tone of voice, for real. He should have clued in.) He didn't. By the time they got to the laser tag building, he was pretty angry. Then he realized it was a surprise party. He wasn't really impressed, and, as a Pacifying Strategist, it took him a bit to calm down. Strategists do not like surprises. They like the process. Tell them what you are doing, and let them enjoy the anticipation. Strategists are into long-term planning. They do not need instant gratification. They enjoy the process of planning and following the plan.

Two months after the surprise party, Todd bought Cindy a diamond ring. But he couldn't buy it outright. So he put it on an installment plan. Then he told her that he had bought it, but was making payments. As a Strategist, he was enjoying the process so much he thought Cindy could enjoy it along with him. Cindy is an Enthusiast Activist. She wants instant gratification. He was driving her crazy. Every once in a while he'd mention that he was getting closer to having the ring paid off. Cindy was ready to explode. She just wanted the ring! Then, in September, he told her that he had the ring paid off, but, because it was so expensive, he would give it to her for Christmas, thinking that she would enjoy the anticipation. Instead, not only was he keeping her on tetherhooks, knowing that he did have the ring but wasn't going to give it to her, he had also ruined her Christmas, in September, by taking away the surprise of opening her Christmas present!

Strategists enjoy the process. They are on the indirect side of the chart. Strategists like to be diplomatic but their focus is on getting the job done. Pacifists are also on the indirect side of the chart, but they are people-oriented, as described next.

Chapter 9
The Pacifist

Primary Driving need: To get along

Our Pacifists are completely focused on getting along with others and creating a peaceful environment. In fact, their motto is Peace at any price. They are always taking other people into consideration and wanting everyone to feel good and to get along. These are our nurturers. They love taking care of other people and seeing that others' needs are being met. Pacifists are sensitive to body language and to the unconscious signals that other people give. Pacifists will approach anyone who is having a hard time to see how they can help. Our Pacifists are our rescuers. They can always be found doing things for other people, trying to get people to make up and get along.

Secondary Driving need: Security

More than any of the other quadrants, our Pacifists need security. They hate change. They will have learned how to do something one way 20 years ago, and still want to do it that way. You will hear comments like, "That's the way we've always done it." "It's worked for us this way for five years, now."

Pacifists are the most resistant to a change in routine. They want routine. They create routines and they stick with those routines, forever. Pacifists are the most rigid quadrant with regard to vents and situations, yet they are the most flexible with people. They are rarely spontaneous. In school, these children have the hardest time if the teacher changes the schedule, unexpectedly. These are the children who have the hardest time adjusting to a substitute teacher.

Doug shared a common problem that parents of Pacifist children face. Doug, an Enthusiast, would be bopping around the house getting different things done, before heading out shopping. At the last minute, when he was ready to walk out the door, he would scoop up Brian, his two-year-old son. Brian would start screaming and Doug didn't have a clue what the problem was. The problem was that Brian was a Pacifist, and an unexpected change will upset him. Doug learned pretty quickly that he needed to give Brian a five minute warning. "Five minutes and the TV goes off." "Five minutes until bedtime." "Five minutes until it's time to come in for dinner." That five-minute (or 10-minute) warning made all the difference. To this day, Doug has to talk with Brian's teachers during the first week of school. Brian is in Grade Six, now. Doug usually starts by saying, "You've probably noticed that Brian doesn't handle a change in routine very well." (During the first week of school, what routine is there?) The teacher always responds, "I've noticed." If the teacher has made the mistake, for Brian, of saying that "this is the way we'll be doing it from now on," and then changes the routine, Brian will quietly point the teacher had said they were going to do it the other way, "from now on."

General characteristics

Pacifists are very quiet people. We will often label them as shy. They walk quietly, they talk quietly, they dress quietly, and they even drive quietly, because they hate public attention. These are the people in the office who never speak up in a meeting. They often have great ideas, but will not share those ideas in a group. If you really want to include the Pacifists, get their ideas before or after the meeting, and present their ideas to the rest of the group (giving credit to your Pacifists, of course!) Quit trying to force your Pacifists to speak up during a meeting—you are simply creating a dangerous situation for them.

These are our gentle people. They are gentle with people's feelings, and with other people, physically. When I shake hands with a Pacifist, I know it. They shake hands gently, because they do not want to hurt my hand. I am always careful to be more gentle when I shake their hands, as well. They do not like being hurt. As children, they are less adventurous, choosing crafts over climbing on the playground. They choose activities that are safer, less likely to end in pain. Pacifists tend to stay away from contact sports and often express interest in the arts, drama, and music for their extracurricular activities. These children dislike engaging in rough physical play with their siblings, and they are more sensitive to pain. They will cry over something that an Enthusiast or Activist child would not even notice.

One client shared a situation where June, a Pacifist, was leaving her secondment position, to return to her original position. She had been in the secondment for a year. When someone was leaving this particular office, everyone would sign a card, give flowers and a gift, have a cake, and a farewell party on the afternoon of the last day. A week before the party, June went to her supervisor, in private. June said, "I know everyone knows that I'm going back to my original department next week. And I've really enjoyed working here. You have all been so wonderful to me. I know I shouldn't bring this up, but you are probably planning on having a going away party. Everyone here really enjoys these parties, and I think you really should have it. I just don't want to be there,"—at her own farewell party!

Even that much attention was too much for this Pacifist. So, they went ahead and had June's farewell party without her. However, one of her office friends stopped over at her house that evening and dropped off the card and flowers and gift and half of the cake. No public attention for the Pacifists.

Along with the strong aversion to public attention, our Pacifists do not accept praise very well. When you thank them for doing something, or praise them for a job well done, they reply will be, "Oh, it was nothing," or "Frank did all the work," and they will actually hand the praise over to someone else. They minimize their own efforts.

Our Pacifists are extremely reliable people. If they tell you they will get back to you about something, they will. And they have no problem doing things your way, because they want you to feel good about the job.

Pacifists are polite, courteous, and diplomatic. They find nice things to say, or do not say anything at all. They have known since birth how to listen. They genuinely care about how things are going in your life. They want to know if there is anything they can do for you to make things better in your personal and professional life. Pacifists cooperate with others, and work very well in a team environment where everyone is sharing the goals, and jobs, of the team. The Pacifists are steady, reliable workers. They will come in early and go home late, regularly, to ensure that everything gets done.

Pacifists are nice, quiet, genuine, caring people. This was the teacher that everyone loved—he or she couldn't keep discipline in the classroom, but most of us loved him or her so much, we didn't create too much chaos. They listen. I'm an Enthusiast and I have a basic driving need to talk. Pacifists have known since birth how to listen. I have never met a Pacifist I did not like because they listen to me! Sometimes, they listen to me to the detriment of the conversation. An Enthusiast will ask a Pacifist a question. The Pacifist will start to answer. The Enthusiast will interrupt what the Pacifist is saying, and the Pacifist allows the interruption.

The rest of us sometimes, especially Activists, see our Pacifists as doormats. We can walk all over them. Activists have absolutely no respect for Pacifists because Pacifists always give in. Activists see Pacifists as weak.

Pacifists will get to an appointment up to two hours early. They loathe being late, and plan their time to ensure they have plenty of time to ease into a situation. They also would never be impolite enough to arrive late.

Pacifists talk about what's happening in your life, and how you feel about things. Pacifists like warm fuzzies and group hugs. They are the people in the office who can rub your shoulder, or give you a hug and you accept it, because you know they are genuine. They are naturally touchy-feelly and understand, instinctively, that a touch makes a connection and calms people down. A touch from a Pacifist is rarely threatening. Rather, it is comforting.

Pacifists will often dress in a more comfortable way, even in the office. Women will wear cardigans in the office, instead of a suit jacket. Men will wear sports jackets with patches on the sleeves, instead of a more formal suit. Everyone knows they can go talk to a Pacifist. In the office, in friendships, and even with more casual acquaintances like a group of parents gathered to watch the kids do something, anyone who needs to talk about a problem will gravitate towards the Pacifist.

The Pacifists strongest sense is the sense of touch. They like to touch others. Our Pacifist middle son likes to be petted and to have his back scratched, daily! They may be extra sensitive to rough materials or obtrusive seams in their clothing. These people will touch others. They are kinesthetic learners, generally. (Kinesthetic learners, are hands-on learners.) They like to do what they are being taught, instead of hearing about it or looking at pictures. Pacifist babies are the most likely to put everything into their mouths. Even Pacifist adults will be seen to chew on the ends of pencils and pens. Pacifists are lured towards anything that looks like it might be soft to touch; baby animals, fur rugs, or velvet.

Challenges

No Conflict Pacifists will do anything to avoid conflict. They will always give in, go along, do it the other person's way, to ensure that everyone stays calm and happy. In relationships, this creates problems, because even Activists have moments of wanting real agreement. If we have learned, over time, that our Pacifists will not tell us what's on their minds, we are left guessing. If you won't tell me who you are, what you believe in, and what makes you feel comfortable and uncomfortable you are an unsafe person. As an Activist, I often see diplomacy as lying. Speak your mind. If a Pacifist goes along with a decision, or says something nice about a situation, and two to six months later, tells me they were actually thinking something different, I may think that the Pacifist did not tell me the truth at the time. Therefore, I am learning to not trust the Pacifist.

No Decisions Pacifists prefer not to make decisions because it might hurt somebody's feelings. So, our Pacifists usually rely on Enthusiasts or Activists to make the decisions. You might have taught Pacifist to do something three years ago. In an effort to ensure that you feel good about it, he or she will ask you how to do it, every single time. It might even be a daily chore. We begin to think that Pacifists are not very intelligent. Of course, they are intelligent. They are simply fulfilling their primary need to get along by checking with you each time.

No Change Pacifists, of all the quadrants, are most resistant to change. They want everything to stay exactly the way it is right now, because that gives them security. They feel safe when they have routines to follow.

No Self-Direction Pacifists have a hard time setting personal goals that have nothing to do with anyone else. Most of the activity in a Pacifist's life revolves around other people. Pacifists help others. When they decide to do something, they will have taken into consideration everyone else in their lives, and base their decision on how other's will react to it, as opposed to what the Pacifist really wants to do.

Hardest thing to teach a Pacifist

Pacifists will not become assertive. Pacifists do not share with other people what they want. They do not stand up for themselves. They will not tell you what their boundaries are, and what makes them truly happy.

One four-year-old Pacifist child, after seeing the commercials on television for children who are starving to death in the Third World went up to his bedroom to pack all of his clothes and toys to send to those impoverished children.

Our middle son is a strong Pacifist. Our oldest son is an Activist. Continually, we step into their discussions and insist that our Pacifist child is allowed to keep his own possessions. I have seen him giving his older brother his allowance. "He wants it, mom. It'll make him happy," he reasoned.

In our house we often discuss what the kids want to be when they grow up. Our Activist oldest son is planning on becoming a millionaire and taking control of the world. Our Pacifist second child has decided that he, too, wants to become a millionaire so that he can make sure that everyone in the world has food, shelter, clothing, and presents at Christmas.

Last Hallowe'en I went trick-or-treating with our three children. Our oldest son only went to five houses because he was feeling ill. Our middle son, the Pacifist, only went for another 15 minutes, then went home to spend the evening with his older brother. Our six-year-old daughter, the Enthusiast, went for another two hours. She was playing a game where people give you candy. Life was grand! When I got home, I found that our Pacifist middle son had given his older brother all of the candy he had collected.

It might seem wonderful that our Pacifist children are so caring—and it is, on the one hand. But if we don't train them how to take care of themselves, they will become doormats. I am constantly teaching our middle son that he can take care of himself and give others what they want. He should not give to others and end up with nothing himself. We will never be able to train our Pacifists to take what they want regardless of the other person. Their basic driving need is to nurture others. But we can teach them to compromise so that both get something they want. My boys decided to put all of their Hallowe'en candy into a large bowl and share it. Of course, their Enthusiast little sister was having none of this sharing, and hid all of her candy in her room!

Personal space

A Pacifist's desk space, or personal space, will be as tidy as possible, but cluttered. They cannot say, "No." So in the office, they will have stacks of work to get through, because they have taken on everything everyone has every asked them to do.

Pacifists in the office have the candy dish on their desks. One Pacifist I met had four candy dishes on her desk! They have little stuffed animals sitting on their computers. Pacifists will either have a plant on their desk, or they will be taking care of the plants in the office. Pacifists have family pictures on their wall. They will have pictures of the family pet and other people's families and family pets. The Pacifist likes the kitten and puppy calendars.

Employment

Pacifists are attracted to the nurturing professions: teacher, preschool teacher, nurse, social worker, and psychologist. In a more corporate environment, Pacifists are attracted to Human Resources, although they need to understand that Human Resources people often have to take care of the negative aspects of Human Resources in the office—including downsizing, etc. Human Resources employees often know something negative is coming down the line, and have to protect confidentiality and not share it with those it will affect, until the right time. This aspect of Human Resources will deeply affect our Pacifists, and they wake up at 2:00 a.m. worrying about the people who will be affected. Pacifists also enjoy routine office work. They enjoy support positions: secretary, paralegal, administrative assistant. Our 18-year-old Pacifists, who have few job skills, will be attracted to positions like daycare worker, data entry clerk, factory worker, seamstress, chef or cook.

How the Pacifist gets angry

Anger is attacking someone. Pacifists never attack. Never! Instead of attacking, our Pacifists immediately identify the fear or the pain they are feeling, and they cry. They have discovered the miracle flush for the adrenaline, tears. They feel the fear. They do not stand and attack. Ever! If a Pacifist attacks, he or she has gone to one of their other quadrants to enable the attack. They are passive and will give in to a more aggressive quadrant. But, if this person eventually blows up in a rage, he or she has stepped into one of the other quadrants to do so; Activist, Enthusiast, or Strategist.

Pacifists do not get angry; they get sick. They will feel resentment, which they never show. They will complain to themselves, never out loud. The adrenaline is released time and again because they are very sensitive and, inside, are reacting to every situation around them. Because they are reacting to every situation around them, and judging most of those incidents and situations to be unsafe, they are constantly releasing the adrenaline into their systems, but never truly flushing it out. If there is a genetic weakness in the body, the chemicals beat a pathway to that genetic weakness until, finally, our Pacifists are seriously ill. (Deepak Chopra Quantum Healing; Louise Hays, How to Heal your Life). They might not get seriously ill, but they seem to pick up every bug, and always seem to have a cold, or be down with the flu.

Working with the Pacifist

1. Talk softly. Pacifists react very strongly to loud noises. Loud noise means danger. Many Pacifist children will scream and cry when the household fire alarm goes off (because the oven ate another casserole!) Pacifists only like an open work environment if everyone gets along.

2. Pacifists need time to answer your questions. Do not jump in with your own thoughts. If you do, Pacifist will never talk. Pacifists have been interrupted so often, that, as they get older, they do not offer any comments at all, because they expect to be interrupted. So wait for their response, quietly.

3. Be polite, courteous, and diplomatic. Greet them with a, "Good morning." Say, "Please," and "thank you," when asking them for anything. They will work so much better with you if you treat them as a valued team member.

4. Use Pacifist language to really create a bond with the Pacifist: gentle, get along, teamwork, guaranteed, stability, always done it, feelings, agreement, consensus, everyone, peace, cooperate, soft, personally, etc.

5. Get their ideas and suggestions in private. Praise them in private. In fact, the best way to give praise to a Pacifist is in writing. They will keep that Thank you card forever. You can even go one step further, by sending that card to their home, so that their family sees it. Be specific about the situation, and very specific as to how their actions helped out the rest of the team.

6. Teach your younger Pacifists to take care of themselves while they are taking care of others. As a supervisor or manager of Pacifists, you may have the opportunity to coach adult Pacifists to protect their time, or to say "No" when asked to do a job that A). they should not take on, because it is someone else's responsibility, or B). they will not be able to fit it into the already overwhelming schedule .

7. In a decision-making process, give your Pacifists time to make the decision. I had one client in London, England, tell me, after I had taught the Communication Styles, that I had just explained why he got out of management. He had been in management for 10 years, and finally left, because making decisions was so very difficult.

I don't share this to encourage all of our Pacifists to get out of management. Pacifist managers, need to realize that, for them, decision-making and dealing with problem people is very difficult. When making decisions, keep in mind what is in the best interests of the organization. This helps ease the decision making process.

8. If there is a change coming down the line, tell your Pacifists as soon as you know. They need a lot of time to think about how the change will affect them, and they will also consider how the change will affect everyone else involved. If it is going to affect anyone in an adverse way, you'll see the Pacifists spending more time with those people. As with Pacifist children, give a warning that routines are going to change.

9. Give the Pacifists lots of pats on the back for making good decisions. This will lead them to gain confidence that they can work more independently.

10. If you are making a team decision and need the Pacifist's inputs, go get everyone else's agreement first. When you talk with the Pacifists, let them know that everyone else is already in agreement. If you don't, your Pacifists will be going around talking to everyone before they can participate in the decision.

Common situations

Situation:

One couple, Sheila and Bill, went to Hawaii for their honeymoon. They were able to go scuba diving, on a very shallow dive, without taking lessons. On the one-hour boat trip to the dive site, someone walked them through an instruction manual. Much of what the instructor talked about were the dangers of doing something wrong. Sheila, our Enthusiast, started getting a bit scared, then decided everything would be fine. She knew she would have an instructor watching out for her the whole time, and she stopped listening about halfway through the training. Bill, our Pacifist, paid attention, saw the huge risk involved, and when they got out to the diving site, refused to dive. In a later discussion, Bill said that he would do some reading on scuba diving, so he could really understand it. Then, he would take lessons, and, next trip to Hawaii, he would be prepared to scuba dive. Pacifists will not take risks, either physically, mentally, or emotionally.

Situation:

Often, in workshops, I will have the participants divide into their dominant quadrant groups; Enthusiasts, Activists, Strategists, and Pacifists, will gather in separate areas in the room. The assignment is: you are coworkers. One of you will have to go to Hawaii for that three-week convention. The group has to decide who gets to go. The Enthusiasts never get around to deciding who's going because they get too caught up in the conversation.

"Hawaii. I love Hawaii. All that blue water. Speaking of water, last night I put my three-year-old in the bath. There was water all over the place.

Oh, baths! I have to stop by the store on my way home and pick up some soap. I was at that store just last week and they had a great sale on ginger. They have great sales. I made a great batch of ginger snap cookies a few weeks ago. Burnt every one. Have you been to that new Chinese restaurant? I just love ginger beef..." Anyone lost? Enthusiasts think by association. Their conversations are perfectly logical, from their point of view. If you find this kind of conversation annoying, you are not an Enthusiast, but the other person sure is.

The Activists take two minutes to make the decision about who is going to Hawaii, and sit there for the next hour impatiently waiting for everyone else to finish up. The Strategists are constantly calling me over to get more detail with questions like, "Jeanette, are we sailing to Hawaii, or flying?" etc. The Pacifists never make a decision. I have actually done this as a two-hour exercise, and still, the Pacifists will not make a decision. Every single one of them wants to go, but not one of them will say so, because that would hurt everyone else's feelings.

Another exercise I do is to have all of the quadrants list what really works for them in conversations with people from the other quadrants, and what they really dislike in those conversations. The Pacifists will not do the dislikes list, because someone in the room might be hurt.

Situation:
Four friends go out for dinner. Each quadrant is represented. The Activist looks at the menu and is ready to order immediately. (If your aren't careful, your Activist will order for you, too.) And Activists order the same thing every time, because "it's only food, after all. Let's eat and get on to our next task."

The Enthusiast is having too much fun talking to ever get around to looking at the menu. The waiter will come back again and again and the Enthusiast will say, "No, we're not ready to order yet. But you can bring us another round of drinks." Be careful with the Enthusiast, or you'll never get to eat.

Never take a Strategist to a restaurant with a long menu. They will read each item, and they'll listen very carefully when the waiter explains the specials. Then, the Strategist will be calling the waiter back over to the table asking, "What comes with this entre?" and "could you explain Special #2 again." At closing time, your Strategist will still be collecting details, and you'll be starving.

The Pacifist will be very courteous and polite. He or she will sit at the table listening to the conversation. He or she will read through the menu when everyone else does. He or she will then close the menu, put it down, and turn to everyone else at the table and asking, "What are you going to have?" The Pacifist will order what someone else is having.

What kinds of foods do each of the quadrants like? And how do they eat? Pacifists like food to have the same consistency. They don't like soups with chunks of stuff in them. Pacifists like comfort foods, like mashed potatoes. Enthusiasts like to work for their food—eating lobster and crab with their hands. They like sharp, strong-tasting food, and foods that have a combination of consistencies. Strategists will eat one food on their plate, until it is gone. In fact, their tendency is to put only one food at a time on their plate. They hate messy dishes, and eating with their hands. Activists will eat anything—after all, it's only food. But the Activist wants to think he or she is getting good value for the money. They like all-you-can-eat buffets.

Situation:

When we first meet people, we are most at ease with people who come from our dominant quadrant. They speak our language. However, these relationships do not last very long. Think about two Enthusiasts being best friends: both of them talking, neither one listening. I had that happen to me, and the relationship didn't last. I didn't get enough air time, and I had all kinds of things I wanted to say!

Two Activists have major conflicts within a very short time as they both try to take control and make the other person do it their way! I've seen my oldest son do this. Initially, he and another Activist boy in the neighborhood were inseparable. After two days, my guy stormed into the house saying, "I'm never talking to him again." Because my children have been fully exposed to this information, I was able to talk with my Activist son about his friend. I explained that they were both Activists, both trying to take control. At times, each of them needed to give in and do it the other person's way. They are not best friends, but they have been able to maintain a friendship by understanding how to work together.

Two Strategists don't look like friends at all. One Strategist works alone in her corner, and the other Strategist works alone in some other corner, in some other office. The only time they talk is to get more details from each other. Where's the friendship?

Two Pacifists can never make a decision. "Í don't know, where do you want to go for lunch? I don't know, where do you want to go for lunch? I don't know, where do you want to go for lunch?" They starve to death, because neither wants to make a decision.

The best team is a group of people who come from each of the different quadrants because they balance each others' strengths and weaknesses. The hard part is learning to work with others and allow them their processes, when their ways of doing and being are so different from our natural inclination.

In order to work with others, step into the middle. We do this naturally in many situations. We know that there are some people we can slap on the back and joke with. There are others, with whom we would never be this informal. We have all noticed, throughout the description of the four quadrants, that we have characteristics from each quadrant, and, although there is one quadrant that we would say is dominant, we do not have all of the characteristics of that quadrant. We are a combination. We have whole brains; we have all of the quadrants in us. In different situations, we will show different sides of ourselves. We naturally bring out the different sides of ourselves to deal with those different situations. However, I also believe that we will deliberately seek out situations where we can express those different sides of ourselves. Many of us recognize that we are different at home than we are at work, and different at church than we are when we go out with friends or when we go to a committee meeting. We seek to

Express all aspects of ourselves, maybe to assure ourselves all parts of us are acceptable.

In dealing with others, we need to step into that middle circle as much as possible to ensure cooperation and good communication. When standing in the middle circle, we can respond to a person or a situation in a way that will gain cooperation. If we retreat to our dominant quadrant, we are likely to escalate the problematic situations and create conflict. We create resentment, confusion, and miscommunication if we stay in our dominant quadrant to deal with every situation.

We have been stepping into the middle circle in many situations, instinctively. With this body of information you can now consciously respond to someone, based on which quadrant they use to communicate. We begin using our thinking brains to help us in communication, as opposed to allowing our safety brain to determine how to respond and react.

Personality conflicts disappear when you know the words to use, and the way to express yourself to make an immediate connection with everyone, in every situation. However, most of us will never be able to do that in all situations. In situations that our safety brain judges to be unsafe, we go back to communicating from our dominant quadrant. Even though I know I will be creating conflict instead of cooperation, there are still many times that, in a stressful situation, I will favor Activist mode, becoming pushy, loud, and more abrasive. I know this creates long-term bad feelings, yet, sometimes it feels like I have no control. My safety brain took over too fast, and too completely. But, more and more often, as I get more practice stepping into the middle circle, I am able to stay in that circle even when stressed.

I know how to talk my way out of getting a speeding ticket. I used to be a Customs Officer, and, with the knowledge and practice I have in communications, I have talked my way out of getting quite a few. However, one Sunday, my flight left Calgary a couple of hours late. When we arrived at the other end, we sat on the tarmac for over an hour before getting to a gate and off the plane. I still had a four-hour drive in front of me, and it was already 10:00 p.m. I was looking at getting to bed at 2:30 a.m. (after ironing my suit) and getting up again at 5:30 a.m. unless I got to my hotel earlier. There isn't much traffic at that time of night, so I was traveling slightly (read way) over the speed limit. Of course, I was pulled over. I knew how not to get a ticket. But I was tired and irritated and stressed and now the police officer was wasting more of my time! So, instead of stepping into the middle circle and dealing with the police officer in an effective way, I was completely in Activist mode. I think I actually said to the officer, "Just give me the ticket so I can get going."

Most of us have been in shopping situations with people who come from the opposite quadrants. Any big-ticket item is bound to bring out the Strategists in full force. Buying a house, a car, or furniture takes months with a Strategist. The Strategist will be collecting details and visiting all of the stores that carry that item. I have learned to let my husband do his detailed analysis. He does the research. He chooses which will be the best buy. During this process my only input is the features that I consider non-negotiable. When he has completed his analysis and made his decision, then I step into the process. I'm the one who negotiates for the best deal. Time and again, by recognizing and working with our strengths in this way, we have gotten marvelous deals. I never expect my husband to negotiate price. If he has decided to buy something, he will simply pay whatever price the salesperson demands.

One parent said her middle son, who is a pacifying Strategist, will go see a movie, and come home to describe the movie to her detail by detail. She hates this. She wants to go see the movie, too, and her son ruins the movie for her by describing it detail by detail. Her son, being a Strategist, doesn't hear her when she says, "Don't tell me about it. I want to go see it, too." To Strategists, having someone describe the movie to them first, would be great, because then they would have enough detail to be sure they would enjoy the movie. Our solution was to start sending her Strategist son to tell her Strategist husband about the movie. They would both enjoy that.

A quick exploration of this material, with regards to marriages and committed relationships, should prevent many divorces. In love relationships, we are attracted to people who have strengths where we have weaknesses. Opposites attract; now we know why. The very characteristics that attracted you to your partner are exactly the same characteristics that start to drive you crazy, the day after you commit to the relationship. I distinctly being attracted to my husband because he had so much knowledge, he seemed to know something about everything. And he thought things through, completely, before making a decision. Shortly after we got married those two things started driving me crazy. I couldn't share any new information with him, because he already knew everything! And, he kept thinking everything through, completely, before making a decision.

Stay married to the same person. There is no point in divorcing because you will find yourself attracted to the same type of person—maybe even exactly the same person—next time.

The question we need to ask ourselves is, "Why do those very things that attracted us to our partners irritate us after we have committed to the relationship?" When I see my husband thinking things through, completely, one of my 80,000 thoughts per minute is, "I don't think things through, completely." Every time I see my husband's strengths, I remind myself of my weaknesses. I cannot be a weak person, because if I'm weak, I'm not a safe person—or so reasons my safety brain. In our society, we have been trained to look at that other person and tell them, "Stop doing what you are doing, so I don't have to feel this way." So, we point our fingers at our spouses and go to defense-attack, trying to get them to have no strengths. We cannot change someone else. What we should be doing is getting to work on ourselves.

This is where your thinking brain comes in. Realize that whatever it is you see in that other person that irritates you is merely a reflection of you. So, instead of releasing the adrenaline, and going into defense mode, get to work on yourself. Once I realized this, I started looking at my lack of interest in thinking through all the details. Instead of pointing my finger at my husband, I realized I had a couple of choices: I could either accept that the way I make decisions works for me and not judge it as wrong. Or, I could get to work on it, and take more time to look at the details before making a decision. I did a bit of both. Now, when I see my husband taking his time, and looking at all of the details, I don't get defensive. You will have the same experience. Get to work on those things in yourself, that drive you crazy when you see others doing it, and those behaviors will stop driving you crazy.

So, stay married. There is no point in getting a divorce. Get to work on what you consider to be your weaknesses. In the next level we will take a look at this idea that others are simply mirrors of us, in a lot greater detail. In Level V, we will also look at the statement—Stay married. There are abusive relationships that we should abandon. However, many spouses find themselves returning to those relationships time and time again, instead of ending them. Why? That question, and some solutions, will be addresses in Level V.

Once you have shared this body of information with the people you live with and the people you work with, it makes it very easy to get past the barriers of the different quadrants. You can look at your coworker and say,

"Alan, you are being way too much of an Enthusiast here. The details are important, so we need you to listen," or Alan might say, "Kathy, you're being too much a Strategist. We don't need all the detail. Let's just get it done." I hear and use conversations like this all the time with people who have integrated this information into their everyday lives.

The Golden Rule creates personality conflicts, if you follow it to the letter. Instead of treating others the way we want to be treated, in all communication, we need to consider the other person's dominant Communication Style, and communicate with each person from their dominant quadrant. There are no personality conflicts if you use this information in all of your relationships to create cooperation instead of conflict.

LEVEL IV

Make Them Calm Down

Introduction

Make Them Calm Down

We cannot directly calm other people down. But we can affect their need to attack by showing that there is nothing dangerous about us. Level IV will explore specific short- and long-term techniques, strategies, and actual formulas to use to avoid situations that create the need to attack. Instead, we can gain cooperation from people. Each chapter in Level IV focuses on a different technique for dealing with others when they are in defense-attack. Each chapter gives the details to make the technique effective and real life examples to show how and when to use the technique.

Each of Chapters 10 through 17 examines a different way to show others that we are safe to be with. If we can show someone who is raging that we are truly safe to be with, their anger can deflate in seconds, and the person becomes rational and ready to look at solutions.

Chapter 10
They are Right, You Know

They Are Right

The people we have to deal with, whether they are family, friends, coworkers, casual acquaintances, clients, or customers, get angry because they have judged something to be unsafe. They have activated their defense mechanisms and have made the decision that attacking, and maybe even attacking us, is the way to get to safety. Whatever they saw that they judged unsafe has nothing to do with us. It might be something they saw out the window or something that they are remembering someone said to them three weeks ago. Maybe we remind them of somebody from their childhood who was unsafe to be with, for whatever reason. Whatever the reason, it has nothing to do with us. Even if the reason they judge us to be unsafe is something we said, their judgement that we are unsafe still has little to do with us, because it is a judgment—something that comes out of their head. We cannot change that we remind them of someone. We have no control over other people's thoughts. Although Level IV is titled Make Them Calm Down, there is no way to calm other people down. We cannot control how other people think or act. We cannot control what they say, how they say it, or what actions they take. We cannot crawl into other people's minds and bodies and give them the thoughts we want them to have, and make them say the words we want to hear, and manipulate their hands and feet so that they take the actions we want them to take. All of these things are completely impossible.

What we can do is affect how others perceive us. We explored some of this in Chapter 3, where we dealt with body language. There are many things we can do with our body language to show others that we are safe to be with. We also mentioned in Chapter 4 that, in order to keep other people's gateways open, we want to be able to answer "Yes" to all requests, and that it is the picture we draw after saying "Yes" that will be challenging for us. Remember when you are using any of the techniques, you must be genuine. You must really believe the words you are using; otherwise, you risk becoming more dangerous to the other person, instead of less. The other person will realize, from your body language, that you are not being genuine—that you are trying to manipulate them.

There is a difference between manipulation and good communication skills. Manipulation is getting what you want, regardless of the other person. Good communication skills take the other people into consideration and give them something that they want, so that they will give you what you want. In Dr. Stephen Covey's *The 7 Habits of Highly Effective People*[1] he calls the first lose-win. They lose, I win—manipulation. The second is win-win. They win something; I win something. We both walk away from the conversation or situation feeling that we got something out of it that was of equal value to what the other person got out of it.

Why are difficult people difficult? Because it works for them. They are living life in the way their safety brain dictates is safe, otherwise they would not engage in that behavior. People do not engage in unsafe behavior. We do or say only what is safe. Children may do or say things that are not safe, just to try them out. They have seen someone else, real people or television people, doing or saying those things, and they looked like safe things to do or say. They try out the behavior or words, especially at home, testing whether the behavior or words really are safe for them to use. If, as parents, we show them that those are inappropriate words and behaviors, they will stop doing them. Of course, we need to ensure that we are actually showing them that those words and behaviors are inappropriate. If they have learned in the past that we do not mean what we say, then they may know that it is safe to ignore the message we are giving them about this particular behavior, and keep engaging in it. If children continue to engage in the behavior you have said or shown them is inappropriate, on some level the message you have given them is that it is safe behavior. At that point, as parents, we need to assess what messages we give the children, and how we give those messages, so that we start to understand how to calmly give them messages that they acknowledge, understand, and with which they follow through.

By the time people have become adults, the ways they know to keep themselves safe are pretty deeply engrained. If you question the way someone has done something, the intrinsic message you are giving is that the way they did it the first time was wrong. However, the way they did it that first time was right for them, otherwise they would not have done it that way. It was the safe way, in their view. By the time someone does something, they already know that it is the safe thing, the right thing, to do based on their emotions, their expectations, their background, their intention, their thoughts, and the separate elements in the situation. Their safety brain has told them to do or say it. If, even in a very subtle way, you tell them it was the wrong thing to do they will immediately decide that this conversation with you is unsafe. They slam down the gateway, and might even attack you, to get to safety. They may start arguing to try to get you to agree that they were right. If you do not agree, if there is nothing that they can say that will get you to agree that they were right, then they might take it one step further. They might use their body language, their 55% of communication, to try to get you to agree that they were right. The exact behavior that you are wanting them to stop will get worse, as they try to prove to you that it was the right thing to do. How

long can that go on? One lady in one of my training sessions said, "40 years!"
I didn't ask for details.

Here are some of the phrases we use to tell others they are wrong:

> You are wrong. Have you thought of this (other thing)?
> That won't work.
> We've always done it this way.
> Look at what you've done.
> Bob isn't going to like that.
> How could that possibly work?
> What are some other ways to do it?
> You did a good job, but...
> That doesn't make sense.
> You need to think this through.
> You haven't thought this through clearly.

We might think we are putting our words together well, with some of
the above phrases, yet others can perceive that we have told them that they are
wrong. Of course, we can be a lot more obvious, sarcastic, and cruel when we
tell others they are wrong, in which case, we are attacking, as well.

So the first thing we want to be able to do, in all conversations, with
everyone (unless we want them to get defensive and go into attack mode) is
to tell them that they are right, *because they are*. The idea of right is that they
did or said what was the safe thing for them to do or say. They have their
reasons for doing or saying what they did. They have justified their own
actions. Many people have a problem with thinking that those irritating,
offensive, and even evil people that they have to deal with are right. We need
to fully understand and integrate that they are right, from their point of view.
If you cannot actually use the word "right" with them, because you just
cannot quite bring yourself to believe they are right, then use other words.
When we tell someone they are right, we are not telling them that it is OK to
repeat their actions. We are not telling them that it was all right with us that
they did or said what they did or said. What we are doing is understanding
their words or actions from their point of view.

We can say things like:

> You are right in what you did/said.
> I know you had good reasons for what you did/said.
> I understand why you did/said that.
> I know what you did/said was right for you.
> I can see why you did/said that. What you did/said was
> reasonable, I can see that.
> I would have done the same thing.
> I'd like to hear why you did/said that.

Some examples:

That difficult person that you have to deal in the office is right in his or her behavior. He or she has reasons for doing it.

Your mother or mother-in-law was right to have said what she said. She had her own personal reasons, and good reasons for her, to have said that.

Your spouse was right to have done what he or she did. He or she had very strong reasons for doing what he or she did. We don't like what that person did, but we can acknowledge that he or she had reasons for doing it.

Charles Manson was right to have murdered all of those people. The actions were horrid. We would never condone murder. Yet, he had reasons for doing what he did.

We are not agreeing that what these people did was nice. We are not agreeing that they should do it again. We are not agreeing that what they did was moral, legal, or ethical. We know we would never do or say what these people did or said. We know that what they did was, in some cases, horrid and awful. However, we are acknowledging that they had made it right, safe, in their minds, before they acted. We are acknowledging that they had reasons for doing what they did.

In our personal lives we can use this concept to avoid conflict. In your own real-life situations with the people in your life, all you need do in a conversation is to acknowledge that you know they had good reasons, from their point of view, to have done what they did. That is all you are agreeing to. And, you will find that agreement to be enough to help those other people raise up their gateways, calm down, and get back to rational thought, instead of defense and attack mode.

This has happened to many of us with children or partners or coworkers or friends. The exact behavior that we want them to change gets worse. Of course, we then get angry because they are obviously doing it just to defy us. The relationship becomes unsafe. We activate our defense systems and go on the attack to regain our position. Instead, we need to realize that they have engaged in behavior that they are simply not conscious of. Their safety brain is trying to get them to safety. The safest thing for them to do is to get you to agree that they were right. That way, you are showing that they are still accepted in your pack and they are still safe.

We have an alternative to the (potentially 40-year) conflict. We can shorten the discussion down to five seconds if we call them right. When we call someone right, they maintain access to their thinking brains. There is a strong likelihood, although there is no guarantee, that, as soon as you tell them they are right, they will admit their mistake and seek to correct it.

Not everyone will go to defense-attack when you imply that they have said or done something wrong. Some people understand that you are simply voicing an opinion and are able to let you have your say without getting defensive. But, in this chapter, we are specifically talking about the people you have to deal with who do get angry and attack.

When we call someone wrong, they will try to defend their original position. When we tell them they are right, they may immediately switch positions because they did not have to defend the old one. In one training session, Gwen gave an example that in her office they had had a longstanding problem. They finally brought the entire staff together to brainstorm some solutions. Gord had an idea that everyone loved immediately. As everyone started getting enthusiastic about Gord's idea and building on it, Gord was trying to point out all of the things that would not work with his own idea. The reason he was open-minded about his own idea, and able to think logically about why it might not work, was that his gateway was up and he had full access to his thinking brain. If someone had told him that his idea would never work or had immediately started pointing out to him all of the reasons why it was a bad idea, Gord may well have tried to defend his idea and persuade everyone that it would work.

I have used this technique with my children, especially my oldest son, many times. (I won't let him read this book, because he might see this and stop responding to the technique!) If I tell my oldest son that he is right, in whatever it was he said or did, he responds, "Yeah, mom, but it wasn't a good thing to do. Sorry." When I forget to use this technique, and instead tell him how wrong he was, the argument can go on for days as he tries to persuade me that what he did or said was the right thing.

We have an old phrase for this technique—reverse psychology. When I think of those words, I think of manipulation. It was a game that I think I was told to play on my kids when they were really little. If we told them to do exactly what we didn't want them to do, then, out of the need to defy us, they would do exactly the opposite. Tell them, "Go ahead. Stay up all night." Supposedly, they would go to bed immediately. It did not work for me when I tried it, so I gave up!

Instead, we use our understanding of the bridge between the safety brain and the thinking brain. We want their safety brains to judge what we are saying to them as safe, so that they will keep their gateways up and maintain full access to rational, logical thought. Then we can have an objective conversation about consequences and alternative words or actions instead of an argument.

Call people right, because they are. It is a very strong technique in having people stay calm in our presence, and think through the consequences of whatever we are discussing with them. If people are really angry, fully in attack mode, and we tell them they are right, we have opened the possibility that they will immediately calm down and begin to think the situation through, as opposed to staying in attack mode.

If the word "right" still does not work for you, here are some alternative words to use to gain the same results: correct, appropriate, suitable, proper, convenient, rational, reasons, motivation, logic, reasonable, explainable, given your understanding, in your view, from your standpoint.

You understand the concept. Use words that make the statement genuine, for you.

Chapter 11
Pure, Clean Listening Skills

If we fully listen to others, in a way that shows that they are completely safe in expressing whatever they need to express, we are showing that we are completely safe people to be with. If others know that we are going to tell them they are right, they can start looking at the situation rationally, instead of having to defend themselves from us telling them they are wrong. They will stop attacking us because we are truly safe people to be with.

However, that is not usually what we do. Instead, in most conversations that we have with one other person, there are three conversations going on. If we talk to Ed, and Ed is the one talking right now, most of us are not actually listening to Ed. Instead, we have a conversation with ourselves. While Ed is talking, we say to ourselves, "I wish he'd shut up and go away so I could get back to work," or "I really have to go pee. I wonder how I can end this conversation gracefully," or "Oh, that happened to me just last week. If he'd shut up I could tell him how to fix it." We have probably all noticed ourselves doing this. While the other person is talking, we think up the things to say next, or we form our arguments to shoot theirs down, or we make other casual or sarcastic comments to ourselves. Not many of us have ever stopped to realize that the other people we speak with are talking to themselves, too. They say to themselves, "She's looking bored, I'd better wrap this up," or "I didn't say that quite right," or "I have to remember to pick up the kids on the way home." We have all done this as well. So, we talk to ourselves, and they talk to themselves. The third conversation is the words we are voicing to each other. Dr. Stephen Covey says in *The 7 Habits of Highly Effective People*[1] that we use a high percentage of what we say out loud for autobiographical comment.[2] Someone says something and we respond, "That happened to me last year, and here's what I did," or "My mom was just like that," or "My kids used to do the exact same thing," or "I went to that same sale," or "My car did the same thing and..." We take the comments that others voice and we think about how they apply to our own experience and then we voice our own experience. That is called autobiographical comment. The problem with autobiographical comment is that when we make them, we prove to the other person that we were not really listening to them. We were talking to ourselves. With some people, when we show them we were talking to ourselves instead of really listening to them, they understand that they were not important enough to be really listened to. Unsafe conversation, slam goes the gateway and attack—they get angry and make an irritable comment or even fly into a rage. In order to show others that they are important and to truly listen to them, we are going to follow four new rules when listening:

Rule #1: Turn off the voice. From now on, when we are listening to others we are no longer allowed to talk to ourselves. Instead we must completely focus on the other person and what they are saying. The easiest way to turn off the voice is to follow rule number two.

Rule #2: No solutions. No advice We are no longer allowed to think up or give solutions or advice. There are four very strong reasons for not giving solutions and advice.

A. When we give solutions and advice we are holding the other person incompetent. When someone comes to us and asks for advice, their implied message is that they are not capable of thinking this one through themselves. When we give them our solutions and advice we are agreeing that they are not capable. When we give others solutions and advice we are saying, "You're right. You don't have a good idea in your head. Here, use one of mine."

Many of us feel that the people we work with, and even supervise, often behave like a bunch of children. People in the office can be petty, demand attention, and ask dumb questions when they already know the answers. Sometimes we feel that the adults, or near adults, we live with act as though they are two years old. If we want them to be responsible and capable, we need to allow them to be competent. Encourage the people you work and live with to think through to their own solutions and advice. When people come to us asking for advice, I think they are asking for the wrong thing. They should be saying, "Can I use you as a sounding board," or "I just need to hear myself talk this one through." Instead, we ask people for their advice and, in the process, we give the message that we are incompetent. When they jump in with their advice and solutions they are, in effect, agreeing that we are incompetent.

Sometimes, when we ask someone for advice, we really want to hear someone else's thoughts on the subject, because we really are stumped. We have been trying to think up a solution and just can't. However, even in this type of situation we do not want the other person to tell us what to do. Rather, I think we want a smorgasbord of ideas to choose from or we want a direction in which to start thinking. Often people have asked me for advice, and I find out that they have also asked eight other people. That's great. What these people are doing is getting ideas. From there they will make their own decision. This situation is different than not trying to think through to a solution.

If someone comes to us four or five times asking for advice about something, and we give it, it is likely that we have helped them establish that pattern, permanently. The pattern is that they do not have to think this one through for themselves. Forever more, they know they can ask us about this situation and we will tell them what to do. We have held them incompetent enough that they now hold themselves incompetent in that area. Do you have someone who asks you the same question over and over and over, when you think that they should know how to do whatever it is, because you have already told them a million times? You may have contributed to this situation by holding them incompetent the first few times they came to ask you about it.

This is one of the reasons that children and teenagers get so angry when we tell them how to do something. They understand that the implicit message we are giving is that they are incompetent. Much of the process of going through childhood is to try to become more competent, but we keep taking that away from them by telling them how to do things.

When my oldest son was a baby, I was a single parent. I used to leave the house at 6:30 a.m. I would push Brett to the daycare in the stroller, then I would continue on my five-mile walk to work. The easiest way for me to get out of the house on time was to dress him. Brett did not learn to dress himself until he was almost five years old because I was doing it for him. It was easier. I also resented it. "He's almost five and can't dress himself. I have to do it all." It took me a long time to realize how I was contributing to that situation.

Six years later, I was married with three children. Our youngest child learned to dress herself by the time she was 18 months old. Really. (No, this is not a boy/girl thing.) I would leave her clothes out for her and without assistance she could get into everything correctly. To this day, she dresses herself. (And at six-years old, you should see some of the outfits she chooses!)

People are amazingly competent. Children are competent at far earlier ages than we sometimes give them credit. Hold people competent. No solutions. No advice. Let them work out the solution for themselves.

B. The second reason for *No solutions, No advice* is that our advice for others is based on fantasy. When we give others solutions and advice we are pretending to be them; pretending that we were in that situation; pretending that this is what we would have said or done. Our advice for others is based on pretense—it is based on fantasy. Often, when we think about the situation and try to imagine really saying or doing what we are recommending, we realize that we probably would never say or do what we are telling them to say or do.

When we give others solutions and advice, whose experience do those solutions and advice come from? Ours. Whose background do those solutions and advice come from? Ours. Whose dominant Communicate Style do those solutions and advice come from? Ours. Who are the solutions and advice for? Us. If the advice comes from our experience, our background, and our dominant Communication Style, the only people those solutions and advice could fit are us.

C. People won't take our advice, even when they have asked for it. Many of us have had the experience of people coming to us and asking for our advice. We give it. They agree that that is exactly what they will do. Our advice was perfect. Then they walk away and never do it! How frustrating! Why should we keep giving our advice when they never follow through on what they said they were going to do? Look at the anger that can come from such a simple situation! Our frustration is indicating to us that we are no longer seeing this relationship as completely safe and we have gone into attack mode.

From the other person's perspective, the advice sounded really good. But, as they walked away and started processing it, at some level, whether on the level of the safety brain or the thinking brain, they realized that they could never actually do or say that. They realized that they actually could not follow through on the advice we had given. Of course, they never come back and tell us why they did not take our advice, so we get resentful. Realize that others often will not follow through with the advice we give because they cannot.

When people come up with their own solutions and advice, it comes from their background, their experience, and their dominant Communication Style. They can follow through with their own advice because it would work for them.

D. By the time someone is willing to talk about a problem, they often have their own solution. But instead of letting them talk through to their solution, we keep distracting them, "Have you tried this…" and they have to leave their train of thought and respond, "I did try that and it didn't work because…" Then they get back on track and we distract them again, "How about this…" and they leave their train of thought again and respond, "That would never work because…" By the end of the conversation we have distracted them so often they will never get to their own solution. If we would just let them talk until they get to their solution, the conversation would be finished, and they would have a solution with which they would be able to follow through. Listen without giving solutions and advice, and people will get to their own solutions.

Those are four very strong reasons for not giving solutions and advice. So, instead of even thinking up solutions and advice, turn off that little voice, and pay full attention to what the other person is saying.

Rule #3: Ask Questions Ask questions to get them to talk about the situation fully. Ask questions about anything you want more details on. If they have not fully explained something, ask about it. Get them to give you full details. As they give you full details, they will start understanding the situation better themselves. Often, they will start to find their solution on their own, as you ask questions.

You can use your questions for a couple of specific purposes, as well. Sometimes, people have been held incompetent for so long that when you give them the opportunity to think problems through themselves they don't know how. If you ask them how they think they can solve it, their response is, "I don't know." Use questions to direct them to a solution. "What's the first thing you could do?" or "How do you think it should be handled?" or "How have you handled this kind of thing in the past?" or "If you were the boss, how would you handle it?" Think of your person, and think up some real words that you could use with them to direct them to a solution. This is one of those situations where, if you know this person well enough, you can anticipate their responses and pre-plan what you are going to say. The key is, continue turning it back to them until they start coming up with their own solutions.

Even in a training situation you can use this technique. Many people have said that we could not use these kinds of listening skills in situations where we are training children or people who are new to the job. I challenge that. If we can take the time for them to look at the situation and think about how they might handle it, even if they have no previous experience with this kind of task, they can often figure out how to do it. Sometimes, they come up with a new way of doing it that is better than the old way. If you successfully use this technique during training so that they are coming up with realistic and good ideas, you will find that it takes significantly less time to train them than someone who has been told how to do everything. Give it a try and see if it works for you in situations in which you are training others.

Of course, if you give an Enthusiast this kind of open space to talk, they will talk forever and never look for a solution. If you have an Enthusiast use questions to direct them to a solution. "How are you going to handle it?" "What's the first thing you could try?" "What are some potential solutions?"

Help other's think through the consequences and effects of any solutions they come up with. If you see that the solution they have reached will not work, keep that realization to yourself (I was really tempted to say, "Don't tell them it is wrong," but then what picture would I have been drawing for you to follow through on?) Instead, use your questions to get them to think their solution through. You can say, "How do you think that would affect the company (or unit or work team or department or family)?" or "What are some of the positives from this solution? What are some of the negatives?" or "How do you think management would react to this?" Get them to think it through. You are holding them competent and teaching them to think through to the consequences of their solutions. This is an excellent skill to teach others whom we want to trust. We will know that they are making good decisions, working independently, and getting the job done.

Rule #4: Use True Empathy True empathy is different from merely saying, "I understand how you feel." I took that course, too, and that statement has never worked for me, either. I think (or say), "You don't understand how I feel," and the situation escalates. Instead, imagine yourself in the other person's shoes and think, "If I were Ed and that had happened to me, how would I feel?" Then voice those feelings to the other person.

When we use true empathy, we show others, with our body language, our words, and our tone of voice, that we really do understand how they feel. This technique enables others to deflate their anger within seconds. We are not engaging in autobiographical comment. What we are doing is imagining that we are them; imagining that the situation happened to us, as them; then thinking about how we would feel if we were them, in that situation. When we put those feelings into words, we reflect back to them some of the feelings they might be having, but we show only a bit of emotion. "I would be furious if that had happened to me." Use a mildly irritated tone of voice. "You must feel like she's out to get you," or "I would be so hurt if I were you." Put a little emphasis in your voice, not a lot.

When you reflect their feelings back to them, one of two things will happen. They will either correct you or they will agree with you. Even if they correct you, your comments show that you are thinking of them, and they will probably not get angrier. Instead, they might simply correct you and explain why they feel what they feel. They might correct you in an irritable and frustrated tone, but their anger will not have escalated.

There is a difference between autobiographical comment and true empathy. Autobiographical comment is saying to someone, "Oh, that happened to me, too. And if you'll just listen to me, I can fix you!" Whereas, true empathy is trying to understand how they feel and reflecting those feelings back to them, in a small way. I learned about true empathy from Noelle Nelsen, author of *Winning, Using Courtroom Lawyers' Techniques to Get What You Want in Everyday Situations*[2] (only a lawyer could think up a title that long!) A good lawyer, who often wins in the courtroom, is a master communicator. This person, with no personal contact, is able to convince those twelve jurors that he or she, out of everyone the jurors have seen, is the safest person, is the person who has the most believable story. Those are the skills of a master communicator. Noelle Nelsen's book is an excellent read for good communication skills.

Two days after I read about this type of empathizing in her book, I had a chance to use it with my husband. (I made one small mistake the first time I used these skills that I'll help you to avoid.) My husband came home from work complaining about his job. He is not one to complain about something like work, so I knew it was really bothering him. In the past, whenever he had brought up work and complained about it, my advice had been, "Quit. Find another job." He hadn't taken my advice up to then, and there was little to indicate that my advice was welcome in this situation. So instead of giving my advice, I thought of the empathizing skill. At dinner, he was still complaining about work, and after he made a particular comment I said, "You must feel so disheartened. You must feel like he's just out to stab you in the back." (The words "stab you in the back" were words that he had already used, so I knew they were O.K.) It was amazing watching him deflate. With just that one little comment from me, said in a slightly irritated voice to show that I was feeling it, too, my husband felt totally validated, and simply let all of the anger go. It was my next statement that was a bit of a mistake. He calmed down so fast that I got excited and said, "Honey, do you know what technique I just used on you?" Well, fooomph! It was like throwing a match into a gas can. He just exploded! (Sometimes I get a little carried away! Wait a couple of days before you share things like the techniques you have used.)

The key to true empathy is, when you imagine yourself being them and in a particular situation, your body language will actually start to reflect the feelings, and so will your tone. You will be validating them with your body language, your tone, and your words. This is an extremely effective way to show that you are truly listening to them. It beats having a conversation with yourself, doesn't it?

Here is a small exercise that you can do, using all the rules of Pure, Clean Listening to experience what it feels like to be listened to this way, and to practice these pure, clean, listening skills. Find someone with whom you can have an eight-minute conversation. You need to have a timer that you can set that will indicate with a noise when time is up. Each of you needs to think about a problem that you can discuss with each other. There needs to be a partner A and a partner B. Set the timer for four minutes. Partner A starts by discussing his or her problem. Partner B gets to listen. Here are the rules again, for listening.

Rule #1: Turn off the voice.

Rule #2: No solutions. No advice.

Rule #3: Ask questions—here is one question that is not allowed, "Have you tried this…?" That would be advice disguised as a question.

Rule #4: Use true empathy, if you have the chance.

You may be tempted to interpret these rules to mean that, when you are listening, you should not say anything at all. That is not true. In fact, if my husband tries that on me I explode, "Show me that you are listening!" You should ask questions, get them to fully explain the situation. Make full eye contact. Nod your head. Get involved in what they are saying. Make appropriate comments. However, no solutions, no advice.

So, partner A starts by talking about his or her problem for four minutes and partner B gets to listen. When the timer goes off, reset it for four minutes and switch. This time, partner B gets to talk and partner A gets to listen.

When I do this exercise in a group, and talk about it after the exercise is over, I get a variety of responses to the question, "When you were talking, why did it feel good to be listened to that way?"

I really felt listened to.

I felt like they were on my side

I got to take my time and think.

I didn't have to rush to say everything.

I didn't understand the problem, clearly.

I had a chance to really listen to myself.

I realized it wasn't much of a problem.

I realized I already had a solution.

I just got to talk about it.

I felt that they were not judging me.

That last statement "I felt that they were not judging me" is interesting. It comes up every time I have groups do this exercise. Of course they were judging you. In fact, the only reason they listened to you was because I told them they had to. Their biggest judgment was, "Do you ever have problems!" However, the feeling that they were not judging you is very important. Why do we feel they were not judging us when they listen to us this way? To answer that question we will look at situations when we have used these listening skills in real life. When have you ever listened to someone like this—giving that person your full attention; only saying things to show that you are fully listening, or to ask questions to get full information? There are three different circumstances when we would use these listening skills.

1. We listen like this when we are very interested and in full agreement. If we were not in full agreement we would be interrupting, "Yeah, but…"or "Wait a minute…"or "What about…"

2. When we want to fully understand the situation so that, if necessary, we can intervene.

3. When we respect them enough to let them vent.

If these are the three times when we have used these listening skills, or others have used these listening skills with us, our assumption is that they are doing so for one of the above three reasons. As we discussed in Level III, we assume everyone is exactly like us and therefore, has the same reasons we have. So, when someone uses these types of listening skills with us, we feel that we are not being judged, because we assume they are listening like this for one of the above three reasons.

We have used these listening skills before. This is really important. We already understand that it is very hard to get our safety brain to stop an old habit and start a new habit, because of the safety factor. One easy way to get the safety brain to help us establish a new habit is to link the new habit to the old habit. If the new habit is actually very, very similar to a habit that we already have, then it is almost like our horse is actually walking an old path, instead of trying to make a brand new path through the meadow. You have used these listening skills before. You already know how to do all this. Now we can expand the circumstances to include everyday conversations, conversations where, in the past, we might have jumped in with solutions and advice.

If it feels good for us to be listened to this way, it will feel just as good for others. These listening skills make us very safe people.

Many of us felt really good listening like this, as we went through this little exercise with partners. It felt really good to relax and just listen, knowing that we did not have to think up any solutions or advice. People who feel good listening this way, have a strong element of Pacifist in them. Pacifists have known since birth how to listen. For the rest of us, we still have blood dripping down the back of our throats because we were biting our tongues so hard to keep from giving advice. We are not Pacifists. And we need to practice pure, clean listening a lot!

One of the common comments I get from people, when they first hear about pure, clean listening is that listening to someone this way is going to take so much time. It would take less time to just tell them what to do, so they will go do it, and we can get on with what we were doing.

I agree. In the short term, these listening skills take time, especially if the person you are dealing with has a deeply engrained pattern of getting others to tell him or her what to do. Over the longer term, people become used to trusting their own judgment, making their own decisions, and thinking things through. You have helped them mature, so we no longer feel that we are dealing with two-year-old adults. The second element to remember is that when we use these listening skills, we are showing those other people that we are really safe people. That means that they no longer attack us.

We are not going to use pure, clean listening in every single conversation. There are going to be times where it is not necessary. You know the person you are dealing with is competent and capable. This person will not go on the defensive if you give them some advice. Of course, with these people you do not often have to give them advice. When you have a crisis or a deadline to meet or there is a time crunch and there is no time to listen, just tell them how to do the job so its gets done.

The point of these listening skills is, the more often you use them and the more people you use them with, the safer you will be. Others will attack you less often because you are a safe person. Someone who is already in full attack mode will usually calm down very quickly when you use these listening skills. You become a safe person and will have less conflict in your life.

The first time I used this with my husband, he was very angry. I arrived home two hours late, it was late at night, and I was on my rollerblades. He had been wondering which hospital to call first. Initially, I simply walked away from him and his anger. Then, realizing that there was something new I could try, I sat with him, apologized, and listened. Less than 45 minutes later he looked at his watch and said, "What happened here? Has time stood still?" We had covered more in that 45 minutes than had taken us six hours in the past. Our previous conversations had been filled with autobiographical comments, taking the conversation off in tangents, and getting defensive. Often we never even finished conversations. I used the pure, clean listening and we actually worked a couple of issues right through to solid solutions.

Not only will pure, clean listening defuse even the most defensive person, it will also save time.

Chapter 12
Quit Taking Away Their Emotions

One of the most crucial times to use the pure, clean listening is when people are showing their emotions. However, this is usually when we tell people they are wrong. When we try to get people to stop showing their emotions we are telling them they are wrong to be who they are. We do this especially when we try to get people to calm down when they are angry (they are showing the emotion of fear) or when they are crying.

Here are some of the phrases we use to try to get people to calm down:

Calm down.

Cool off.

Have a seat.

Can I get you a drink of water or some coffee?

It's OK. It was no big deal.

Let's talk about it.

Simmer down.

You don't have to get angry about it.

What can you do to fix it?

Take a valium.

Relax, it's not that bad.

We'll fix it.

I understand how you feel.

Let it go.

He or she didn't mean it.

He or she wouldn't do that.

Are you sure that is what happened?

With all of these phrases, we are trying to get them to calm down so that we can work through to a solution. We want to fix the situation so they stop being angry. Unfortunately, the implied message is that it is not OK for them to be angry or to show their emotions. They are wrong to have these emotions. Many of us have used some of these words with an angry person, and, with almost every word we said, they got angrier. Yes, they may well get angrier, because, added to what they had already perceived as unsafe, now we are unsafe people to be with, too. Not only were they on the attack because of something else, now they have to protect themselves from us telling them they are wrong to have thought the original situation was unsafe.

When we try to calm people down, it is as though they are big, red balloons that are blown up as full as they can be. When we try to calm them down, it is as though we have taken a pin and tried to pop them. We want them to instantly let go of their emotions and only show us the parts of them that we want to see, instead of the parts of them that they need to show us. We are telling them that they are not OK. Let people have their emotions and express what they are feeling. Get them to talk about it. Use the phrases from Chapter 10: Tell Them They Are Right. Use the pure, clean listening. Call them right by letting them show their sadness, their tears, their fears.

If you are really uncomfortable when others show their fear through anger or through crying, go back to Chapter Two. That is where we realized that, when others in our packs indicate that there is danger, we want to activate our defense mechanisms so that we can get to safety, too. That is where our discomfort is coming from. We can control our own need to go to defense-attack simply in realizing that, while this person is raging, they are the only ones who have perceived danger. We do not need to get defensive.

Instead of trying to pop other people and force them to conceal their feelings, let others deflate themselves. Let them fully talk about the situation until they calm down and are ready to solve it. If we allow people to express their feelings, they will let those feelings go. Allow them to show you their fear, through their anger, and accept that people do feel fear in all kinds of different situations. Some situations that you would never consider to be dangerous, they have found so dangerous that they are raging.

One of the absolute hardest times to let others have their emotions is when their issues involve us. It is very hard to be objective, to use true empathy, and not let our safety brains get hooked into judging the situation as unsafe, when they are talking about us. However, this is exactly what we need to do. When we try to fix situations, give solutions and advice, even when they are discussing or complaining about situations that involve us, we are falling into two traps: the first is the trap of trying to take their emotions away from them; the second is the trap of holding them incompetent. We need to prove that we are completely safe to be with, so these people can feel safe with us, instead of defensive.

When someone brings up an issue that involves you, concentrate on using pure, clean listening, especially Rule #2: No Solutions. No Advice. I remember phoning a friend to ask him for some wild meat. Everyone in my primary family has hunted for meat at one time or another. I have given up hunting in recent years, but I still love venison. I offered to help Jack with cutting and packaging the meat, in exchange for some of the meat. He got quite offended and told me that I was offering to help with the easy part. I did not say anything as he continued the attack, because my mind had gone blank. I was quite taken aback by his anger over the request. He phoned me back about 30 minutes after that conversation to tell me how offended he was that I would even consider asking for some of the meat.

What was truly interesting to me was that he was offended that I had even asked. My husband and I have always taught our children that they are allowed to ask for whatever they want. Of course, the person they are making the request to, has the right to say, "Yes," or "No." We have had to remind our children on many occasions that, "Yes, they get to ask and we get to say 'Yes' or 'No.' And the answer here is, 'No.'"

For some reason Jack went to defense-attack when asked for some wild meat. With the improved communication skills that I now have, I would get him talking about why he was so offended. At the time, my mind went blank as I went into defense mode and turned off access to my thinking brain. When people get angry and attack us, we can keep from activating our defense systems by recognizing that we have not caused them to attack. Nobody can make anybody else angry. People get angry because of their fears.

One really interesting part of getting people to talk about what is bothering them is that, if they can actually voice the fear that is fueling their anger and look at it rationally, they will often let that fear go. Usually these fairly small fears are released by acknowledging them. It is as though, when we actually give voice to the fear, we are releasing it from our minds with our words. The fear flies out of our mouths, along with the words, and it is forever gone.

Joe Paterno, football coach for the Pennsylvania State University football team and author of the book *Paterno*, said, "People resent not having their say, but they don't mind not getting their way, if they have had their say." [1] This is exactly what I am referring to. When people have a chance to voice their objection, their fear, they will often just let it go.

We have probably all done this. Someone asked us to do something and we refused. Then, this wise person got us talking about why we could not do it. We listed all of our objections, and by the time we had listed our last objection, we said, "OK, sure. I'll do it for you." If we get them to voice their objection, they let it go.

One of the hardest times to keep from getting hooked when someone is discussing a problem, is when that someone is really close to us. I am getting better at it with my kids and even better at it with my husband, but it seems that between spouses or life partners, getting hooked when our spouses need to discuss a situation that involves us can be extremely difficult. Some of these issues are the minor irritants that escalate into full-blown rage because, instead of letting that person voice their fear, we got hooked and go to defense-attack. Imagine each of the following comments being said by your partner, child, or close friend, in an irritated voice:

        Get your feet off the coffee table.

        Why can't you put your shoes away?

        Leave (that child) alone. It's not a big deal.

Clean up after yourself.
Why can't you help out more?
Can't you see I'm watching TV? Leave me alone.
Why can't you put the toilet seat down?
Why are you driving home this way.
I'm not your maid.
Put your dirty clothes in your laundry basket.

Fill in your own comments. What are some of the small things that happen around your house that drive you crazy? Being driven crazy means that it is such an ongoing, constant occurrence, that every single time you see it you get irritated, annoyed, or in an outright rage. What are some of the things your partner says in an irritated or angry tone that irritate you? They have gone to defense-attack because they see something to fear. We do not need to respond with anger. We often respond with anger because we get hooked. We see that the other person sees something unsafe and we activate our defense systems and attack. Or, it could be that this issue has come up so often in the past that as soon as we hear the beginning of the same issue, we know where it is going, and we go on to defense-attack. If your partner shows fear, over such a small, everyday occurrence within a household, surely it is worth getting them to talk about it and work it through so they can let it go. Instead we tell them they are wrong to bring up issues that involve us. We tell them they are wrong through our defensive-attack, or we try to fix it with solutions and advice. Each of these responses shows our spouses that it is unsafe to discuss issues with us that involve us because we will go to defense-attack when they do. This is a very dangerous pattern to establish with spouses or life partners, with children, and with anyone else with whom we are close. If we make it unsafe for them to discuss issues with us that involve us, they either stop discussing the issues, and, therefore, the issues never get resolved, or they go discuss the issues with someone else.

When people show you their fears, especially by being angry, listen. Let them talk. Validate them by taking the time to listen. Show them that they are OK because you will accept them and all of their emotions. Show them that you are a safe person, because they can show you who they truly are, and you will accept them. You can keep people from attacking you by allowing them to have their emotions.

You can help them express their fear and other emotions by using the next technique.

Chapter 13
Constructive Criticism Doesn't Exist

There is no such thing as constructive criticism. In fact, constructive criticism is an oxymoron. An oxymoron is two words used together that mean the exact opposite; "yeah, no," or "same difference," or "clearly misunderstood," or "pretty ugly," or "terribly pleased," or "plastic glasses." When we use these phrases we have a definite meaning. However, if you look at the two actual words in the phrase, they are opposites. If we take the literal meaning of each word, they do not belong together.

I consider constructive criticism to be an oxymoron. These two words should not be used together, as there is nothing constructive about criticism. When we criticize people we are telling them what they did was wrong. That is not constructive. In fact, we have just opened the possibility that they will go on the defensive and shut off access to their thinking brains. However, there is a way to give feedback about something someone has done, so that they stay open to our suggestions.

Like Best; Next Time (LBs and NTs) is a short, easy phrase to use in giving feedback, that allows the person to see some positives, and they stay open to our suggestions.

"Brett, what I *liked best* about you spilling your milk, is you ran immediately to clean it up. *Next time*, put your glass above your plate."

"Susan, what I *like best* about this report you did for me is that it is very well organized, you have formatted it so that it is easy to read, and you have included all of the necessary details. *Next time*, could you also add a table of contents and a reference list, and we also need to ensure that the grammar and spelling are correct."

Do you see, in these two examples, how we have used *like best, next time?* Instead of getting angry and attacking a child at the table for spilling his milk, which guarantees that the child will slam down his gateway, get defensive, and shut off access to his thinking brain, we find something nice (be genuine) about what has happened. Then we add to the statement by drawing a clear picture for them to follow through on *next time*. Their gateways stay open because we started off the statement with a positive. There is nothing to get defensive about. They hear what we have to say. Then we engage their safety brains in doing the situation differently by drawing a clear picture for them to follow through with, next time.

In the second example, we are dealing with the work site. Point out the positives of what they have done with the *like best*. In the *next time* statement, ask for the changes you need. What if there will not be a next time?

What if we need this report corrected, because we want it to go out with the grammar and spelling corrected?

"Susan, what I like best about this report is that it is very well organized, you have formatted it so that it is easy to read, and you have included all of the necessary details. When you get it back to me at 11:30 a.m. could you also add a table of contents and a reference list, and we also need to ensure that the grammar and spelling are correct."

There is always a *next time*. The next time might mean that this task needs to be redone, so the next time includes a deadline for when you need it back.

Like Best, Next Time is a very small, simple formula to use, and we get great results with it. Instead of having people get defensive with us and attack because we have told them what they have done wrong, we change this to what they did right, and then suggest a different way, or add some corrections, for next time. It is a small, simple, and very powerful formula that we can use to avoid anger and conflict and gain cooperation. The added benefit to using this formula is that we do not get angry and attack them. Because we are looking for the positives, we help our safety brain avoid judging the situation as unsafe, so we avoid going on the attack. We can calmly and rationally point out the positives, and ask for something different, next time.

Chapter 14
Strong Boundaries Create Safety

When we set strong boundaries with people, so that they know what to do to be safe with us, then they feel safe. It is interesting to note that Pacifists will give in on everything because, by giving in, they are avoiding conflict and confrontations. Yet, Pacifists can find themselves attacked again and again, and more and more often, by different people. They are not safer because they give in, they are more dangerous and, therefore, more prone to being attacked. If we never tell people what our boundaries are, then they cannot feel safe with us. They will keep testing different boundaries with us to see if we will take a stand, to see if we will show them how to be safe with us. They do not test the different boundaries to see how much they can get away with. They test the different boundaries to try to figure out which ones will stand firm, so that they can start to feel safe with us. In the long run, always giving in causes more defense-attack, not less.

An excellent way to show people that they are safe with us is to tell them what our boundaries are. Then, we need to make those boundaries solid and firm. These boundaries never change. When someone knows exactly where they stand with us they can feel safe. Many of us have lived or worked with someone who was very moody. We never knew how to approach that person because from moment to moment, hour to hour, day to day, they would react differently. We could say exactly the same thing, in the same way, to that person two days in a row. The first day they would laugh and make it into a joke. The second day they would fly into a rage. After a while, we simply did not want to have anything to do with them because of the inconsistency. We could not figure out what was safe with that person. They had no solid boundaries.

When we are up front with people about how we need to be treated, we are setting boundaries. When we let people know immediately if they have crossed a boundary that we have never discussed with them before, we are setting the boundaries. When they try to push that boundary—and throughout relationships we often try to push all the boundaries at one time or another—we let them know that the boundary still stands. People know exactly how to be safe with us.

All of us have a family member or friend who is always late, regardless of what event was planned and how many people were there. The first time that person was late we should have told them, calmly, pleasantly, and firmly, "When we make a date I need us to both be on time." So many people get resentful and angry because that person is never on time and the situation has gone on for months or even years. In fact, Charlotte has been getting together with a group of moms once a month since these six women met in prenatal class ten years ago. Originally, with small children, they brought the children. They do still bring the children, on occasion, but now it has become more of a moms' day or night out. Jessica has consistently been late since their very first meeting. Everyone could count on Jessica being up to one hour late. Everyone resented Jessica for being late, and felt that Jessica was showing a lack of respect for them and their time by being late. But nobody said anything. For Charlotte's last birthday the other ladies bought her dinner and tickets to the opera. The rest of the group wanted Jessica to be on time. So Charlotte told Jessica that the dinner reservation was for 6:00 p.m. The reservation was actually for 7:00 p.m. Jessica, this one time in their entire relationship, showed up on time. Nobody else was there. She left before the others got there. To this day, that relationship has not been repaired.

There is no rational reason to let something like this go on so long. Have that one-on-one conversation: "When we get together, we all need to be on time. Can we all agree to these rules?" It really is not that hard, yet we think we are preserving the relationship by not setting boundaries. Instead, we are jeopardizing relationships by not setting boundaries.

In our family, I was the parent who was very volatile. Sometimes the kids could do something and get away with it. The next time they did it I got defensive and attacked, yelling and screaming at them. For parents, when we start talking about strong boundaries with no exceptions, the popular catch phrase is "be consistent." In our family, we learned this lesson with our oldest son. We saw the inconsistency come to the peak of destruction when our oldest son was in grade six. He was volatile and raging a lot in the house. He would question every single statement we, his parents, made. There was no safety in our house, for him. Any decision we made could change. We would often make plans and set goals and decide how we were going to do things differently, and, like good parents should, we would tell the kids what the new plans were. Within minutes or days we were back to doing things the old way. All of the kids knew that the boundaries were flexible to nonexistent. The one thing they could be sure of was that any little thing could set mom into attack mode, and they could not guess what that little thing would be. I remember growing up in a house very, very similar to the one we were running. No safety.

Our oldest son, being an Activist, was the one who had the strongest need for strong boundaries. There were no boundaries that he could count on. He constantly felt the need to defend himself. We changed. We set strong boundaries that were not flexible. We wrote down the new procedures and the consequences so that we could look at what we had decided and ensure that we followed through. I started looking that young man in the eye and saying, "Not negotiable," or "Do you really think that there is anything you can say right now that will make me change my mind?" We showed the kids that they were safe because there were rules that always had to be followed; procedural rules (put your shoes away), politeness rules, respect rules, and chore rules. We are consistent. All of the kids started behaving better, but we especially saw the change in our oldest son, who was our barometer with this issue.

Being consistent means setting strong boundaries that never change. We have far fewer challenges and arguments about rules because the kids have learned the rules don't change. *No* means *no*. We have far fewer rages and temper tantrums because the kids feel safe. Our house is a far happier now because we all feel safer.

I was talking to a mom who has a five-year-old son and an 11-year-old son. Her oldest son was invited to a sleepover. The mom was having a hard time deciding whether to let him go or not, because when the oldest goes on a sleepover, the youngest cries. She decided that if the youngest son started crying, then she would not allow her oldest son to go on a sleepover. I looked her in the eye and said, "It sounds like Billy is holding you hostage with his tears." Her oldest son heard the comment and said, "Yeah, mom, and that's illegal." We are not doing the kids any favors if we let them set the rules. They have no idea what is appropriate and what is not. It is our job, as parents, to teach them. If the children are setting the boundaries, or pushing boundaries, and we let them, the children feel unsafe. Does Billy get to feel sad when his older brother gets to go on a sleepover and he doesn't? Absolutely. Teach him that emotions are OK and how to deal with them, instead of trying to fix the situation so he never learns.

We are also not doing our children any favors when they sometimes have to follow a rule and other times do not. In doing this we have shown them that there is something they can do to make the boundary go away. If too many of the boundaries are sometimes there and sometimes not, then the kids do not feel safe. They cannot follow the rules because they do not really know what the rules are.

In our house, boundaries do not change. Bedtime is bedtime and it is the same time each night, weekday or weekend. You do your chores, and each child's chores are written down, or you face the consequences and you still have to do your chores. Our children are not allowed to have sleepovers on Saturday nights, because then they are still too tired for school on Monday. They are only allowed sleepovers on nights where they have two days to recover for school. Rudeness earns a timeout. Those are a few of our rules. We are consistent and firm with our rules, and the kids have responded by being happier, feeling more secure, and being more cooperative. They treat each other nicely, as well. In fact, our children are such good friends that, instead of sibling rivalry, our biggest problem is that they play too much instead of doing their chores. (You might not consider this to be a problem, but we do!)

Before we started setting consistent, strong boundaries, anger, tantrums, whining, and raging were what we could expect from the kids. They felt unsafe most of the time. Our oldest child, who is our Activist, was often in attack mode. Our middle child, our Pacifist, was as quiet and cooperative as possible, trying not to be seen. Our youngest child, our Enthusiast, broke every rule we made, then lied about what she had done. Make the rules in your house strong and inflexible. Initially your kids will push those new boundaries, or the old ones that you are now enforcing, because you have changed. In the long run you will have a happier, less angry, more cooperative family.

In the office, people who feel unsafe show it through lack of moral. They do things like:
- come in late and go home early.
- take more sick days.
- are unmotivated, and do sloppy work.
- can be rude to each other and clients and customers.
- gossip and complain about everything.
- are insubordinate, and actually refuse to do something when asked.
- are sarcastic.
- are angry, frustrated, irritated, and annoyed at different times.
- have far less tolerance for each other than they used to have.

If you have an office where many of these behaviors are happening, you have low morale. Low morale is evident when people test all of the boundaries, in one way or another, trying to find safety. They are not trying to push the boundaries over. They are actually testing the boundaries to see which ones still stand, so that they can feel safe. In this day of downsizing and outsizing and resizing and whatever-sizing, people are losing their jobs. The people who are still with the company have as hard a time, and often an even harder time, than those who left. The people who have left have closure with the old job and the chance at a new beginning. The people who are left are unsafe. They are thinking, "Who goes next?" "When will we lose our jobs?" "Now we have to do the work of three people, and if we don't do a good job, and get it all done (which is absolutely impossible) they will lay us off, too."

People are angry, irritable, frustrated, and annoyed—defense-attack—because they feel so unsafe in their jobs. Management needs to ensure that these people regain the feeling of safety so that they can become more productive.

If layoffs are not the issue and you have poor morale in the office, you are still dealing with people who are not feeling safe. Maybe some of the basic boundaries have been tested and found flexible. One of the common complaints I hear is that someone in the office comes in late and goes home early. This is one of the basic boundaries in the office. This is one of the inherent elements of receiving a pay cheque. The hours that people work are usually even written into the contract when they are hired. If someone is seen to come in late and go home early, the rest of the staff at the work site now know that one of the basic boundaries of work is not really a boundary. It is as though one of the foundation walls of the building has been taken away. The entire structure is now unsafe. Everyone will watch to see what other boundaries no longer exist. Soon, other people try to come in late and/or go home early. People will start testing both the written and unwritten boundaries:

Hours of work
Sick days
Dress code
Length of coffee breaks
Length of lunch breaks
Professional behavior
Courteous behavior
Temper tantrums in the office
Respect to clients
Solve your own problems
Deadlines
Error-free work
High production
Timely responses
Productive meetings

We might think we like to get away with breaking boundaries, but at a deeper level we really do not want to be allowed to come in late and go home early, for example. We want the boundaries of work hours to be firm. Sometimes we think we are doing people a favor by letting them push the boundaries. We make allowances for one person because of extenuating circumstances; we have managers who come in late because they have scheduled meetings first thing in the morning somewhere else; we have managers who leave early, because they have scheduled their meetings for later in the day. If the rest of the staff does not know about the extenuating circumstances, or they do not know that those managers are attending meetings, then all they see is a boundary that moves or falls over. What can easily happen from there is that people begin to test other boundaries, mostly to reassure themselves that this work site is still safe, and we have a work site with low morale.

With our Pacifists who give in rather than create conflict by standing their ground, although our Pacifists are very nice people, they are not necessarily very safe people. When we tell others what we need from them and what we do not like, we are telling them how they can feel safe with us. If we never, or rarely, tell others what our needs are, or we give in when they attack us, we are showing that we either have no boundaries, or that the boundaries we do have are only boundaries some of the time. We then become unsafe people to be with and we find ourselves being attacked more and more because those other people do not feel safe when they are with us. Tell people when they push your boundaries that that boundary still stands and it is not going away. You can tell them nicely. You can use kind words. But tell them.

In one job, I organized someone's farewell party. The staff all contributed to the two sleeping bags we bought for Steve, as he loved camping. During the gift opening, a 54-year-old male manager made a comment that suggested I had bought those two sleeping bags so that I could share them with Steve. I was furious, and embarrassed that everyone else had heard the comment. I don't recall what I said at the time, but I do recall going into his office the next day, looking him straight in the eye, and calmly saying, "You can apologize now for that comment you made yesterday at the farewell party." He did. And that was the end of it.

Set the boundaries up front. If someone crosses one of your boundaries, you have to let them know. Otherwise, they will never understand that they are crossing one of your boundaries and the behavior will continue.

My husband is far more the Pacifist in our relationship than I am. When he finally decided to become less diplomatic and start voicing his needs, I could not believe it. I thought, "Who is he to take a stand now! This isn't the way we have been doing our relationship and you'd better change back, bucko!" I did not say those words out loud, but I could hear them loud and clear in my safety brain. I went to defense-attack trying to get him to change back. At times I raged. He continued setting his boundaries, and now I now feel far safer with him, I respect him, and my behavior has changed.

It really can be that simple. We want to feel safe in our closest relationships. Show your partner, children, friends, and coworkers that you really are a safe person. Voice your boundaries. All of us need to voice our boundaries kindly, nicely, gently, and firmly. Tell others what they can do to ensure they are safe with us.

Chapter 15
The Public Secret

Almost all of us have a Public Secret person in either our family, our work site, or both. These are the people who consistently engage in behavior that bothers us and everyone else in the pack. We even gossip about this person to each other, behind the person's back. We might even jokingly comment on it to the problem person: "Hey, Darla, did you have two flat tires on the way to work, today? (Darla is frequently late for work and always has an excuse.) "Dad, could you just find something nice to say about that person?" (Dad is the negaholic and it drives the rest of us crazy.)

This person who engages in the unacceptable behavior is your Public Secret. Everyone in the pack knows about this person and his or her behavior. In fact, we share a common bond against this person because of that behavior. We gossip about it. We joke about it, even with the problem person. However, no one has ever "caught" the person. If this person has never felt "caught" in this behavior, in such a way as to make it unsafe to engage in the behavior, it will continue. Catching someone involves a serious conversation with the person about the behavior asking them to help you come up with some solutions that might work.

Think about having this conversation with someone. We can see that it will be a fairly uncomfortable conversation to have, because we are making the relationship unsafe for both of us. This person may attack us. This person may never again have anything to do with us. This person may try to get revenge on us by making our lives miserable or sabotaging us in some way. However, if the conversation goes well and our problem person agrees to make the change, or even just hear us out, the new relationship might include: increased trust, more open communication, behavior that works for both of us or for all of us in the pack, increased productivity in the office, better morale in the office.

In the office, the best person to have this conversation with the public secret is the supervisor. Often the behavior in question ignores boundaries that are actually in writing, such as hours of work. These types of issues need to be discussed between staff and supervisor. As coworkers we have little power and little authority to address these situations.

We do not catch our public secret by joking with them. A teacher at a Senior High School that I did some training with did a lot of tutoring at lunch time. Russell, another teacher, often commented that Mona was wasting her time. He would say that the kids were just lazy and stupid and they would never get it. (Nice guy, huh?) We did some brainstorming about some of the things we could say to him. We gave her all kinds of great ideas. Mona finally said, "You mean I shouldn't just tell him to 'screw off because he's such a pig'?" No, she should not tell him that. When she made this comment to Russell, he would walk away chuckling. Mona had helped turn the whole situation into a game. Russell is obviously in Enthusiast mode when he comes to her making those comments. He will play this game forever, because Enthusiasts play the game to play the game and get attention. If Mona truly wants him to stop making the comments, she needs have a private, serious conversation: "I feel really offended when you make those comments. I know I have been making a joke out of it, but I'd really appreciate it if we could both stop. Thanks." A calm and pleasant but serious and firm comment like this ends the game.

You will need to do the same with your public secret. Have a calm and pleasant but serious and firm discussion with this person. Tell them what the problem is and let them know that it is no longer appropriate.

As a coworker, you could have this conversation with the office public secret, but only if his or her behavior directly affects how you do your job.

Your public secret can easily be the person who goes on the attack in the office. This person is obviously scared of many things. We do not want to talk with these people because they have already shown that they are willing to attack. We do not want to escalate the problem by trying to point out to them that their anger is inappropriate. They will probably fly into a rage and we will be the target. Yet, if no one has ever had a calm, rational discussion with them pointing out that their attacking behavior is inappropriate, then it is safe for them to continue the behavior. In the office, this discussion is best done by the person who is being attacked. There may be many people who the angry public secret feels safe to attack. Then each one needs to have the discussion with the public secret pointing out that his or her behavior is no longer acceptable.

The public secret is someone who is creating difficulties for everyone else in the pack. Yet, if you do try to get that person to change his or her behavior, the rest of the pack is now going to be against you. If, prior to talking with the public secret, you tell the others what you are going to do, they will try to talk you out of it. There are two reasons. First, you are changing the rules. The pack will now be unsafe because, even though things might get better, the rules have changed. Second, you have shown that you are an unsafe person. All of the other members of the pack will be wondering when you are going to confront them with one of their behaviors.

You can still have the conversation with your public secret. Afterwards, you will need to re-establish with everyone in the pack, including the public secret, that you are a safe person. Joke with them. Show interest in them, personally. Casually point out some of your weaknesses. These are all ways to re-establish yourself as a safe person.

Hubert was the public secret in his family. He try to make his wife and adult children feel guilty if they refused one of his requests. Hubert phoned his oldest daughter and demanded that she contribute $50 to a wedding gift for one of her cousins. Valerie said, "Dad, I'd prefer that you ask me for the money instead of telling me to give it." Hubert was slightly taken back, as this was the first time Valerie had stood up to him in this way. He then proceeded to tell her how she owed the money because the cousin had given her a wedding gift. At which point Valerie said, "Dad, it sounds like you are trying to make me feel guilty. I'm willing to contribute the money, but I would prefer to be asked, and I don't need you to try to make me feel guilty." Valerie said that her heart was in her throat the whole conversation, it was so hard for her to stand up to her dad. Hubert got defensive with Valerie and ended the conversation on a defensive note. Valerie sent a cheque for the $50. Six months later, Hubert phoned Valerie about an upcoming 45th wedding anniversary. Hubert said, "I'm not asking you for money, I just want some ideas about what to get." Hubert no longer tries to send Valerie on a guilt trip, nor does he demand what he wants. He asks. Confronting the public secret gets results. Take your stand. Be calm. Be firm. Be objective. Catch the public secret and that behavior ends.

Confronting the public secret may sound easy as we read this. However, as we start to imagine actually having the conversation, we begin to have serious doubts about whether it is worth it, because our safety brain is against the whole idea. The technique in the next chapter is a great way to ask someone to change his or her behavior.

Chapter 16
Give It to Them in Writing

When we have a discussion with a problem person and we want them to change their behavior because of the way it is affecting us, we can gain their cooperation.

The In-writing Formula
1. Validate—say something nice about them. Make it genuine.
2. Say "I have a problem."
We say "I have a problem" because they do not have a problem. They are the problem, but they do not have a problem. Difficult people are difficult because they are engaging in behavior that is safe for them. It is not a problem for them. We are the ones with the problem, so admit it right up front.
3. Next say, "I need your help with a solution."
We have already discussed why we get their solution instead of giving them one of ours.
4. Give a deadline for the discussion.
Write up the entire problem using this formula, then give it to them. Here is how it might look.

In one of my past jobs I would get to my desk at 6:30 a.m. The next person came in at 7:00 a.m. She was a supervisor and I was not; however, she and I both reported to the same person. We had an open office design, which meant that most people walked right by my desk to get to theirs. When Jane walked by my desk at 7:00 a.m., I would look up with a smile on my face and say, "Good morning." Jane would walk straight past my desk without even acknowledging my presence. No smile. No hello. No nothing. For the first week of work I tried every morning to get her to respond. By the second week I was looking at my watch. I would go get a cup of coffee at 6:58 a.m. so that I would not be at my desk when she came in. By the third week I was thinking of quitting my job. I was thinking, "What had I ever done to her? Nothing! Why was she treating me this way? I hate this place! I hate this job!" (And those were only some of the things I said to my husband that third week!) At the beginning of the fourth week I decided to e-mail her.

Dear Jane:
You have given me a lot of ideas in the past couple weeks that will help me to do my job better. I really appreciate that. Thank you. Validate and make it genuine—she had and I did.
I have a problem. And I fully described the problem. *It feels like you*

have a closed door policy. Something about her door being closed all the time! After I fully described the problem I reiterated, *I know this is not your problem; however, I'm having a hard time with this. Could we please meet before Friday so I could get your help with a solution?* There has to be a deadline, otherwise that person may never respond and the letter and the problem will float out there forever.

I put the whole problem in writing to her for a couple of very strong reasons. I had had three weeks to realize there was a problem, mutter about it, complain to my husband, and then decide to solve it. What we normally do when we have a problem like this is mutter and complain about it and then finally decide to do something about it. When we decide to do something about it, we screw up our courage to face that person, then we catch the person in a private moment where there isn't anyone else around. "Jane, could I talk to you for a moment?" We vomit up the entire problem at her feet, then hold out a hand, snapping our fingers, basically saying, "OK, come on you've had your two seconds to think about it, let's have some solutions." We dump the problem in their lap when they did not even know there was a problem and expect them to be able to think it through in two seconds and come up with a solution. We have had three weeks to think about it. They get two seconds.

Putting it in writing gives them the same privilege that we have had, the privilege of time. It does not need to be the same amount of time that you took, but they do need some time to think about the problem and start to look at solutions.

The second reason to put it in writing is that they are going to get defensive and probably angry. It does not matter how nicely we put our words together, although please do try to be as nice as possible. As soon as they figure out that they are part of the problem, they are going to see that the relationship is unsafe. They will get defensive and maybe feel the need to attack. If you are standing there, they will attack you. At that point we have a confrontation. It will be very difficult to walk away if they are raging at you. Instead, let them get defensive and attack a piece of paper. It is much safer for the relationship. Putting the problem to them in writing first is guaranteed to be more effective than trying to talk with them face-to-face first. When you do finally get together for the meeting, you will probably both be a bit nervous, but open to resolving the issue.

When I walked into Jane's office on Thursday for our meeting, she said, "Jeanette, could you kick the doorstop away from the bottom of the door, please." I did and the door swung shut. She said, "I don't have a closed door policy, it's just that the door wouldn't stay open on it's own. After I got your e-mail, I went home and made a couple of doorstops." Whew. That was a good start to the meeting. I was really glad that I had said, "It feels like you have a closed door policy," instead of "You have a closed door policy." Be careful with the words you do use in that letter. Then she said, "When I got your e-mail I was hurt and embarrassed and angry and ashamed and angry…" I think she said angry about ten times. I had seen her angry on the phone with another supervisor. In a very loud and angry voice she shouted, "Oh yeah, if you think you can do that to me and my people you just wait to see what I can do to you!" I was pretty clear I did not want her angry in my face—I probably would not have a face left.

After the meeting, nothing changed. I would still look up at her when she walked by. I would smile and say, "Good morning, Jane." And she would still walk by my desk without any acknowledgement whatsoever. However, during the meeting she did share two things with me that made a difference in how I perceived the situation. She said, "Jeanette, by the time I get in at 7:00 a.m. you are already in the flow of work. When I walk through the door I want to go straight to my office, close the door, and have my coffee and muffin while I read my e-mail. Then I'm ready for people."

I had never even considered that because I am such an Enthusiast, I always want people around me. When she said it, though, it sounded fair. She gets to do her life her way. The second thing she said made sense to me, too. She said, "I don't wake up until my tenth pot of coffee." For me a tenth pot is Saturday morning. I get it. I get it. She had a couple of reasons for doing what she was doing. If I had never written her the e-mail, I would never have found those out, and I would probably would have let her get to me, forever. I would have been in attack mode whenever I thought about her or saw her. That would have been a total waste of energy, and I would have felt and been much less safe.

Why would I keep looking up and smiling at her and saying good morning even though I knew that she was not going to respond? That is who I am. I like smiling at people and acknowledging them. I do not have to let the way people respond to me, affect who I am. Jane and I were never friends, but we did work together professionally. Our styles were too different and I did not have the understanding I now have of why people are the way they are. So, I was never fully comfortable with her, and she probably was not comfortable with me, either. But we could work together.

If you need to ask people to change their behavior, use the In-writing Formula to get the best results. Make sure that you put a deadline in the letter. You can do this with people in the office or in your family. I see many families with grown children who could solve many of the problems they have with each other by putting it in writing, then getting together to have calm, rational, solution-oriented discussions. One of the biggest things holding them back from the discussions right now is that they imagine saying something to each others' face, and their safety brain prevents the discussion. They figure there will be a confrontation, which is unsafe. It can be so much easier than that.

Family dynamics are difficult to change because those patterns are some of the deepest. However, we can change them. By the time you get together, the defensiveness is past and both of you are ready to look for solutions.

Some people object to putting it in writing, especially in the office, because then that letter can be used against them, especially in a union environment. I see exactly the opposite. The letter says:

1. I like you.
2. I have a problem.
3. I need your help with a solution.

This shows you in a good light. You are willing to admit there are good things about that other person and you are willing to try to solve the problems you encounter. If the letter comes to the union's attention, you will look good, not bad.

You will be using the In-writing Formula fairly often if you decide to implement the next technique for yourself personally, in your family, or in the office.

Chapter 17
The Talk-first Policy

When we have a problem with someone, we must talk to them about it first. We do not talk to coworkers and feed the office grapevine. We do not gossip with others about the person and the problem. Instead, we need to enable ourselves and everyone else to take responsibility for our problems and deal with them immediately and directly.

When we talk to friends or coworkers about the problems we have with other people and we have no intention of solving the problem, we are gossiping. Gossip is a clear indicator of poor self esteem. When we gossip about others—Have you heard what John is up to now—the implicit message is, "We would never do that." We are talking negatively about the other person to make ourselves look good. If we have to tear others down to feel good about ourselves, then we do not feel very good about ourselves. There are better ways of feeling good about ourselves. If you start to identify who you are, what you like to do, and start becoming that person, you will not need to gossip about others to feel good.

If we refuse to solve problems with our difficult people, every time we think about that person and that problem, we will activate our defense system. This happens when others talk to us about their problem people, too. When we listen to their defensive tone of voice, we hear the irritation and anger. Sometimes they even start talking about attack actions. They start talking about getting revenge. When we allow people to talk about problems they have no intention of solving, we are helping them remain fearful. We enable them to be defensive, and even go into attack mode, instead of using that energy to solve the problem. If they actually solved the problem with a win-win solution, the problem would be fixed and they would feel more competent. Then, the next time they faced this type of problem, they would feel more able to solve it.

An offshoot of listening to others gossip, is that the gossiper now knows that he or she can no longer trust us. If we will listen to them rip someone apart, then we will probably listen to others rip them apart. Gossip is a lose-lose-lose situation. The person gossiping, loses. The person listening, loses. The person being gossiped about, loses.

Take responsibility for yourself and your problems. Enable others to take responsibility for themselves. When my children come to me and talk about each other or their dad or a friend, I say, "Are you ready to solve this problem?" If they are ready to look for a solution, I will listen for as long as they need me to listen while they get to their solutions. However, if they are just gossiping with no intention of solving the problem, I have no time for them and will not listen.

With people in the office, you can do the same thing. Many of us let coworkers gossip to us again and again about the same people. First, they are wasting time. They are wasting their time because they have no intention of solving the problem and they are also wasting your time. Second, when we listen to them, without asking them how they are going to solve this particular problem—or even forcing them to solve the problem if we are in a position to do so—we are helping them to avoid solving their problems. If you are in a position to implement the Talk-first Policy, do so.

The policy simply states that *people talk first about a problem with the other person or people involved in the problem.* Present this to everyone at your work site and get everyone involved. We will no longer be wasting time gossiping. We will be solving problems immediately when they occur. What this really does is make the office an incredibly safe place to be because instead of letting problems fester until they explode, they are taken care of while they are new and small. Sometimes a person feels that they need to talk with someone else before they talk with their problem person. We can allow them to talk with us as long as they are looking for a solution, instead of avoiding dealing with the problem.

We can implement the Talk-first Policy in a small way if, when someone comes to us to gossip, we simply look at them and say, "It sounds like you have a problem with Kathleen. You need to talk to her about it. I can't solve it for you." The most assertive way to get a gossip to stop is by getting up, standing beside him or her, putting two fingers, very gently, on his or her elbow and saying, "It sounds like this is a real problem with Kathleen. Let's go talk with her right now about it." Your problem person will go with you for about four steps and them start stuttering and stammering about having to get back to work. You have just shown that you are willing to take action on problems. They are gossiping to you because they do not what to take action on their problems. They will no longer come and gossip to you, guaranteed. They may be gossiping to others. They probably will not start solving their own problems, but at least you will not have them interrupting you with gossip anymore. (Of course, they may start gossiping about you!)

We all have different boundaries and nobody reads minds. The first time someone does or says something that crosses your boundaries, say so, otherwise, how will they know? If you do not feel safe having that conversation alone, have someone in authority be present during the discussion you have with your problem person. Tell others your boundaries, otherwise they cannot know that it is a boundary for you.

This is all the Talk-first Policy is, letting others know what does and does not work for you. If you need to use the In-writing Formula to start the process, do so. If you need to talk with someone else to make sure you are clear about what you want to say, do so. If you want someone to witness the discussion, get someone. But talk first to the person you have the problem with and start enabling those around you to do the same thing.

In Level IV we have discussed eight different techniques that we can use to help others stay calm or calm down. Each of the techniques will also show others that we are safe and that they do not need to attack us. We might even show them that it is unsafe to attack us. The eight techniques we discussed were as follows:

Chapter 10, They Are Right.
Chapter 11, Pure, Clean Listening
Chapter 12, Quit Taking Away Their Emotions
Chapter 13, Constructive Criticism Doesn't Exist
Chapter 14, Strong Boundaries Create Safety
Chapter 15, The Public Secret
Chapter 16, Give It to Them in Writing
Chapter 17, The Talk-first Policy

Choose one. Think about an actual situation in your life where you can use this. Concentrate on it, and take it step-by-step over the next 21 days. Think about it, at least once a day for the next 21 days. Take one small step with the chosen technique each day over the next 21 days. What you are doing is embedding the technique in your safety brain as a new habit. If you were to do this with every one of these eight techniques, in less than six months you would see a wonderful difference in how people treat you. They would no longer attack you. They would know that you are a safe person. They might get angry in your presence as they try to work through problems they have with other people, but you would know that they are not attacking you. You would not freeze. You would not want to get away. You would not feel the need to attack them. Instead, you would be able to listen calmly and objectively to them as they search for their own solutions. It sounds like an ideal life, right? It is possible. It could be your life if you are willing to work with your safety brain long enough to get it to form the new habits.

LEVEL V

What Can I Do
About Me?

*I have gone to look for myself.
If I get back before I find me,
please have me wait.*[1]

Introduction

What Can I Do About Me?

Where do the fears that generate our anger come from, and how do we get rid of them? In Level V we will explore some of the thoughts we have about others, and how those thoughts trigger our fears. If we can change those thoughts, we will not have the fear. If we do not have the fear, our safety brain will not activate. We will stay calm and deal with people rationally and calmly, instead of defensively, by attacking.

Level V is much more sensitive material than the earlier levels, simply because we are starting to look at the root of our anger. We are going to explore what we fear and why. We will explore how we have been hurt, and we will re-experience that pain. These next few chapters can bring up very strong emotions in people. We can feel a great deal of pain, sadness, loneliness, and confusion. Sometimes we can be reminded of extremely painful incidents that were long forgotten. If you have never worked with any of your really painful issues before, get a professional counselor, or therapist, or psychologist, or psychiatrist to help you through. I do not have an advanced degree in any of the counseling professions. I can tell you how it looks. I can show you some places inside yourself to go. I can share with you some techniques to working it through, but I cannot directly help you. When I first started working through my painful issues, I did work with a group therapist, and with individual psychologists. I could not have done it alone. I had been protecting myself from feeling that pain for so long that I had absolutely no clue of how to deal with all that pain when I felt it. When the pain came, it was overwhelming. I could have hurt myself very badly if I had not had someone helping me.

We started dealing with what we think about others in Level III with the four different Communication Styles. That information allowed you to get past some of your defense and attack behavior with the simple realization that people do things differently. We do not need to assume they are out to get us. They do things differently because it works for them. If what they do does not work for us, we need to decide how we are going to handle the situation. We can decide without going to defense and attack.

In any relationship we have four choices:

1. We can try to change the situation, which is what the whole book suggests.
2. We can accept the situation, which is what we did in Level III; we accepted that people are different and need to be dealt with in different ways.
3. We can leave the situation—we can always leave a relationship or quit a job.
4. We can complain about the situation for the rest of our lives.

In this level we are going to explore each of these four choices. We will explore more of the thoughts we have about others that lead us to think they are out to get us, so we attack. And by the end of the book, option #4 "complaining about it for the rest of your life," is no longer an option.

Chapter 18
You Agreed to the Rules

Leanne had a long distance relationship with Calvin. Leanne lived on one side of the country, Calvin on the other. They spent a lot of money paying off telephone bills. They sent a lot of e-mails. They almost single-handedly supported an airline because they flew to see each other so often. For that first Christmas, Calvin bought them an all-expense paid cruise. (At that point I hinted to my husband, "Nice Christmas present, huh?" He did not take the hint!) While Calvin and Leanne were on that boat in the middle of whatever ocean they were cruising, Calvin informed Leanne, "The former love of my life that I said wasn't in my life anymore, well, she kind of is." Ah. Many people at this point would advise Leanne to throw him overboard and enjoy the rest of the cruise. Good advice. But their relationship did not end that way. In fact, Leanne went home and started talking with her friends. "Should I stay in this relationship or not?" (Was staying in the relationship an option? Not to me, personally.) However, Leanne did actually choose to stay in the relationship. In fact, three years into their relationship they are talking about getting married. If they do in fact get married, Leanne has no right to go to Calvin in five years, furiously angry, and tell him, "You have been fooling around on me the whole time. I'm leaving you." Why not? Because she accepted the situation or she knew about it from the beginning. Let's get just a bit more responsible here: she has no right to do that in five years because she agreed to the rules, right from the beginning. Unlike most relationships, he actually told her what the rules were. And she agreed to them, right?

And so did you.

Whatever your problem is and whatever the relationship is, you agreed to the rules. However long the relationship has been going on, whether five minutes or five years or fifty years, you agreed to the rules. Whoever the relationship is with, whether a coworker, an employee, a boss, a child, a spouse or life partner, a friend, a sibling, a parent, a client, a customer, you agreed to the rules. You are not a victim. They are not doing it to you. When we pretend to ourselves, and to others, that we are victims in our relationships, then we have absolutely no safety. If we are victims, they can do anything they want to us, and we will let them. When we pretend to ourselves that we are victims, we are defensive a lot. We go on the attack often, trying to regain control over ourselves and regain our safety.

You agreed to your part in whatever the situation is. You agreed by using your 55% of communication—using your body language. The first time they did whatever it was they did—they were rude to you, they demanded that you work more than the time you are paid to work, they told you to do something that you did not want to do; they were late for a date—whatever the situation is, you went along with it. In going along with it, you agreed to the rules. Take responsibility for your part in the relationship. There is no relationship if there is only one person. There are two people in any relationship and each person has full, 100% responsibility for his or her actions and words, or non-actions and non-words. And each owns 50% of the relationship. You agreed to the rules.

What is the hardest thing in the world to do? Go back into the relationship and try to change the rules. It does not matter what the rules are right now. It does not matter how much you tell yourself that you do not like what is happening. It does not matter how much you complain to others about what that other person is doing. Whatever the rules are, however you have been living that relationship, it is safe. Your safety brain is going to make the thought of trying to change the rules as uncomfortable or as impossible as it possibly can so that you leave it be. However much you tell yourself you hate the way it is, your safety brain likes it because it knows what to do and what to expect in return.

When these relationships last for a long time, we build real resentment towards the other person. We feel defensive and in attack mode whenever we think about that person or that situation. We complain bitterly to our friends. In our minds we make up situations where we get to attack them and make the situation better. Of course, making up conversations in our heads without ever taking action does not change the situation, and so we continue living the relationship and resenting it. We need to acknowledge that we agreed to the rules.

In the back of our heads, in that 80,000 words per minute, we have a little black book. On each page in the little black book we have the name of someone with whom we have a relationship. There would be a page with my husband's name. Each child has a separate page with his or her name on it. Parents each have their own pages; siblings, coworkers, supervisors, or managers that you have to report to, the building's janitor, if you encounter this person occasionally and chat, your bank teller if you see this person often enough to chat at the bank. Each person that you have any sort of relationship with has his or her own page. On each person's page you also have written down the rules for how each relationship should be.

Maureen started working with the company three weeks ago. Today, she walks up to my desk and… "Oh, did you just see what she did?" Well, I quickly grab the little black book in the back of my mind, flip to Maureen's page, and put a big ticky (check mark) on her page. "I can't believe she did that!" Five days later she walks up to my desk and she does it again. Flip to her page, Well, ticky! Two days later she's back at my desk and she does it again. Black book, Ticky! Two weeks later, she does it again, Ticky! Ticky!

Ticky! Each time she engages in that awful behavior, we put a ticky on her page. We fill up space after space, and row after row on her page with little tickies.

How many of us keep score? This is what we are talking about. Keeping score. Each time that person engages in the behavior that we do not like, we make a note of it. We keep score. In fact, after a while we begin to watch for that behavior, just so we can keep score.

We only forgot to do one small thing. We forgot to read the rules to her from her page in our book. We forgot to tell her the first time she offended, that her behavior did not work for us. In not telling her, we agreed to the rules. So now, hidden from her, we keep score and build up our resentment. We pretend we are victims, letting her do it to us, instead of realizing that we have an equal say in our relationship with her.

Now it is three years later. Maureen is still working with the company, and yesterday, we put the last ticky on her page. That's it. She has no more chances. We have had enough. We slam the little black book shut, figure out how to say it to her and, when we catch her alone we say, "Maureen do you have a minute? Great. Listen, I really enjoy working with you. You are so efficient, and you're always in a good mood. That's really great. There is just this one little thing that has kind of been driving me crazy since you started here." I am trying to find a fairly nice, yet realistic way of having the conversation with her. Could you imagine actually saying something like this to her? And I have even started off with saying something nice about her. If we have a conversation like this with her, what is the implicit message that we have just given her?

"Maureen, don't ever trust me again. Because I will lie to you for up to three years at a time."

When we tell someone that something has been driving us crazy for a month, a year, eight years, or forty years, we have just told them that we have been lying to them the whole time. When we refer to any situation that we have allowed to go on for any length of time, without having told the other person when we started having a problem with it, we are telling them that we have hidden something from them. We have not been telling them the truth, right from the start. And, in telling someone that we will hide problems from them, we have broken trust. I do not know about you, but for me, it is extremely hard to rebuild trust.

I have done it with my mom. We broke off an contact a few years ago, and I let it go on for eight months, because it felt good. However, knowing that it is extremely difficult to break off relationships with your primary family and ever feel safe again, after eight months, I took the first steps to fixing that relationship. It was not easy to make the first move, but I did it.

The relationships we have with our primary family are vital to our feeling of safety, because those are the people that taught us how to be safe in relationships. It takes a tremendous amount of time, energy, and hard work to heal if we break off relationships with our primary family. Many people break off those relationships and never heal. Which means they carry added defensiveness with them for life. Sometimes, for some people, those relationships were so horrid and debilitating, we do need to end them. We can heal after we end them. However, it does take a lot of energy and hard work.

The issue with my mom was not that bad. So, after eight months, she and I fixed it. My husband and I have broken trust again and again in our relationship. We have said things and done things, intentionally and unintentionally, that have broken trust. However, because we are committed to our relationship and our love, for life, we fixed it. We talked those issues through. We accepted those issues, and then we fully let those issues go. No emotions were left over, except love for each other. With friends and coworkers, though, I am one of those people who, if a good friend or a coworker crosses that line, if I feel that that person has broken trust, the relationship is over as far as I am concerned. I might have to continue working with that person, professionally, but I will never again have a personal conversation with that person. For me, when someone breaks trust with me, and that person is not family, I end the relationship. (I still have some areas to work on.) I know that there are many, many other people who are like this with relationships.

You do not want to be the one to give the message, "Do not ever trust me again, because I will lie to you for..." Many of us have already had conversations like this with people. We have broken trust. Be careful to never do that again.

There is a way to change the rules in a relationship without breaking trust. First you say, "It has been working for me up until now." We can say this honestly because we are acknowledging our part in the relationship. We need to understand, for ourselves, that the point when the rules in a relationship no longer work for us is when we are willing to do something to change the rules. We are willing to say something to that other person. When we are willing to say or do something in a relationship to change the rules that is when the old rules stop working for us. Until we are willing to take action, the old rules are working for us. So, admit it when you have the conversation with this person. Be honest. "It has been working for me up until now. It does not work for me anymore." Only after we admit our part in the relationship can we then let them know that we want to change the rules. They may agree to participate in new rules. They may not. That would be their choice. If they will not agree to new rules, if you gave it your best shot, and they refused to help change the situation, you still have three choices left. You can accept the situation, you can leave it, or you can complain about it for the rest of your life.

You agreed to the rules in the situations and relationships that you are in. That simple acceptance that you are 100% responsible for your part in every relationship puts you back in control of yourself. You are not a victim. When we switch from victim thinking to responsible thinking, we get rid of our anger. If we are in control, and can change the rules in a relationship at any time, then we have no need to be defensive. If we are fully in control and making choices, then we can choose differently at any time. There is nothing to fear because we can choose differently at any time. In each and every relationship you are in, you agreed to the rules for some good reasons. Now, you have decided that these rules do not work for you any more. You are going to engage the other person in a discussion, with one of the techniques from Level IV, give it your best shot, and try to get the person to agree to a new set of rules.

It is also perfectly OK to decide that, although you have been complaining about the relationship a lot to yourself and your friends, you are not planning on doing anything about it. You might decide that you will never do anything about it—then get out of the Negative Thought Cycle that we examined in Level II. You may decide that at some future date you will change the rules, but not now. Then you have just decided to accept it, at least for now—so stop complaining about it. Complaining about a relationship takes us into the Negative Thought Cycle where we may find ourselves ending a relationship that was, in fact, a good relationship.

The other reason we need to stop complaining is explained in Chapter 19, Stop Asking Permission. Besides, your friends are getting really tired of your complaining.

Chapter 19
Stop Asking Permission

I often have people come to me at the end of a training day to catch me alone because they have a really personal situation they want to share with me. Bonnie caught me at the end of one Wednesday and told me about a situation with her aunt. On the past Friday, Bonnie's 20-year-old dog had died. She was still pretty sad about it. On Saturday, Bonnie's aunt had phoned to find out if Bonnie had received the bouquet of flowers that her aunt had sent. In the course of that conversation her aunt accused Bonnie of being a lesbian (who knows how the conversation got there!) Bonnie was terribly offended. Instead of commiserating with Bonnie for her loss, the aunt had phoned with a personal, and totally inappropriate, agenda. Bonnie said that her aunt did this kind of thing constantly and that nobody in the family talked to the aunt anymore (small wonder).

Bonnie then said, "Tonight, after the training session, I'm going to phone my aunt and end the relationship. I don't ever want to talk to her again." Even though the aunt had been a very important part of Bonnie's life as she was growing up, Bonnie had had enough (keeping score). Why was Bonnie telling me about the situation and about her decision? She was asking my permission. She wanted me to agree that she was making the right decision. Even though she knew it was not the right decision. How can I say that Bonnie knew that it was not the right decision? Because she was there talking to me about it. She was asking my permission. If she truly felt it was the right thing to do, she would not be so worried about it that she had to talk with me, almost a stranger, about it. She would not need anybody's permission. She would simply do it.

One strong reason that Bonnie felt that she needed to end that relationship was that the rest of her pack (her family) had shown her that everyone in this pack ends their relationship with the aunt. It was a safe thing to do. As well, maybe she would not be fully accepted into the family pack until she, too, ended that relationship. Bonnie's safety brain was recognizing the pack behavior and trying to ensure that she would continue to be accepted by the larger pack. She might even have received advice from others in her family to end that relationship with her aunt.

I do not give permission and I did not give Bonnie permission. Instead, I said, "You are asking me for permission to do something you know you do not want to do." She started crying and agreed that she really did not want to end the relationship as her aunt had been like a mother while Bonnie was growing up. Bonnie was really upset with her aunt and could not see any other way to deal with it. She was grieving for her dog and this situation with her aunt was an added emotional burden that she just could not handle. Bonnie's solution was to phone the aunt, let her know how upset she was, and tell the aunt that Bonnie would contact her in a month or so to discuss it, because she was just too emotional to do so right now. For Bonnie, it was the right solution, because she came up with it.

When we talk with people who are not involved in a situation we are gossiping. Gossiping is complaining about a situation with no intent of doing anything about it. Gossip is a clear indication of poor self-esteem. Instead of feeling good enough about yourself to deal with the situation, you talk about the other person negatively, to show your listener that you are better than that other person. If you find yourself talking about the same situation over and over with others, and you have not taken any action to solve the situation, you are gossiping. If you find yourself talking about someone in the same way, from different situations encountered over months or years, you are gossiping. You have no intention of taking action. You are asking permission to keep doing the relationship exactly the way you are doing it right now. You are trying to get the other people to tell you that you are right in how you are dealing with the situation. After a time, when a friend or coworker continually complains about the same person or situation and shows us quite clearly that they have no intention of talking action, we get impatient. We become unwilling to listen because we know that the conversation is pointless.

The interesting thing is that you know you are not right. It is bothering you. If you knew that you were 100% right, it would not bother you. You would feel good about the situation or relationship and not need to ask others' permission. Your part in the relationship is bothering you. You know that because you are defensive and feel the need to get your thoughts and actions justified. You have tens and hundreds of casual and intimate relationships about which you have never gossiped. There is no defensiveness attached to those people, and you feel no need to talk about them. Why do you need permission for some relationships and not for others? Your part in the relationships that you gossip about over and over is bothering you. So you need to have others tell you that what you are doing is OK, so you can continue doing it. You are asking permission.

Stop the gossip. Stop asking permission. Decide to take action. Or, decide to accept the relationship. You are not a victim. You are agreeing to the rules in that bothersome relationship. Complaining only serves your safety brain's need to keep you stuck doing that relationship exactly the way you are right now, until you die. Do not fool yourself that you are talking about it today because you will eventually do something about it. It's gossip. Your safety brain is trying to fool you, so that you make no changes.

I used to spend so much time doing this. Every gathering we left, family, friends, or casual acquaintances, as soon as my husband and I were in the car I would start saying, "Did you see what so-and-so did…" and "Did you hear what so-and-so said," and "I can't believe what so-and-so said…" I was clearly showing my own low self-esteem. As my belief in myself grew, as I began to hold as a truth that I was a good and worthwhile person who deserves the best, once I started believing in myself and feeling better about myself, I cut way back on gossiping about others. (I do still engage from time to time, but about 1% of the time, instead of 99% of the time.) Now, when we leave a gathering we will discuss the interesting things we heard and thought. We will discuss how much fun we had. We will talk about other plans or about the kids, instead of engaging in the gossip.

In order to write this book I had to get out of the house. I have a home office but it is so easy to do laundry, or make a sandwich, or start and finish reading one of my trashy novels instead of writing. So, I would take my laptop and go out to coffee shops and the big bookstores with coffee shops in them, to sit all day and write. There is something about sitting in a bookstore watching people spending money on other people's books that I have found really motivating in getting this book written. What is fascinating is to eavesdrop on other people's conversations. Almost constantly, I would hear the people next to me (men talking with men, women talking with women, and men and women talking together) asking permission from the person they were with, to keep doing their problem relationships the way they were doing them. The complainers would get quite vehement if their listener would not agree that they were in the right, in the problem relationship. One lady was talking about ending a marriage and cited a totally irrelevant novel she had read about a child being kidnapped, to gain her listener's sympathies and agreement. (Did I ever want to jump in! But I didn't.) Defense-attack came up almost every time the listener would not agree that the gossiper was in the right.

Often, we have chosen exactly this person to gossip to, and ask permission from, because we are pretty convinced that they will give us permission. Or, we respect this person so much that their agreement will really make us right. When they refuse to agree, we become defensive. Many times we engage in defense-attack when this specially chosen person will not give us the permission we seek.

We ask for permission. What really scares me is that many people will complain about their marital problems with friends. They complain to friends so that they do not have to take action. Many times, the friends will recommend actions that are totally inappropriate. Remember, when people are simply complaining they are trying to look better than the other person. They make the other person look worse than he or she really is. They build themselves up to look better than they really are. People do not tell the full, unadorned truth when they are complaining. They either leave out things that would make them look bad, or they actually make up little lies about what they said and did, so that they look good. Either way, far too many people talk themselves out of marriages and relationships that are good and could easily be fixed. But the gossip made it worse.

I have made it an iron-clad rule for myself that I never talk about my problems in my marriage with anyone but my husband (and the three million people who are reading this book and who take my training sessions!) You will notice that all of the marital problems I have discussed in this book happened in the past, and they have all been worked through and fixed. I have been sharing real life situations so that first, if you have been engaging in any of these behaviors you know that you are normal, instead of aberrant, and second, now you know you can solve them, too.

It is far too easy to fall into the Negative Thought Cycle when complaining about your marriage or intimate relationship. Talk about it often enough with the focus on the negative and you could well talk yourself out of a marriage, for no good reason. Stop the gossip. Stop asking your friends and life partners and family and coworkers for permission to keep doing your problem situations in the same old problem ways. Allow yourself to talk with someone about a problem only if you are brainstorming solutions or working up the courage to deal with a problem and change the rules in that relationship.

When we engage in asking permission, we find ourselves defensive and angry, and we can easily attack the friend we are complaining to, because they will not agree that we are in the right. Stop. Focus on the positives. When you get together with friends, talk about all that is wonderful in your marriage instead of gossiping about problems. Talk about how supportive he is. Talk about how much fun she is. Talk about what a great mother she is. Talk about how great he is in bed. Focus on the positives.

Take care of the little problems before they grow up.[2] If you take care of your problems instead of letting them build and keeping score, you won't have any problems to talk about. You will feel in control of your life. You will be in control of your part in all of your relationships. When you are in control, you feel safe. There will be far less need to attack. Your life will be great and you will have to talk about the positives because that is all there will be. One way to ensure that we have a great life is to get past any guilt we are carrying from past situations and relationships.

Chapter 20
Assumptions Create Road Rage

The kids were throwing a football to each other right outside the living room bay window. We told them to take the ball across the street to the playground, so that the bay window would stay in one piece. We went back to what we were doing, and two minutes later heard the sound of the shattering bay window resound throughout the neighborhood. We rushed out the front door, saw the bay window in shards, and yelled at the kids, "What happened? I just told you to take that ball across the street. What is the matter with you? Now look what you've done!" How many of us would react like this? Most of us. How many of us would rush out the front door, see the destruction, make sure the kids were OK and then very calmly say, "OK, guys, we have two problems. The first is that you disobeyed me. The second is this broken window. What are you guys going to do about this?"

We can react in either of these two ways. We can react with anger or calm. Why do most of us react with anger? When would you ever completely ignore something that someone had just asked you to do? Maybe because you could not care less about them, or maybe you have your own agenda that is far more important than theirs, or maybe you want to get even with them over something. Think of your own reasons. Imagine, from your own life, when you have stood listening to what someone is asking you to do, and you agreed that you would do it. Then, as soon as they walked away, you went ahead and did what you wanted, totally ignoring what you had just agreed to do. This is what the kids did—they deliberately and totally ignored what we had just asked them to do, and we even gave them a good reason to follow through on what we asked them to do. We mentioned that we wanted the bay window to stay in one piece. We look at what they have done and, in our 80,000 words per minute we quickly think, "When would I ever do this?" If it is for a negative reason we recognize the danger in this situation and we go to defense-attack.

We do this often with other adults. When other adults do things or say things, we assign them one of our motives. Then we get defensive and attack based on that erroneous thinking. And that thinking is erroneous because we actually have no idea why they did what they did. We cannot crawl into their heads and read their minds and their motives. If we would stop to ask, we might find that there is absolutely no reason to go on the defensive. Use the pure, clean listening that we learned about in Chapter 11 instead of jumping to a wrong conclusion and attacking.

Leo is a teacher who attended a *Parenting without Anger* course I gave a couple of years ago. In Calgary, our playground driving zones are in effect from 8:30 a.m. until one hour after sunset. During those hours the speed limit through playground zones is 30 kilometers per hour. Outside of those hours the speed limit is 50 kilometers per hour. Leo gets furiously angry with people who go 30 kilometers per hour through a playground zone when the playground zone is not in effect. As a teacher, he is very aware of playground and school zone speed limits. Leo has gotten so furious with other drivers that he has actually pulled them over and has told them that they should be driving faster. Leo knows this law and he assumes that everyone else knows it too; therefore, if they are driving that slowly in front of him, they are doing it to him deliberately. Hence, defense-attack.

We are funny creatures. We assume that other people have the same knowledge and reasons and experiences that we have. When they do something we assign them one of our reasons and then we get defensive and attack, instead of asking them about their reasons and dealing with the situation calmly.

Another situation where we do this is when we experience road rage. That idiot driver speeds up, cuts in front of us, and we have to hit the breaks or we will backend him. If we get angry in this situation, we are seeing the physical danger and we release adrenaline into our system so we can keep ourselves safe. However, if we start muttering, yelling, gesturing, or cursing at this person, we need to check out the motives we assigned to that other driver. For me, driving is a race. If there is anyone in front of me, I am not winning. (How many of you are like that?) Those other drivers cut us off because they are trying to win. They did it deliberately! Maybe you are not in a race when you are driving, but if you experience road rage you assumed they did it deliberately.

Did you know that your face is posted in every bathroom around the world, and under it is the caption, "When you see this person driving, you must cut them off." I don't think so. Maybe they were late for something important. Maybe there was a pregnant person or injured person in the back seat. Maybe it was just an accident and they started moving over without shoulder checking. Maybe they did shoulder check and you were in their blind spot. Have you ever cut someone off for one of these reasons? Yet, we assume they cut us off for one of the negative reasons instead of one of the positive reasons. (Negative Thought Cycle). They did it deliberately. Defense-attack.

When you start going into attack mode, because you are sure you understand the other person's motives even though you have never asked them, STOP! You do not understand their motives. You are assigning them one of your own. We judge others based on their actions, and how we perceive their actions, rather than on their intent. Ask them about their intent.

In doing so, you will be stopping your anger, turning on your thinking brain, and listening for their true intent instead of assigning them one of yours.

We also activate our defense systems and attack for exactly the opposite reason as we will see in Chapter 21. At some level we believe that, instead of us being able to read their minds, They Can Read Our Minds.

Chapter 21
No Guilt

How many of us made a mistake last year? All of us. How many of us made the mistake on purpose? None of us. The definition of a mistake is that we did not make it on purpose. It was an accident. How many of us were treated as though we made the mistake on purpose? Many of us were treated by others as though we made the mistake on purpose. How many of us treated ourselves as though we made the mistake on purpose? Most of us treated ourselves as though we made the mistake on purpose: "That was a stupid thing to do," and "I should have known better," and "If only I had taken more time," etc. We treat ourselves as though we made the mistake on purpose and then we beat ourselves up for it. We carry guilt for having made the mistake.

Mistake = miss take = it was only a miss. Take Two.[1] Just like in the movies: Take Two. You get to try again.

Guilt is carrying old situations around with us wanting to do them over again in a different way. Redoing the past, winding the clock back and having the opportunity to undo the situation and do it a different way is impossible. It is a total waste of our lives to engage in this kind of thinking. We often go to defense-attack when we think back on situations that we feel we did not do well. I think that anger comes from the realization that we cannot undo that situation. It is done. It is over. When we use our imaginations to go back to that situation, our safety brain understands that we are asking the impossible. If we are asking the impossible, then we, ourselves, are unsafe to be with. Anyone who asks us to do the impossible is unsafe. So we slam the gateway shut because of our own thoughts.

Guilt is thinking, in retrospect, that you could have done something differently. You could not have done it differently. You did not make a mistake. You have never made a mistake in your life. You have done every single second of your life in exactly the right way. I can prove it. Because that is how you did it. There was no other way to do it, so stop imagining that there was another way to do it. You did exactly the right thing. The proof is in front of you. That is how you did it. Let go of the guilt.

Every action you have ever taken, every word you have ever said, everything was exactly the right thing to do and say. Would you do it differently if it happened again, today? Possibly. Because you have different knowledge now. You have more experience. You would probably have slightly (or greatly) different emotions should the same situation occur today. However, today is not yesterday. Yesterday, whenever it was that you said the thing or did the thing that you regret, you did or said exactly the right thing with the information you had, the emotions you were feeling, what your safety brain was telling you to do, and the experience you had up to that moment. You were right. *Call yourself right because you were.* No guilt. Every second you spend wallowing in guilt is a second that you are not spending doing your life differently, now. Get past it. Get over it. Call yourself right. You were.

One of the real dangers of carrying guilt is that we tell ourselves that we were wrong to do what we did. When anyone tells us we are wrong, we get defensive because the conversation is unsafe. Slam goes the gateway. We launch the attack. If we call ourselves wrong, we attack ourselves. When we attack ourselves we think: "It was such a stupid thing to do. I could have done this, or this, or this. I should have said this. Then he would have said that. Then I could have said this. It was so stupid. I did the same thing with so-and-so last year. It was stupid then, too. What's the matter with me? I did the same thing with that person at university. And remember those other stupid things I did in university. Boy, am I ever stupid. I never change. It's hopeless. Then there was the time when I was 13 years old and I did that. Oh, and remember all of those other situations in my teens when I was really stupid. And then there was that time when I was 2 years old…" Does this sound familiar? We start by calling ourselves wrong about one thing, and end by dredging up every single thing that we can remember doing wrong in our whole lives. We dredge up all those negatives from our past. We have all been there. We have all done that. And none of us like it very much.

The other thing that can happen when we call ourselves wrong is that we start trying to prove that we were right. We engage in a short argument with ourselves, trying to persuade ourselves, with words, that we were right. If the words do not work, then our safety brain uses stronger tactics to prove we were right. We use our body language to prove that we were right. Those exact actions that we want to change become worse as our safety brain tries to prove that we were right to engage in them in the first place.

Many of us have done this with some of the simple goals we set. We decide we are going to lose weight. For the next three days we pig out on everything in sight. The exact behavior that we want to change gets worse as we try to use our body language to prove that we are right to weigh what we weigh.

We decide that we are going to follow that exercise regime and get into shape. For the next week our safety brain has us lying around even more, watching even more TV, as we try to prove to ourselves that we are right to be in the shape we are in.

We tell ourselves that we are not going to get angry with the kids anymore. It is wrong. They do not deserve such a nasty, attacking parent. And over the next two weeks we attack them with our anger even more often as we try to show ourselves that we were right to have been treating them the way we were treating them. It seems like such a convoluted situation. When we call ourselves wrong we attack ourselves, and the exact actions or words we want to change get worse as we try to prove that they were the right things to do or say.

Every action we have ever taken in the past and every word we have ever said were exactly the right things to do and say with the information we had, the experience we had, the emotions we were feeling, and the thoughts our safety brain was feeding us to keep us safe. When we accept this, we can let go of the guilt. We can stop trying to change the past. We can stop fighting against ourselves. We can stop wasting our time and energy in the past, and start focusing on the present and future. The best way to get out of the guilt and call yourself right is to use *like best, next time* on yourself.

"What I *liked best* about screaming at the kids is that it was a lot shorter than before. I've made progress. *Next time*, when I feel that anger starting to bubble, I will walk away." Concentrate on finding a realistic *like best*. You must pat yourself on the back. If you start off by telling yourself how wrong you were, slam goes the gateway. Defense-attack. We want to change that pattern.

Some of the key words to listen for that will let you know that you are trying to change the past are *could'a, should'a, would'a, if only*… When you use these words, know that you are engaged in the absolutely useless exercise of trying to rewind the clock and do the conversation differently. Think about the last time you were in a fight or an argument. Two days later, or two hours later, you thought to yourself, "That's what I should'a said." You are imagining the situation, imagining yourself using different words and different actions. What a useless waste of time. Instead do a *like best, next time*. "What I *like best* about that argument is that I did not say anything hurtful. *Next time* I will…" We have the same benefit using the *like best, next time* with ourselves that we have when we use this formula with other people. The *like best* is a positive that helps us to keep our gateways up. Then, because we are imagining the situation, we come up with a real life, realistic *next time* picture that gets stored in our safety brains to follow through with, next time. It is a very simple, very powerful phrase.

I did a small calculation. I thought that if we only spend ten minutes per day trying to change the past: "I should'a fixed that zipper, yesterday," and "I could'a done the grocery shopping on the way home from work. Now, I'm just too tired," and "I could'a been kinder when I said that to the kids," and "If only I had finished all that work yesterday," and… (Personally, I think we spend a lot more than just ten minutes a day trying to change the past.) But, if we only spend ten minutes a day trying to change the past, over the course of our lifetime we will have wasted five years of our life trying to do the impossible. We will have wasted five years of energy feeling guilty and having nasty thoughts. Instead we could use that five years of energy to get something that we really want in our lives, like happiness, or wealth, or a long vacation in Hawaii. Instead of wallowing in how we *should'a* done it differently last time, we could take even 30 minutes of that wasted time and figure out how to do it differently, next time. Notice that in the last two sentences I have used could. It is perfectly acceptable to use this word when focusing on the present and future. The waste of time comes when we focus on the past. The words *could'a, should'a, would'a, if only,* are used most of the time, not all of the time, when trying to change the past. Simply note when you use them. Look at how you have used them. If you were using them to imagine an old situation, replace those words with the formula *like best, next time.* If you were using them to form a new picture of the present and the future, go for it.

Let go of the guilt. You were right to do every single thing that you have ever done. You were right to say every single thing that you have ever said. *What I like best...next time* will allow you to get on with the life you want to live, instead of the life you did not want to have lived. *Life is what's coming. Not what was.*[2] You will be happier, less defensive, and far less prone to attacking others when you let go of the guilt over what you have done and said in the past, and instead, work towards doing things differently next time. Work forwards, not backwards.

Chapter 22
They Can Read Our Mind

If he loved me he would buy me flowers.

If she loved me she would stop nagging me while I watch football.

If he loved me he would know that when I am crying because I am feeling like this, he should hold me in his arms, but when I am crying because I feel like that, I don't want him to touch me (even though they look exactly the same to him). If he loved me he would know.

If he loved me, he would tell me more often.

If she loved me she'd know when I want to make love.

If he loved me he'd know when I want to make love.

If she loved me she'd know I hate doing the yard work.

If he loved me he'd help me out more around the house.

If she loved me she'd know to leave me alone when I am feeling like this.

If he loved me he would have bought me that sweater.

If she loved me she wouldn't spend so much money.

If he loved me he would spend more money on me.

If she loved me she'd encourage me to take time out for myself.

If he loved me he'd give me a night off from the kids.

If she loved me she wouldn't try to make me talk about work.

These are some actual comments that I have received when I have asked participants in my courses to finish the phrase, "If she loved she would…" "If he loved me he would…"

We feel deeply hurt and express it with fury when we expect to be shown how much we are loved with a certain gesture or certain words and those gestures or words are not forthcoming. At a very deep level, we think that those people who are most important to us know how to talk with us and how to show us their love without being told. Sorry. Mind readers are rare to nonexistent. We need to tell others what actions we need and what words we need so that we feel completely safe with them. Tell them. In a calm, peaceful moment, tell them. "Honey, I really feel loved when you give me flowers unexpectedly," or "Babe, I really feel like you care for me when you let me watch the football game without any interruptions," or "I would really feel good if you would take the kids one evening next week. I'm really feeling the need for a night off." In fact, in my marriage, we have gotten to the point where I can even ask my husband for the words I need to hear in any given situation.

At one point, he had done something that was really thoughtless (a rare occurrence). I was starting to yap, yap, yap and attack, attack, attack, and I heard that little voice in the back of my head say, "All you really want is for him to say he is sorry." I stopped my attack and said, in a fairly angry tone, "I want you to say your sorry." Wonderful man that he is, he acknowledged that it was his fault and very genuinely said, "I'm really sorry." I thought it over, checked out how I was feeling inside to see if the hurt was gone. Nope, it was still there. So I said, "Nope, that didn't work. You have to say it a number of times." Incredibly, he managed to say, "I'm sorry," four times in a row, and made each one of them sound genuine and sincere. That worked. I let the hurt go. The situation was over.

OK, this situation looks a bit ridiculous. I needed his cooperation in this conversation and he was willing to give it. I was hurt, and instead of attacking as per usual, I was able to look at the hurt and understand the words I needed to hear in order to let the hurt go. He did not and could not know the words that would end the attack if I did not share them with him.

Many times, we are not able to end the attack ourselves. Our safety brains have gotten us too engaged in the defense-attack to be able to get out of it on our own. But, if we are vulnerable enough with the other person to ask for the actions and words we need to end the attack, and if the other person is willing to help us, we have a quick end to the attack, because we are addressing the fear.

Many of us have received gifts from our loved ones and felt incredibly hurt that they would buy us such an unwanted gift. How do they know what to buy you unless you give them a list? In my family, we do this. We draw names for the Christmas gift exchange and with that person's name comes a list of what he or she wants. My husband carries around a list of items he has heard me say I want. I do the same for him. Unexpectedly, for no reason at all, he will buy me something from that list of things he knows I want. I get an incredible feeling of being loved when I receive a gift that I truly want.

Where is the spontaneity? Where is the spontaneity of receiving a gift that you have not had to ask for? Where is the spontaneity of hearing the exact words you need to hear without ever having to have told that person? Better to ask the question, "Where is the mind reader?" If you expect spontaneity without ever telling that person what you need to receive or hear, you are expecting them to read your mind. When you do not get it, you feel hurt. He or she doesn't love me. You attack. Far better to start asking for what you need to receive and hear in order to feel cared for.

I had a discussion with my kids about this not long ago. I ended up being mom's taxi for an entire day, and not getting done anything on my list. By the end of the day I could feel the resentment starting to bubble and I tried to think objectively about why I felt the need to attack. What I said to my kids, after my internal check, was, "It is not your right to have me drive you where ever you need to go. I do it as a kindness. I don't have to. It is a gift I give you. There isn't much you can give me in return. You can't give me that time back. You can't pay me for my time (because you would be paying me with money that I had given you!) The one thing you can give me back, to help me feel that it was worth my while is a really genuine 'Thank you.' Give me a kiss. Give me a hug. Tell me how much you appreciate me taking time out of my day to drive you around." They have started doing this, and I feel great when they do. No resentment boiling. No thoughts of all the things I had planned to do with my day.

Instead of expecting them to read your mind, you need to read yourself. It simply comes down to knowing yourself well enough to know what you need to hear, what you need to receive, and the actions that you need made towards you. Other people are not responsible for your feelings and they are not responsible for reading your mind. In fact, they always have the right to say "Yes" or "No" to any request. If they refuse to help you, you can then decide what to do about that. But if they are willing to help you feel loved through giving you the words and gestures you need, it makes the whole process so much easier.

Another way we expect people to read our minds is when we increase our expectations and think the other person knows about those increased expectations, without us ever having told them, as examined in Chapter 23, The Expectations' Explosion.

Chapter 23
The Expectations' Explosion

I wonder how many times, over the years, I have said to my husband, "You don't listen to me. Why can't you just listen to me?" But I do remember the last time I said that to him. I had been travelling a lot and had gotten home late Friday night, from a two-week trip. I was tired. Mid-Saturday, I was cleaning up the kitchen muttering to myself, "Why do I have to clean up their mess? I haven't even been in the house for two weeks, and here I am cleaning up this pigsty. Mutter, Mutter, MUTTER. Theode!" And I started ranting. He listened. He made eye contact. Frustrated and hurt I said, "Why can't you just listen to me? You don't listen!" I will never forget his response, "I don't know what's the matter with me. I keep trying to listen. I just can't seem to get it right." He said it in such a defeated tone of voice. And I just stopped. I had no idea what was happening here. This was a man with very high self-esteem, yet he sounded so defeated, disheartened, and hopeless. We talked about it and realized that we had had many conversations over the years as to what good listening skills were. The first time we talked about it I told him that listening, for me, was someone not saying anything, but just letting me talk. But when he tried listening to me that way, I told him, "You don't listen to me. Why can't you just listen?" The next time we had a conversation about what listening was, I told him that he had to agree with me. He should say, "You're right Jeanette. That guy really was a dumb jerk." So he tried that and my response was, "You don't listen to me. Why can't you just listen?" What had happened over the years was that each time I gave my husband a new element to add to his repertoire of listening to me, he would try it. Instead of seeing that he was trying, I would adjust my definition of listening, see what was missing, and expect more, without even realizing that I was doing so. I would not recognize that he was trying to do as I had asked. I would only see what was missing. Then, I would say the exact same words, "You don't listen to me. Why can't you just listen?" He thought he was trying and getting it right, I kept telling him he was not even close. And now here he was, ready to give up.

When we ask someone for something, it is abstract. We tell them what we want and some of the elements, but, because we ourselves do not understand all of the elements we want included, we don't tell them everything. When they do it for us, we see what is missing. It's like we have asked someone to bake a cake. We don't have a recipe, but we know we want a chocolate cake. The other person has never baked anything before. When they ask how to make a cake we tell them to put in eggs, flour, chocolate, milk, mix it all together, and bake it for 45 minutes. They put in a dozen eggs in the shells, a spoonful of flour, a cup of chocolate, and pour in some milk. They mix it up with a spoon and put the whole bowl in the oven but they never turn on the oven. We have a mess. Whose fault? Ours, we forgot to give them exact measurements, tell them all of the ingredients, tell them how to mix it, and how to bake it. The other person willing tries to give us what we want based on their expertise, knowledge, and the few instructions we gave. If we don't give them all the instructions, they cannot meet our expectations. We don't understand that we did not give them all the instructions. When we re-explain what we want, we still do not include everything. They do not understand why we are upset, and we think they are incompetent.

We will ask a child to clean his room. We will actually accompany him to his room and tell him what to do: "Put all of your dirty laundry into the laundry basket. Hang up all of your clean clothes. And, for goodness sake, pick up all of your toys off the floor and put them away." When we check up on the cleaning job 20 minutes later we say, "This isn't clean. Look at your desk. Get those books and papers put away neatly. And what have we lost under your bed this time? Get all of this put away. And make your bed. This isn't a clean room. Clean your room!" He had done the first three things we had asked, and done them well. But we see all of the things that he had not done. We raised our expectations. He's thinking, "What's the point? I can't ever get it right anyway. I might as well not even try." And we are thinking, "What's the matter with this kid, anyway. Why can't he even clean up his room!" We are angry and in attack mode because he did exactly what we asked instead of anticipating our raised expectations. Start examining the words you use when asking for something, and look for what you have not explained.

This happens in the office as well. Many of us have had a direct supervisor ask us to complete a project. We listened carefully. We understood what they asked for. We did exactly what they asked for. We took the completed project to that supervisor and he or she ripped it apart. "This part is missing. This has to be done over, right here. And where is the…? This part here is all wrong. You're going to have to do it over." On the way out of his or her office, how did we feel about ourselves? We feel really incompetent, and think, "Why did I even bother? I can never get it right." The supervisor was thinking, "If I want it done right, I'll probably have to do it myself. What's the matter with him or her? Why can't he or she get it right?"

We did get it right. Our kids did clean their rooms. My husband was listening. The person did follow our instructions to bake the cake. The problem is the Expectation Explosion. When we ask for something, it is abstract. When we get the finished product, whether being listened to, or a clean room, or a finished project, we see what is missing. We do not realize what we did not ask for. Our expectations have gone up.

There are two simple solutions. As the person giving instructions, admit that you might have made a mistake in what you asked for. "I know I asked for this and this and this. I forgot to mention this other thing. Would you please add it? Sorry about that," or "I know I asked you to clean up the floor, make your bed, and put away your toys. I forgot to mention cleaning up your desk. Would you take care of that now, and then you're done." Admit that you did not give full instructions.

The other solution is for those who take the instructions. Teach these people to pat themselves on the back. For a while my husband would say, "Honey, I'm listening here, just the way you asked me to. Is it working?" This may sound ridiculous but it works. This type of patting ourselves on the back has two components. First, he told me that he was doing just what I had asked. Then he asked if there was any way he could make it better. This gave me a chance to acknowledge his efforts with a huge "Thank you." Then, I got to tell him how to alter it to work better.

Teach the kids to pat themselves on the back. "Mom, you asked me to pick up all of my dirty clothes, put away my clean clothes, and pick up my toys. How did I do?" This gives us a chance to say "Good job. After supper you can finish by cleaning up your desk, making your bed, and cleaning out everything from under the bed." Everyone walks away feeling good instead of everyone walking away feeling bad.

In the office situation, when you hand in a project, or someone hands a project in to you, use the words, "You asked for this, this and this. That is what I have done. Is there anything that needs to be added?" Teach yourself and others to reiterate that they have done what is asked. Teach them to pat themselves on the back. Then, they can ask if there is anything missing. It is a simple concept that works, and it nullifies anger and resentment that accompanies the Expectation Explosion.

Another simple concept that works is examined in Chapter 24, the realization that You Do Not Rule the Universe.

Chapter 24
You Do Not Rule the Universe

You are about to make a very solemn oath. Stand up. Hold up your right hand. Read the following statement out loud, and fill in the blanks with your information.

I, _____, being of sound mind and body, do solemnly acknowledge, agree, and swear that I do not now, never have, and never will Rule the Universe.

Name:_____ Date:_____

Read it again, and mean it this time!

Now, sit down and sign it and date it!

Olsen sat in the very front row of a training session that had 250 people in it. When I asked for an example of a person that really irritates someone, Olsen said that he worked in a nonsmoking environment. Tina, a coworker, smoked ten cigarettes every day before she walked in that front door of the office. A cloud of smoke entered the office with her every morning and it was driving Olsen crazy. Why was Olsen getting so angry about it? Because, he had decided that Tina was a nonsmoker. Well, how dare she come into the office this morning with that cloud of smoke surrounding her, when Olsen had decided that she no longer smoked! Olsen ran the universe. In his infinite wisdom he had decided what people should and should not do. When they did not fall in with his plans, he went to defense-attack. There were many solutions to Olsen's problem without getting defensive and attacking. He could get a fan. He could get an ionizer machine that is supposed to zap the smoke. He could sit in a different location. He could change the office around and sit as far away from Tina as possible. There were many solutions. The one guaranteed to create defensiveness and attack in us is when we have decided that our problem person will be different tomorrow. We have decided that they are changed. They are fixed. When they dare to approach us the next day, not fixed, well, defense-attack. Somewhere in our heads we have decided that we rule the universe.

We have decided that the kids no longer spill their milk. When they have the gall to spill their milk at the next meal: defense-attack. Our spouses will no longer ignore us when we talk to them. Then they do: defense-attack. A friend will be on time for all of our meetings from now on. She dares to arrive late to our next meeting: defense-attack. That jerk in the office will not be a jerk tomorrow. He has the gall to still be a jerk: defense-attack.

When we come from the mindset that our way is the right way, and we have decided how other people will be, and they do not follow through on something that we never told them about in the first place, we get defensive and attack. This thinking is absurd when we examine it. We do not run the universe. (Come on. Agree with me. You know you have to.) Other people are exactly right in the actions they take, the behaviors they engage in, and the words they use. They get to be them. If it bothers us, we have four choices. Invite them to change it. Accept the situation. Leave the situation. Complain about it for the rest of our lives. The one choice we do not have is to demand that they change. We cannot change other people's behavior.

We can invite them to make their relationship with us better by agreeing to some new rules. We can stop asking permission from others to continue in the behaviors that we actually want to stop. We can rid ourselves of guilt by realizing that everything we ever did was exactly the right thing to say and do, simply because that is what we did. We can concentrate on doing things differently in the future than we have in the past by using *like best, next time*. We need to stop assuming that people can read our minds and, instead, tell them what we need to hear and to receive. When others agree to the changed rules, we need to acknowledge that they have given us what we asked for, then we can tell them what is missing. If we teach ourselves and others to pat ourselves on the back we will stop attacking based on the Expectations' Explosion. And, we do not now, nor have we ever, nor will we ever, run the universe.

Everyone gets to live their lives the way they want. We can ask them to change in their relationship with us to make it a better relationship, but we cannot crawl into their minds and bodies and make them change. We can make it dangerous for them not to change by attacking them when they engage in the old behavior, but this is the least effective way to gain cooperation.

In Level V we have looked at some of the ways we think that have kept us believing that others are out to get us. We have examined some of our thought patterns about others that allow us to engage in defense-attack. Defense-attack is based on our fears. We have to be scared of something in order to feel the need to defend ourselves. Those fears come from inside of us. In Chapter 25 we will look at how we created some of those fears, and how to rid ourselves of them, so that we can truly deal with life calmly and rationally.

Chapter 25
No Buttons to Push

We often accuse others, either to their face or behind their back, of taking control of our emotions. "She makes me so angry," or "He drives me crazy." We talk about people deliberately pushing our buttons. "They know exactly how to push my buttons," or "She knows exactly what to say to get my goat." Well, *they can't get your goat if you don't tell them where it is.*[1]

Others do not push our buttons. We do not have little red, green, blue, and yellow buttons sitting up on our foreheads or on our wrists, so that people can just come up to us and push a button to get exactly the reaction they want. We are not like elevators where someone pushes a button and the elevator goes up or down—no one pushes our buttons to make our temper go up or down. No one can get inside of us, like inside of an elevator, and push the buttons. Our anger is more like a rain cloud. There is nothing we can do to make it rain. Rain dances do not work. We cannot poke a cloud and make the rain come down. When everything is just right for the cloud—the temperature, the amount of moisture in the cloud, the strength of the wind, and whatever else a cloud needs—then it rains. Our anger is like a cloud: when the circumstances are right, we get angry. Nobody makes us angry. We do, however, respond and react to what others say and do. We get defensive and attack because we have tapped one of our fears due to something someone has said or done. Something the person said or did reminded us of a situation that we have learned is dangerous. That other person did not crawl into our heads and manipulate our emotions. That person does not form or voice the words that come out of our mouths. We are not elevators for people to walk inside. We trigger our reactions. We see incidents and hear words, and we judge them to be safe or unsafe. From there we decide whether or not we need to become defensive. These are all choices that we have. These are decisions we make based on what we have learned. These are the paths that we have made in our meadows. These are the patterns that we live.

Farah and Sam have been married for almost 20 years. Farah's parents got a divorce when Farah was in her early teens, about 14 years old. Sam's parents divorced when he was even younger, about 11 years old. When I first met Farah, her oldest son was 13 years old, middle son was 11 years old, and their youngest, a daughter, was 9 years old. Farah was fed up with her marriage. She had a litany of complaints against Sam and was hinting at leaving the relationship. After I got many of the details of Sam's and Farah's upbringing, my first comment about their divorcing addressed the fact that their oldest was 13 years old. Farah knew, from her own childhood, that parents divorce when children are in their early teens. Sam knew this as well. This was a path for each of them that had been grooved really deeply, since they had experienced their parents' divorce.

One would think that an incident that only happens once is not grooved very deeply. If the incident only happened once, then we have only walked the path once. Walking through the grass once only leaves a very faint trail through the grass. For Farah and Sam, their parents' divorces had not just happened once. Those divorces had happened hundreds, thousands, hundreds of thousands of times. When those divorces were first happening, and over the years, they had revisited the incident hundreds of thousands of times, in their minds, in conversations with friends and maybe in conversations with family. In revisiting the divorces in their minds they were reliving the divorces. Many children relive divorces imagining what they could have said or done differently to prevent the divorce. They relive it, experiencing the divorce and the emotions that went with it again and again. Each time they think back to it and relive the situation in their imaginations, they walk the path again. Each time they walk the path in their imaginations, they groove it more deeply. Any incident that engages our emotions strongly so that we imagine the incident over and over, has not happened just once. It has happened as many times as we relive it in our imaginations. Remember, the safety brain does not recognize any differences between reality and imagination or fiction. It only sees pictures. The more clearly we imagine a situation, with all of the sights and sounds and smells and feelings, the more clearly we walk that path again, making it happen again, for our safety brains. The divorces of their parents were not incidents that had happened just once, for Farah and Sam. What they had both learned, deeply, is that parents divorce when the children are in their teens.

When I pointed out this potential pattern to Farah, it really struck a cord with her. She could see that, from both of their upbringings, she and Sam might very well follow the pattern of divorce without consciously meaning to. It was a very strong pattern in their marriage because both of them had experienced their parents divorcing. Being caught in this pattern, both Farah and Sam were engaging in many of the different traps that we have identified through the other chapters in this book. They were often in the Negative Thought Cycle. I talked mostly with Farah, so I know that she often focused on the negatives in Sam, to an extreme. She was talking herself out. She discussed situations between her and Sam where she went to defense-attack, asking for permission to continue thinking the way she was thinking. She definitely spoke as a victim, not taking responsibility for her part in the relationship. She fell into the traps because she was living a pattern set by her parents. Sam had his own part in it, because he was living the pattern set by his parents, as well. They had no awareness of the pattern, they were simply living it. We identified the pattern, and Farah and Sam both worked to ensure that the divorce did not happen. They have made some incredible changes in how they view their marriage and how they view each other. They have made some wonderful changes in how they manage their marriage. Farah and Sam are so committed to making their marriage work that each time they see themselves step back onto the divorce pattern they do something to ensure they get off of it. They have spent time in marriage counseling, which helped them tremendously. They have taken the time to attend relationship courses. However, this past November, when Farah again began talking about how horrid her marriage was, and I pointed out that here we were in November again, and here we were back to the same conversation, she simply said, "I'm not listening to this. I'm tired of always being the one to do all the work. I'm tired of always getting to this point, to these feelings." To me that sounded like her safety brain at work trying to get her to not even look at the pattern because if she sees it she might decide to try to change it. Her safety brain is fighting to get her back on the safe path: marriages end in divorce when the kids are in their early teens. Both Farah and Sam are fighting that message from their safety brains, and they are winning.

We do not have to live the patterns that we learned from our parents, our siblings, our peers, other influential adults in our childhood, and from society. These five packs are our primary packs. These are the packs from which we received our strongest training. We will still be accepted into the pack if we decide to do our lives differently. However, in order to make the changes, many times we have to identify the patterns before we can change them.

Theode and I are committed to each other's happiness and to having a forever-after-loving-relationship but that's not what I grew up seeing. When I was growing up, life was an emotional roller coaster. One day we would be laughing in our family. The next day, there was a lot of anger. Then the next day, everybody would be laughing again. I created that emotional roller coaster in my marriage, as well. There would be times when we were talking about how life was so great. Our marriage was wonderful. Within days and sometimes hours of one of those conversations, I was raging, screaming angry. I would find, or even create, something to be upset about so that I could stay on the path of that emotional roller coaster. Of course, I was not aware of why I was becoming angry. In fact, I could not understand how, after having such a great couple of days, I could be feeling like I wanted to leave. I created those situations so that I could experience the emotional roller coaster. Today, I do not get the need for the emotional roller coaster fulfilled in my marriage. My marriage is really good. We catch our anger. We stop it.

We talk. We try to treat each other with respect and courtesy and love. So, I have to create that emotional roller coaster somewhere else.

That pattern of the emotional roller coaster is so deeply embedded (I can remember it back to when I was two years old), that I need it. Sometimes I create it with my work. While I was writing this book, there would be times when I felt bleak—it would never get done. It was a stupid concept. Nobody would ever buy the book. The odd thing about those thoughts is that I firmly held the belief that this book was needed and that it would be a success. Even in my darkest moments I could tap into those thoughts and feel the Truth of those beliefs. So, why become bleak? Because I needed the emotional roller coaster.

I love to read trashy novels with great sex scenes (Warren Farrell calls today's romance novels "pornography for women." [2] I agree and I love it!) In the past, when I felt a dirth of love in my life, with low self-esteem and a real feeling of not being loved or lovable (even in the early days of my marriage), I read those books for the love. I would read and reread the scenes for the tenderness and the feelings both the hero and heroine received from being loved. Now, I read those same books but find myself reading and rereading for the sadness and the emptiness and the anger and the feelings of not being loved or lovable. I can actually see the change in what I read, because I have a collection of my favorite romance novels that I have been rereading for years. They are like old friends, and I love going back to them and rereading the entire novel, or simply the sections that I need. I now turn to the negative scenes where I once used to turn to the positive scenes. In fact, this was one of the indicators that led to me realize this pattern. How else and where else would I ever realize that I was searching out the emotions of being negative, angry, hurt, sad, and empty, as though I had lost someone I loved, as though I had just had the biggest, worst, marriage-ending fight with my husband (which I could no longer engage in and, with my thinking brain, didn't want to)? However, my safety brain sure did. The emotional roller coaster, for me, is such a deeply grooved pattern that I need to walk this path. I do not walk this path as often as I used to. And, when I do walk that path, I do not have the same consequences that I used to. Still, it is such a deeply grooved path that my safety brain gets me back on it now and then.

I have watched one particular pattern that Gail has indulged, for years, and she still does not even recognize it as a pattern. She simply lives it. She is not happy with it. I can see the anger building. But still she lives it. Twenty-one years ago, I watched Gail cut her father out of her life. It was over a small incident, in the grand scheme of things. But for Gail it was an incident worth ending her relationship with her father. Five years later, her father died without her having taken the opportunity to mend that relationship. In the years before Gail ended the relationship with her father and in the years since,

I have seen her have good friendships with people for short periods of time. Then, for one miniscule reason or another, she ends the friendship. The reasons are not miniscule to Gail, though. To Gail they are very big and very real reasons for ending relationships. I have seen Gail cut off all contact with two of her five children, meaning that she has also ended her relationships with five of her grandchildren. Looking in from this objective side, the pattern is clear, but Gail cannot see it. She is so stuck in the pattern, that she can only live it. She justifies it. She protects it. She denies that she has any part in it. Her son has even apologized for his part in whatever that incident with him was all about, but she finds reasons that the apology is not good enough. Why is Gail living this pattern? Our relationships with our children, our parents, our grandchildren, and our friends are so important that we need to do everything and anything to ensure that we maintain those relationships. Yet Gail does not see that. Why would Gail need to sever her closest relationships, when you and I would never do that? Because Gail needs it. Why? Only Gail knows. She may never get past living the pattern to the understanding that it is only a pattern in her life that and only she can understand and change it anytime she decides.

A great time in my life were the years when I was single and at university. Life was good. I felt popular. I had many friends. Between the ages of 25 to 34 years old, I birthed one child out of wedlock, got married, and had two more children. I was a responsible, down-to-earth wife and mother, concentrating on the wellbeing of my children and husband. I felt old, responsible, and tied-down. Then, I got a job where I felt young, attractive, and free. I dressed in nice clothes and had fun with my coworkers. In fact, I was very attracted to one of my coworkers. I enjoyed that attraction for a short while, then I started to realize that the attraction was affecting my marriage. I never acted upon that attraction. I was never unfaithful to my husband. But, I found myself less interested in spending time with him. I was less patient and angrier, at home. I knew I loved my husband. I knew I never wanted to divorce. So, why was I feeling strongly attracted to someone else? And why was I letting it affect my marriage? I started looking for the pattern.

The pattern: after being at home for so many years feeling like a dowdy housewife and mother, I was now going to work and feeling young, attractive, and free, just the way I had felt when I was going to university. At university I had been single. Somewhere inside me, I felt single again. If I felt single that must mean I could "shop around." That scared me because I knew I still loved my husband and wanted to be married to this man, forever.

The hardest and best thing I have ever done in my marriage was to go to my husband and say, "I need to talk to you about something that has nothing to do with you, but I need your help. I am attracted to this other person. I love you. I don't want to be attracted to this other person. I need to figure out what's going on, and get over it." Can you imagine having that conversation with your spouse? Can you imagine your spouse's reaction? My husband tried so hard to let me work it through without getting hooked. He did get hooked, at times. The process of figuring out what was going on and how to fix it took a few months. These were very tense months in our marriage. My husband questioned his worth as a husband. He questioned his attractiveness. He questioned some of the basic elements of who he was, at different times. He questioned my faithfulness. And I was questioning myself, as well. It was very painful for both of us.

I finally asked myself the right question and figured it out: "What am I giving myself in this relationship that I am not giving myself in my marriage?" The biggest element in that relationship with the coworker was that we had a tremendous amount of fun. In the office we laughed, we told jokes, and we played practical jokes. I was not giving myself any of that in my marriage. We were very serious spouses and parents. We did not have fun at home.

Once I figured that out, as a couple Theode and I started working on how to have fun in our marriage. He often faces water gun or snowball ambushes when he gets home from work. We look for the funny things that have happened during the day, and share them. We tell jokes. Just yesterday our middle son said, "You guys are weird. One minute you're in the middle of an argument and the next minute you are laughing." *We've come a long way, baby.*

Telling my husband about the attraction was the best thing I have ever done in our marriage. It told him that I would talk with him about everything. It told him that he could trust me. It told him that I wanted to work through all problems and have that forever-after-loving relationship with him. Because he was able to listen and support me through it and only got hooked some of the time, he showed me that I could trust him, that I could talk with him about anything that I needed to talk about, and that he was totally committed to our relationship as well.

I share that particular pattern because I think many women go through this pattern. After childbirth and, potentially after being out of the workforce for a while, we can experience being young, free, and "single." When we re-enter the workforce, dress in nice clothes, talk and laugh with other adults, we feel attractive. Somewhere in our thoughts, we equate that feeling with being single, which is obviously very dangerous to a marriage.

We all have patterns and we all live our patterns. All we have to do is start reflecting on our lives and looking for the patterns. We can live without realizing what is happening or, at any time, we can step back and look for a pattern and reveal the path's starting point. We will also see many of the times when we have walked that path, re-enforced the path, and grooved it deeper.

It's like watching the pendulum on a clock. We can predict exactly how far the pendulum will swing, where it will stop, and where and when it will start to retrace its path. It is the same for most of what we experience in our lives. If we care to look, we can see exactly why we do many of the things we do in our lives. We are able to identify why we react in a particular way to certain events if we care to look. We can trace each pattern back to one of the catalytic events that started us walking that path. We can predict how far we will walk on the path, and what events now, and in the future, will have us walking that path again.

If we have had the same discussion with others, if we have had this argument before with our spouses, if we have engaged in just this action/reaction with the children, or friends, or siblings, or parents or coworkers, it is time to look for the pattern. If we have had these same thoughts many times, we need to ask ourselves, "Why? What do we say, what does he or she say? Then what do we say? Then what does he or she say?" Look at the specifics. Stop hiding it. Dissect it. "When we say this, what feelings do we get? Why do we need these feelings? We do this, then he or she does that, then we do this, then he or she does that, then we do this, then he or she does that. Why? What are we getting out of it?" You are looking for the pattern. You are starting to see there is a path that you are following.

If we start to see a pattern, and it is painful and it scares you, that is OK, because your safety brain knows that you can handle it. The reason that we have been walking that path, doing that pattern, is that it is the safe way to do situations like this. Our safety brain will hide the fact that we are walking a path and following a pattern. Only when the safety brain, for whatever reason, decides that the safe course of action is to identify the pattern, deal with it, and get over it, will we be able to see that pattern. Of course, it will be scary when we first start to see a pattern. We were not even aware that it existed. The reason that we have been walking that path is that it was the safest thing to do. That means that doing situations like that in a different way will seem scary at first because they are new and have been judged as unsafe in the past. But your safety brain is on the side of change; otherwise, you would not even be able to identify that you are living a pattern. Your safety brain will not show you anything that you cannot handle. Your safety brain is totally devoted to keeping you safe. So allow the fear, feel the fear, and start looking at the pattern.

This is why Gail cannot see her pattern. It is not safe for her to do so. This is why we can so clearly see other people's patterns, yet when we point it out to them, they ignore what we have said. They twist what we have said to mean something else. They get defensive and attack us. Their safety brain will not show them things that are too dangerous for them to look at. It can be, and often is, painful to look at patterns, but not unbearably so. Because, if you are looking, your safety brain will ensure that it is not unbearably painful.

If we learned some of our patterns from our parents then our children will be learning some of their patterns from us. We know that abusive parents probably had abusive parents themselves.[3] *Children are natural mimics who act just like their parents…despite every effort to teach them Good Manners.*[4] Our children learn from what we do.

By the time the kids are 10 years old they are old enough to have had catalytic events and paths and predictable patterns. Our 12-year-old started going back to some of his old behaviors from last year. Quickly, we identified that he was leading the way, and we were following him, back to some old patterns. Why? He was feeling lonely, as though he had no friends. Those were some of his strongest feelings last year that led to the *year from hell*. Start talking with your children. I did not figure out why our son was going back to some of the old behaviors. I asked him, "What are you feeling? If there were something to be scared of in your life, what would it be?" using pure, clean listening. And he told me. If your child is old enough say, "Here is what I have seen, some of the old behaviors. What's up?" Start talking. Get the kids talking about their feelings. If they can talk about their feelings, they can let them go. You can help them learn a different way to deal with those same feelings. You can teach them that there are all kinds of different ways to deal with situations and feelings. If you can get them talking, they can heal those hurts while they are young, or certainly, younger than you are now as you try to heal yours. They do not need to walk around as adults with the same feelings that we have been carrying. Maybe our parents did not know that they could heal their old hurts. We know. We can heal our pain, and we can teach our children this skill while they are still young.

Will our children have scars from our parenting? Yes. Would you take that away from them? You get to have your lessons, live your life, and have your experiences. Why would you want to take that away from your kids? Some of your best learning has been through your pain. Would you give those lessons back? Maybe we would give the pain back, but would we give the lesson back? In retrospect, is there a different way you could have learned that lesson? No! Because that's how you learned it. Don't try to take this away from your kids based on the fantasy that you could have done it an easier way, and, therefore, you can teach them to do it an easier way. You couldn't, because you didn't. If you didn't, why would you assume someone else could?

If you start changing now, you will be giving your children their greatest lesson of all, regardless of how old they are. We can change. We can change who we are, how we live, how we react, the emotions we experience, and how we do life. If we have taught this lesson to our children, because they see us doing it, then they know now that, at any age, they too can change. Talk about it with them. Tell them they do not have to be 18-, 35-, or 69-years-old to change. They can change anything they want to change in the way they do life, any time they want.

We get angry in the same type of situations, over and over because it is a pattern to get angry in those situations. The children make a mess. We get angry. We tell ourselves not to get angry. We feel guilty about getting angry. We try to make a firm, irrevocable decision that we will not get angry in those type of situations. Next time, we get angry again. It's a pattern. Until you identify the pattern and get rid of the reason why you need to live that pattern, you will continue feeling hurt, getting defensive, and attacking in those situations.

We make the commitment to change patterns for several different reasons. Sometimes patterns change because we have made it more dangerous to continue reacting the same way than to change. One man I talked to, Malcolm, was an alcoholic ten years ago. He and a brother spent a lot of time together getting drunk until his drunken brother caused a car accident, killing himself and a child in the other car. When Malcolm heard about the deaths and the details of those deaths, being drunk became more dangerous than changing. Malcolm stopped drinking and has not touched a drop since then.

Sometimes we change a pattern because the pain of continuing the pattern is unbearable. It is safer to change than it is to do life the old way. It was more painful for me to continue being an attacking parent than it was to change. I changed. Sometimes, as kids, we looked at what our parents were doing and we said, "I will never do that." And some of us didn't ever do that to our kids. For some of us, though, that was the first thing we did to our kids, after they were born. What makes the difference between those who follow through on their vow and those who do exactly what they vowed not to do, as soon as their kids are born? The difference is that, for some, repeating a pattern learned from our parents is safer than trying to change. For others, our safety brains know that it is more dangerous repeating the old pattern than it is to change. Sometimes it isn't a pattern that we learned for our parents. We learned it from TV or from society or from friends. One pattern that girls learn from the media and their friends and society is that girls must be thin, and they must always be thinner than they are. We are so bombarded by that message through newspapers, magazines, advertising, TV, and movies that our mothers have bought into the message, and so have our sisters, our friends, and our eight-year-old girls. We hear all of these females talking about being too fat and needing to go on a diet. How about running around the playground a few times to build muscle instead of worrying about weight?

In the creation of these patterns that we re-enforce again and again, there is always a catalytic event. There is always the first time. Chapter 26 describes how catalytic events are formed and the *Emotional Water Balloons* that are attached to those catalytic events.

Chapter 26
The Emotional Water Balloon

I remember the catalytic event that led to my obsession with my weight. I was about 12 years old. Sam, an older male friend whom I adored, said, "No man is ever going to want to marry you. You're too fat." (I have weighed 125 to 130 pounds since I was 11 years old. I'm 5'3"—I have never looked fat.) But I took that statement to heart. I felt embarrassed, ashamed, humiliated, unattractive, unloved, and unacceptable. What made it worse was that his wife, Sarah, overheard and said, "She is not. Someday you'll make some man a cute little armful." (Looking at it now I have to wonder, a cute little armful of what? Never mind.) First, there was the realization for me that people noticed how much I weighed. Second, this was one of the only times that I can remember Sarah showing me affection. Normally, she left me completely alone. Since that moment my weight has been a huge factor in my life, and is one of the deciding factors as to whether or not I feel acceptable.

It has been a real quandary. I had taken the lesson from Sam's comment that if I weighed too much, I would not be acceptable, especially by men. Of course, this is a lesson that is constantly re-enforced through the media. The lesson I took from Sarah's comment was to be "lovable and acceptable, I needed to be a bit overweight, because she was nice to me, she showed me that I would gain acceptance when others thought I was a bit overweight." Because she was nice to me, she showed me that I would gain acceptance when others thought I was a bit overweight. Every day, since that statement, I have weighed myself (until I started Hap Ki Do—more on that in Chapter 28). When things in my life were not going well, I was able to lose weight. When things in my life were going really well, and I was feeling lovable and accepted, I gained weight. So, everything in life would be going great, and I would gain weight. Being on the emotional roller coaster, when I started gaining weight I would start feeling bad about myself, and was then able to lose the weight.

If you have an issue with your weight, you can identify the catalytic event that started the creation of that pattern. Look for it. Think back: "when I think about being concerned about my weight, what incident can I remember, from before I was 10 years old, that had anything to do with my weight?" Identifying the catalytic event is always a journey into your childhood. Usually, the journey takes you to those years from birth to 10 years old.

For Farah and Sam, their parents divorced when they were in their teens. Some of the catalytic events will have happened in our teens. However, every time you take that journey to your childhood and identify an incident in your teens, go back further. Really think about when was the first time you experienced those feelings. Ninety-nine percent of the time, those incidents happened before you were 10 years old. The incidents that you identify from your teens are usually the re-enforcements of a pattern, not the original event.

Many people, when I ask, "What incident from your childhood do these feelings remind you of?" say that they do not remember their childhood. This is the safety brain working hard to keep you safe. You can remember everything from birth. You have stored it all in your memory. You simply are not accessing those memories. Spend some quiet time thinking about your pattern and search your memories. Go there. Access them. Get to the catalytic event.

Our buttons or triggers are the catalytic events that started us judging certain words, situations, or people as unsafe. When we get angry today, we are protecting ourselves. We are protecting ourselves from our own fears. Something happened in our childhood, maybe once, maybe many times, that scared us. It probably threatened our sense of acceptance into our primary pack, acceptance by our parents, mainly. Now as an adult, when our safety brain judges a situation, a person, or an incident to be like that catalytic event from our childhood, we begin to feel those same emotions that were created by the original incident. Today, those emotions are even stronger because we have re-enforced them again and again. Every time we have judged a situation to be similar to that original incident, we re-experienced the original emotions, just a little. However, those feelings are dangerous. When we feel those same feelings of being unloved, unworthy, not likable, unacceptable, we are completely unsafe. We are as unsafe as we were when that incident first happened, when we were two years old, five years old, or seven years old. Children who are two and five and seven have so little power. They are completely dependent on the adults in their life for their safety. And children can see many incidents as unsafe and dangerous.

As adults, we need to protect ourselves from feeling those original feelings. It is as though there is a water balloon of emotions attached to each incident that, as children, we found to be unsafe. As adults, when our safety brains judge something to be the same as one of those situations, that water balloon starts to surface, trying to splash those feelings of sadness, loneliness, and fear all over us. Feeling those feelings is dangerous. It hurts and we feel totally vulnerable. Instead, our safety brains protect us from those feelings. We get defensive and attack. We might attack that person who reminds us of that event or we might simply experience the need to attack. We prepare to attack and, in our imaginations, we attack.

Each time that we identify a situation that is like one of those original situations, we re-experience, just a little, those feelings of sadness and loneliness and being unlovable and unacceptable. We quickly bundle up the little bits of those feelings and push them away. We are adding more water to the emotional water balloon. You can see that, after a few years, we have added so much water to that emotional water balloon that it is ready to burst. We find ourselves being angry and attacking often, because that water balloon is so full that some of those feelings are overflowing back into our minds and we are experiencing more of them. So, we defend-attack often because we are almost continuously feeling unwanted, unsafe, and vulnerable. Then, that one last thing happens, and we try to stuff one last little bit of those emotions into that overfull water balloon, and it explodes. We defend-attack, big time. We rage. We cry. We remember that original situation and we remind ourselves of all the little situations that have re-enforced that original learning.

It can be a real crying jag. It can go on for quite some time. And it can be extremely healing. In the days and weeks after that explosion, we feel so much calmer. We are able to handle life a lot better. We might go through a few days right after the explosion feeling quite down and depressed. In our 80,000 words per minute, we are processing. We are going over the catalytic events. We are rehashing the emotions. We might tuck as many as possible into the water balloon again, and start the whole process again, which is very emotionally debilitating. Doing this will lead to more and more defensive-attacking behavior.

Or, we might let it go. The goal is to let it go. The goal is to get rid of that particular emotional water balloon by emptying it completely, so that it no longer exists. We might have a realization that what we did was exactly right, and what we said was exactly right. We protected ourselves as well as we could. We were children. We had no other choice.

We did a good job. Now, as adults, we can let it go. If we let it go, we may never again be reminded of that catalytic event by events in the future. It is truly gone. Our safety brain never again sees anything that reminds us of it. Or, we might be reminded of the catalytic event, but with no emotions. We see it and we know that it is no longer unsafe. Or, maybe there will be a little emotion. Maybe a little sadness. Maybe a little guilt. Maybe a little hurt or loneliness. But, if we have started on the healing path, then each time we are reminded, instead of going to defense-attack, we heal. We let ourselves experience that little bit of emotion, and let it go. We acknowledge the emotion. We acknowledge our part in it. We accept ourselves and what we did. And we get over it. Then, those types of situations and incidents in the future stop causing defense-attack because we have let the old emotions go, so we have no reason to defend ourselves. We have fully experienced the emotions and let them go.

The only reason we store the emotions in the emotional water balloon is that we had to hide them away instead of experiencing them. Our parents may have taught us early that it was not all right to fully express all of our emotions, especially sadness, loneliness, feelings of being unloved or unaccepted. If our parents took away our emotions by fixing situations or actually telling us to not show our emotions—"Stop crying. You have nothing to cry about," or "Don't you ever say that you hate me"—we learned to tuck away our emotions. They do not just disappear. They get tucked into an emotional water balloon. When we fully experience those emotions, when we feel them and allow them and show them to ourselves and maybe to someone else who will fully accept those emotions with us, we take them out of the emotional water balloon and let them go.

When Billy was about six years old his mom asked him to walk across the street and buy some milk. He did. On the way back, though, there was a funeral procession going by. He waited until they had passed, then continued home. When he got home his mom told him how embarrassed she was that he had stood there and watched those grieving people drive by. She said it was like he had been prying into their sadness. (I'll bet she doesn't even remember this whole incident. Children will take things to heart that, as parents, we never even realize were significant.) When Billy was in grade 11, a friend told him that she and some other friends had driven by him three times in one day, yelled, waved, honked the horn, and he had ignored them. She was quite hurt. Billy did not ignore them. He actually had not seen or heard them.

Billy now realizes that at six years old he learned to experience shame if he looked in the windows of cars. So, he stopped looking in the windows of cars. He also realized that he experienced a great deal of discomfort looking in the windows of houses. Billy overcame those feelings of discomfort by staring in the windows of cars and houses: "Hah, see. No shame," and at the next house or car, pause, stare, "Hah, see. No shame." It was not one of those things that was a big deal for Billy. So, after playing some with staring in windows, he stopped. (People can have their privacy.) If something in a car window or house window catches his eye, he looks. Otherwise, he ignores.

Some of our behaviors are silly when we look a them. The lessons that we thought we learned as children can look a bit ridiculous when we look at them with our objective adult eyes. Those silly patterns can be easily changed when we identify the pattern and the catalytic event. Other catalytic events are not silly, and not so easily changed.

In one training session with a company in Britain, Elaine told us that she hated the color yellow and the letter "P." Those are strange things to be uncomfortable with because they are so common. When asked, "When you think about the feelings you get with the color yellow and the letter "P," what do they remind you of from your childhood?" Elaine started crying. Her early childhood had been spent in France. When she was about three years old she had gotten a bladder infection. It hurt to urinate. The doctor told her parents that the pain was all in her head. So, every time Elaine complained about the pain, her parents would slap her to teach her not to complain about it. What color is urine? Yellow. In French, Elaine had been taught to refer to urine as "pee-pee." Elaine had taken all of those feelings she had experienced during this time in her life, put them in an emotional water balloon, and instead of attaching them to her parents, or the doctor, she had attached them to the color yellow and the letter "P." Identifying the catalytic event and being allowed to fully experience the emotions that came up allowed Elaine to let the emotions go and begin having no emotional reactions to the color yellow and the letter "P."

A child's logic is amazing. As children, we will rarely attach those painful feelings to our parents because those people have to keep us safe. If we identify our parents as being unsafe, where do we find safety? We don't. So, we attach those feelings to something else.

When Lettie was 12 years old, her mom went to the hospital for a week or so. Before mom returned, as the only girl at home, Lettie had to do a full house cleaning. Lettie even waxed and polished all of the floors. She made the mistake of waxing and polishing under the rug at the entranceway. When mom came in she just about fell. She had had major surgery, and Lettie can now understand the pain mom must have experienced as she caught her balance. Her mom got very angry with Lettie for waxing under the rugs. To this day, when someone does not appreciate Lettie's efforts to keep the house clean, she will go to defense-attack. Her children and husband have experienced this many times. Lettie finally realized that when they do not appreciate her efforts to keep the house clean; i.e. when they make any kind of a mess, she experiences the same feelings that she had during that catalytic event: "they don't love me." The realization that that was where the anger was coming from around her house cleaning issue eliminated the defense-attack behavior in those situations.

In one of the relationship courses Theode and I attended, "Love as it Can Be,"[1] run by Liz Garland and Gordon Tebbut in Calgary, Canada, I discovered another simple, yet deeply-rooted pattern. We were only into the first couple hours of a four-day retreat when Liz started talking about first names, and I started crying. I realized that Theode only used my first name when he was angry with me. Much like my primary family where, being called by your first name by an adult with an angry voice led to discomfort, sadness, and the feeling of being unlovable. When I identified that particular pattern, in the safe environment of Liz and Gord's course, I cried. They encouraged me to experience those feelings. I did. For a few months after that, I was very sensitive to Theode only using my first name when he was upset. Now, two years after identifying that pattern, I noticed the other day that he made a deliberate attempt to use my name in a loving situation, and I was amused and appreciative. I no longer even really notice whether he uses my name or not, because I have no emotions left around it. I have experienced the feelings and I have released them. That emotional water balloon no longer exists.

Our parents and siblings will not remember many of the catalytic events that we experienced in our childhoods. These events that were so significant to us had absolutely no significance whatsoever to the other person involved in the event. Even if we had parents who were great at allowing us to experience our emotions and talk them out, they could not possibly have guessed at every event that we would find catalytic. Now, as adults, having too many full emotional water balloons leads us to a great deal of defensiveness and attacking. It can be almost continuous as we get older and the overflow from all the emotional water balloons becomes constant.

One man, Lenny, had a difficult childhood with an autocratic father. He had sporadically ended his relationship with his father. Lenny was not able to look at those past events to heal. He was still defending himself from the pain. That was three years ago. Today, I occasionally hear about Lenny. He yelled at one of his sons at a soccer game to the extent that the coach evicted him. He has sworn at other kids at the school during school hours and been escorted off the premises. You, I, and Lenny all know that this type of behavior is totally inappropriate and unacceptable. Yet it is less dangerous for Lenny to behave like this, than it is for him to experience those feelings from his childhood.

As parents, we can attack our children often. Our children are great reminders of our catalytic events. They show us what it is like to be a child. When we see the kids doing something that we were punished for we get angry with the kids. They remind us of many of the catalytic events in our lives. We do not want to experience those emotions. The reason we tucked those emotions into an emotional water balloon in the first place is that they were unsafe emotions to feel. Now, instead of feeling those emotions that the children remind us of, we go to defense-attack with them. It is as though there is a big, 18-wheeler truck coming down the street. We step out into the street and then we see the truck. Without thinking, we grab the nearest thing so we can pull ourselves out of the pathway of that truck. Unfortunately, it was not a lamp post that we grabbed to pull ourselves out of the way of the truck. It was a child. And, in pulling ourselves out of the pathway of that truck, we put a child into its pathway. In our need to protect ourselves we put our children in the way of that truck. That truck is our anger. We attack our children. We may well attack anyone instead of having to experience those feelings again. It is the avoidance of those feelings that leads to our greatest anger, because those feelings keep coming up. The longer we avoid them, the stronger they become, because each time we avoid them, we tuck more of them into the emotional water balloon. Each time our children remind us of a catalytic event: the kids spill something, break something, leave a door open, forget to do their homework, get a bad grade in school, miss a goal, leave clothing lying around, or do not feed the dog (this list is infinite), we attack them. Each time one of your children does something that you did as a child and were reprimanded for and felt sad, unaccepted, and unloved, you tap one of your emotional water balloons. The threat of having to experience those emotions has you going to defense-attack. The fuller the water balloon, the bigger the defense-attack.

Find a private moment. Go to those emotions. Experience them. Cry, rage, scream, and remember. Remember them fully. Get rid of them by experiencing them one last time. This whole idea of healing some of the pain that we experienced as children is referred as dealing with our inner child.[2]

One brother and sister experienced a great deal of physical, emotional, and sexual abuse as children. When they approached me and asked to work with me, they flat out told me that they would not talk about their past. They were so scared of feeling that pain that they would not go near it. The brother had a very high-paying job in the computer industry. Yet, he was scared of losing his job because he could not keep an assistant. After just a few weeks of working with someone new, he would explode in anger at them. His temper was very volatile. He would yell, scream, and throw things. They would quit. Other coworkers tried to keep away from him. His company valued him, yet he was so costly in terms of the work relationships in the office that they were willing to pay for help with his anger issues. But, he had so much pain and fear of the past that he would not go to it, and I could not work with him. The only way to rid yourself of the need to attack is get rid of the fear and pain.

Last I heard of the brother, he had changed his name for the third time. Changing his name three times shows that those old emotions keep coming up. They come up and they are strong and they are so very uncomfortable and painful that he cannot go to them. He runs away from his pain by reinventing himself again and again.

Why do we direct our defense-attack at others? If the pain and fear comes from inside us, we need to turn inside, not outside, to get rid of it. Why do we attack others? We turn our anger on them because we feel unsafe with ourselves. The only person we have to live with every second of every day is ourselves. If we feel safe with ourselves, we have a solid basis for dealing with situations from our thinking brains—calmly and rationally. If we feel unsafe with ourselves we will be steeped in defense-attack. It is much safer to turn the defense-attack on others than it is to turn it on ourselves. When we attack others we are basically saying, "You change so I don't have to feel this way." If we can blame situations on others, then we can leave them or try to change them. If we are the ones we feel unsafe with, what can we do? In the past we may have tried to change some things, like our weight or our exercise regime, with little success. If the only way to feel safe is to change ourselves, and we have had so little success with the little things, then our situation is hopeless. We might even have tried to change more crucial things, like our defense-attack behavior, but we were unable to make those changes, either. So, we cannot leave us and we cannot change us. We then engage in even more defense-attack behavior because we feel so unsafe with ourselves. If someone else is available, we may direct the defense-attack on them, because we feel more in control when we are attacking others than we do when we are attacking ourselves.

We cannot escape the pain. We need to go to it, and make our peace with it. You can do this with someone with whom you trust and can be vulnerable, someone with whom you can cry. You can get this support from a professional. The other person's role is to use pure, clean listening. Their role is to help you go to the emotions of the catalytic event. They need to ask questions about that incident from your childhood so that you fully go to those emotions and say everything you need to say about that situation. They need to support you to cry and yell and relive that catalytic event until you are finished, until you have said it all, and expressed it all.

Your role is to express it all. Your role is to relive the emotions from that catalytic event, completely. Imagine yourself as a child, back in that moment, facing the people you were facing, and say what you really want to say. Show them, in your imagination, your pain and frustration. Then say the things you need to say that would be taking care of yourself. In doing this, you will be emptying that emotional water balloon and getting rid of it.

If you do not have anyone you can be that vulnerable with, you can still go through this process. Get a crayon and some blank pieces of paper. Find yourself a private place with no one around. Give yourself an hour or more, if you like. Put the crayon in your nonwriting hand.[3] If you normally write with your right hand, put the crayon in your left hand, and vice versa. Now fully write out everything you want to say to the other people who were in that situation with you. By writing with your nondominant hand you are recreating some of the frustration and discomfort in learning to write that you experienced as a child. When you do this, it becomes easier to bring up the emotions from a catalytic event on your own. Write out every detail. Write out every emotion. Say exactly the words that you have imagined yourself saying to that person or people. Fully express what you were feeling and thinking when it was happening. You will be emptying that emotional water balloon and getting rid of it. We do not send these letters. They are private letters just for us and to us. We need to fully express what we thought and felt when that catalytic event was occurring. You keep those letters for yourself or you can get rid of them in a way that symbolizes your getting rid of that particular emotional water balloon. If this process brings up a lot of pain, get a professional to work with you.

Heal the pain caused by events in your childhood and you begin to live a calm, loving life. You have no need to defend-attack because you have no hidden pain that gets tapped. We have a whole body of information in our society today to help us deal with our inner child. One great book I have encountered is A Return to Love: *Reflections on the Principles of A Course in Miracles,* by Marianne Williamson.[4]

Healing ourselves and our past has less to do with forgiving the others involved in those situations, than it has to do with Chapter 27, Forgive Yourself.

Chapter 27
Forgiving Ourselves

All of our emotions come from us. All of our thoughts and feelings come from us. We are totally responsible for everything we say and do. We have 100% responsibility for our part in every relationship. Therefore, when something goes wrong and we judge ourselves to be unsafe in any given situation, it is because we cannot keep ourselves safe. We believe that, as children, there was something we could have said or done differently to have created a different outcome. Looking back, we can see all kinds of things we could have said or done to deal differently with the situation. We dealt with it wrong at the time. We allowed ourselves to deal with the situation in an unsafe way. We try to reinvent the past. We relive those past situations, trying to create different results. We try to redo them in such a way that we take care of ourselves and keep ourselves safe. We need to forgive ourselves.

With our angry thoughts and words we direct the defense-attack at the other people in those catalytic events. Underneath our attack of other people, we are really unhappy with ourselves. Yet, if we take responsibility for it, we will direct that defense-attack at ourselves and that would be worse. All we need to do is forgive ourselves. Forgive ourselves for being children and not big enough, old enough, strong enough, or wise enough to do the situation any differently.

In our minds, in those 80,000 words per minute we experience, we have an image of who we want to be. We have an image of how strong we are, how calm we are, how lovable we are, how loving we are, how many friends we have, and how we deal with different situations. When we do not live up to that image, whether it is in a situation where we needed to protect ourselves as children, or in a situation where we have an image of our being calm when we weren't, underneath everything else, our discomfort is directed at us. Why did we not live up to our image of ourselves? Why were we not more loving, more lovable, calmer, or whatever? We did not live up to our own picture of ourselves. We need to forgive ourselves. This comes back to something we explored in Chapter 21, No Guilt. We need to accept that everything we have ever done or said was exactly the right thing to have done or said. The proof is that is what we did or said.

There is no point in confronting the other person who was part of that situation. There is no point in trying to forgive them. They acted out of their own best interests and we do understand, at a very basic level, that they are responsible for them and we are responsible for us. There is no point in hammering it out with them or confronting them. There is no point in writing them a letter that tries to lay the blame at their door. They are not to blame for how you handled the situation. They are responsible for them and their emotions and actions. We are responsible for ours.

A discussion I had with a participant just a couple months ago had me reassessing this idea of forgiveness. He felt that there were times that we had to forgive others. As we discussed forgiveness I realized that the only time we have to forgive others is the first time they do something. If we know and they know that what they did was discourteous, impolite, or wrong and they did it anyway, we forgive them the first time. If we have never had the need to express our rules in a given situation, because it has never happened before, then the first time they do it, we forgive them, not us. If a friend makes a date with us, and is late (and they were not kept from meeting us on time by some sort of extraneous incident), we forgive the discourtesy this first time and take the opportunity to lay out the rules in a way that is clear for both of us. If they are late the next time, we can take further action as needed. If we do not take further action, though their behavior bothers us, we need to forgive ourselves not them. We continued living the relationship in a way that violated who we hold ourselves to be.

We acknowledge our part of the situation. We were right in agreeing that they could arrive late. We had perfect reasons for agreeing to those rules, at the time, and the friend being late does not work anymore. So, now we will need to change the rules about being on time, with our friend. It is so much easier to establish clear rules that work at the beginning, instead of having to change the rules later on.

For the big things and the little things, forgive yourself. For the times you lived by rules that were not true to you, and the times you attacked when you held that you were a person who did not attack, forgive yourself. For your reaction to that particular situation, forgive yourself. For your reaction to that particular individual, forgive yourself. For your actions as a child when you were too young, too small, too weak, too uneducated, too unknowledgeable, forgive yourself.

When we accept that we did exactly what we needed to do, given the time, the emotions, the situations, our safety brains, and our experience, we begin to experience less anger. We are safe people to be with. We live by the image that we hold of ourselves. We are true to ourselves. Now, today, if something happens or someone says something, we find ourselves reacting and responding in ways that are true to who we hold ourselves to be. When we start doing this, we let go of defense-attack. We are in control. We are safe. Therefore, we are also safe to be with. We explain to people what our rules are. We live by our own rules. We are not governed by our safety brain. We are governed by our thinking brain.

Forgive yourself. If, today, you do something that is against who you hold yourself to be, acknowledge that you did exactly the right thing for the right reason. Then, start looking for the reason! It is there. All you have to do is find it.

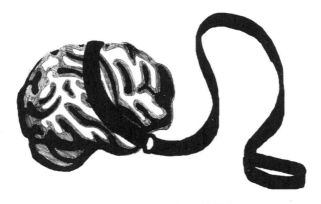

LEVEL VI

Lead Your Safety
Brain to Change

Introduction
Lead Your Safety Brain to Change

If we are going to be *fixed,* no longer angry and attacking, we need to lead our safety brain in a new direction. It would be nice if our safety brain would come along quietly to the new way of doing life instead of fighting every step of the way to continue doing conversations and relationships in the old way. It is possible to lead our safety brains in a new direction without it fighting. In this concluding chapter we will take a look at achieving our goals. How can we set our goals so that our safety brain supports the change, and helps us to achieve it, instead of fighting against it? We'll look at what actions we can take to achieve our goals. All of the information in the world will not change our lives. We need to take action on the information to have things different than they are now.

Chapter 28
We're Fixed

Part I: Achieving our goals

We are all very good at setting goals. "I'm going to lose weight." "I'm not going to yell at the kids anymore." "I'm going to exercise three times a week." "I'm going to take that course." "I'm going to file every piece of paper as soon as I read it." We set goals constantly. Achieving our goals is the more difficult part. Throughout this book we have discovered why achieving our goals is hard. Our safety brain is not interested in doing any part of life in a new way.

There are four key elements in setting a goal that will easily lead our safety brains in the new direction instead of us having to fight to make the change.

Here are the four things that go into setting your new goals:

1. The picture has to be positive.
2. The one sentence statement is a "now" or "present" statement.
3. Write your goals down every morning before you roll out of bed.
4. Every day for at least 21 days; 40 days is better; 100 days is even better.

1. The picture has to be positive. We discovered in Chapter 4 that we have been trained to focus 95% of our attention on the negative and that we are constantly setting negative goals for ourselves. "I'll never be able to do that." "That won't ever work." "Nobody ever listens to me so I won't speak up this time." "I don't remember names." You have actually achieved most of the negative goals that you set. So, maybe we are good at achieving our goals and it's just that we keep setting the wrong goals. If we want something positive in our lives then we need to deliberately set a positive picture. The picture has to be positive because your safety brain is going to make it happen. You want good things to happen in your life, not the bad things.

The vast majority of people that I interact with will say, "I don't remember names." Good picture. They do not remember names. Personally, I do remember names. Remembering names is easy. When I work with a group, I can remember up to 100 names at a time. Everybody can do this. Everything we have encountered, from birth, is stored in our memories. Why can't you access the names of the people you meet? Because you set the goal for yourself, "I don't remember names."

In a training seminar, where the people I am working with do not know each other, I will have people form teams with others that they do not know. When the exercise is done I will challenge them to remember names. For those who do not remember names, their safety brains will help them achieve that goal in numerous ways. When I have people start to introduce themselves the rooms can get very noisy because so many people are talking. As people are turning to each other and starting to listen they may not have heard the first person say his or her name. For many, their safety brains will help them to not remember names by keeping them from saying, "Excuse me. I didn't hear your name. Can you repeat it?" It is such a simple and effective technique for our safety brains to use. If you never heard their name, you cannot possibly remember it. Most of us are not offended if we are asked repeat our name. Why would we feel embarrassed to ask someone to repeat his or her name?

One of the key elements necessary for remembering names is the goal "I remember names." Once you set that goal and start repeating it to yourself, listen to that little voice from your safety brain that gives you ways to remember names. You know many techniques. You simply are not using them. Set the positive goal and watch yourself start remembering names.

"I now earn $10,000 per month." " I now weigh 121 pounds." "I have a forever-after-loving relationship with my husband, Theode." "I am a calm, loving, nurturing mother." "I love myself just the way I am."

We have heard another word for these types of goals. Affirmations. Affirmations are simply positive goals about ourselves and our lives. When you set a positive goal you are giving your safety brain a new picture to work on. In one training session for management, I invited the participants to use these four principles to set some goals and I gave them time to write down some goals. One manager wrote, "I don't procrastinate." Take the "don't" out of that statement and what picture is formed? "I procrastinate." This is exactly what this first principle addresses—ensure that your goals are positive.

The other part of this first principle is to focus on what other positives your goal will give you. When I first started Hap Ki Do, the minute I walked into the building, I was given a real feeling of being accepted. Master Park invited me into his office and welcomed me. When I walked up to the exercise area, two or three people immediately came over and introduced themselves. When we started class, Master Park introduced me to the entire group. Also, I had a senior Black Belt assigned to me—in other settings we would call this person a mentor. I did not have to try to figure out what the rest of the class was doing. The Black Belt who was working with me walked me through everything at a much slower pace, explained things to me, and helped me get a few things right. I worked with a Black Belt for the first three or four classes I attended until Master Park felt that I had caught on enough to be able to follow reasonably well with the class. Master Park does this with every new person who joins. This type of welcome and mentoring gave me, and everyone who experiences it, an immediate feeling of acceptance and being part of the pack. It is a very strong technique to guarantee people feel comfortable and will come back.

Besides the acceptance and mentoring, the physical aspects of Hap Ki Do had me 100% committed to sticking with it within two or three classes. I started analyzing why I liked it so much and came up with the following list:

1. I was exercising regularly (a constant goal over the course of my life).
2. There was enough routine in the exercises to keep it feeling familiar.
3. There was enough variety in the routine to keep it interesting.
4. We learned something new almost every day (I love learning).
5. I was doing sit-ups and pushups every day (I had been wanting to do that since I was 14 years old. I'm up to 75 sit-ups a day!)
6. I am highly competitive. I get to compete against myself, stretch a little further, push a little harder.
7. I get to compete against the others in the class, trying to kick higher, do better, test for my next belt earlier.
8. I am accountable to Master Park, which is very much like being accountable to my coaches in the sports I participated in growing up. That means I can't slack off, because someone else will notice.
9. I get occasional pats on the back from Master Park, just enough to fill my need for attention which keeps me working hard.
10. I can do a full workout when I am on the road. All I have to carry is a sweat suit. No breaks in routine for my safety brain to seize on and get me back to not exercising.
11. I can eat whatever I want whenever I want and no longer worry about gaining weight.
12. I look better because some of the fat has transformed into muscle.
13. I no longer worry about my weight, something I have been doing since I was 12.
14. I'm doing it with Theode and two of our kids, with whom I love spending my time.

The list is actually much longer. The point is, instead of focusing on, "I'm too tired to go out tonight and exercise," I have such a long list of positives, that if I am feeling tired, one of them pops into my mind and I find myself getting ready to exercise, whether I am on the road or at home.

We can set a positive goal and still talk ourselves out of achieving it by falling into the Negative Thought Cycle. Or, we can have such a long list of positives about the goal that if the safety brain tries to talk us out of achieving that goal with one of our old excuses, our list of positives comes to mind and the safety brain sees that the new goal is safer because of all of those positives, and keeps us focused on and achieving the new goal.

2. The one sentence statement is a "now" or "present" statement. If you can state your goal in one sentence, then you are really clear on what it is you want and you have set a really clear picture for your safety brain to start working on. The clearer you are the clearer the picture. The clearer the picture the easier it is for your safety brain to see opportunities to make that picture happen. The easiest way to figure out your one sentence statement (25 words or less) is to think about what life looks like when the goal is achieved. "I talk to the kids calmly, even when I feel like attacking." "I now weigh 115 pounds." "I remain calm and reasonable with Fred, the jerk at work."

If you can see exactly what the end result is, then you are very clear on what your goal is. The goal needs to be about you, not about Fred or the kids. "The kids speak softly in the house." That cannot be a real goal for us, because we cannot step inside the kids, as though they are elevators, and push the button marked "soft voice." Instead, the goal has to be about ourselves and what we are going to do about our part in any situation.

The goal must be a now or present statement. I did not write down, "Some day I will earn $10,000 per month." I didn't say, "I'm going to earn $7,500 per month." When we set the statement in the present, we are lying to ourselves. "I now earn…" That is OK. Lie to yourself. Your safety brain does not see the untruth; it simply sees the picture that it needs to work on.

Have you ever said, "I'm going to lose weight?" Look at those words. What is the picture? "Going to lose…" Sometime in the future. And forever more you will be going to lose weight. Every day, for the rest of your life, your safety brain will be helping you to be going to lose weight. If you draw the picture for it happening sometime in the future, that's exactly what your safety brain will be working on. Instead, use "I am…" or "I now have…" or "Right now, I…"

- Right now, I am calm and productive every moment I am at the office.
- I now deal with all clients and customers using pure, clean listening and understanding what they need and how we can meet their needs.
- I now walk away from a conversation with my spouse when I feel the defense-attack bubbling inside.
- I am calm and kind with the kids.
- I treat my family and friends with respect and dignity.
- I like the person I am.

Go ahead, lie to yourself by putting your goal in the present. And, please, reach for the moon. No intermediate steps. Don't think that there is a first step then a second step. If you do that, your results will be a lot slower. Make the goal as big and wonderful as you can possibly make it. Ignore that safety brain voice that tries to talk you out of saying the goal. Ignore the safety brain voice that says, "Yabbut." "Yah, but you always scream at the kids. You will this time, too." "Yah, but Fred the jerk is such a jerk, you need to get angry at him to get anything done." "Yah, but the kids won't listen unless you're screaming at them." Yah, but. Any time you hear a "yabbut" you are hearing your safety brain trying to get you back to the old way of thinking. Acknowledge it, and continue thinking the new way. "You're right, safety brain. That's how I've been up until now. From now on, I am different." If you give your safety brain a crack by not following through with the new goal on even one day, it will force open a canyon, allowing the old habit to take control again.

Make sure you pay attention to the safety brain voice when it is pointing out opportunities to make the new goal happen.

- That book probably has some ideas in it that will help me make it happen.
- I should make that phone call to see if that client is interested.
- Defense-attack bubbling. Walk away. Walk away. Walk away now.
- I should take each child out for lunch once a month and just listen to him or her.
- We should spend some family time tonight playing a board game.

We do not want to follow through with the little safety brain voice when it is telling us to do things the old way. But we sure want to pay attention and follow through when the safety brain is telling us to do things in a new way. Listen for those new things. Make the commitment to do one new thing a day, or one new thing every two days, or one new thing every week. Whatever period of time seems reasonable to you will be good. But do make the commitment to listen for those new opportunities and follow through on some of them. We never follow through on all of them. But, the more we follow through with, the quicker we will achieve our goal.

3. Write your goals down every morning, before you roll out of bed. Why write down your goals? Part of any time-management information and goal-setting information suggests that you write down your goals. If you just think about them, they are a wish, a dream, and the safety brain can wipe them out quickly. If you put them in writing, you are fully activating your thinking brain. Goal-setting becomes a full brain activity when you write down your goals. We are applying the same concept here as we did in Chapter 3 when we talked about the physical technique we use to get rid of our anger of picking up a pen and writing. We are tricking the safety brain into opening the gateway and letting the thinking brain get to work. The goal-setting becomes a full brain activity instead of just a thinking brain activity or a safety brain activity. Your chances of achieving your goals become far greater. In writing down a goal you have already started doing things differently. The next step is to do something else differently, so that you can start achieving that goal. By clearly seeing the goals and writing them down, you are getting your safety brain to work with your thinking brain to help you achieve the goal. Your safety brain is helping, not fighting.

Why first thing in the morning? This is when you have the most access to your safety brain. Have you ever woken up in the morning and not gotten up right away? You fell back into a kind of waking dream, where you took all of the sounds around the house and put them into the dream? This is the thinking brain and the safety brain working in harmony. Give your safety brain a good, clear picture to work on at that time of day, and watch how quickly you begin to see the opportunities to make that goal happen. Also, you will have a picture that you can work on, and be thinking about, all day. Sometimes I will print a goal on a piece of paper and try to have it in front of me all day, getting my safety brain to work on it and actively think about it, constantly, throughout the day. I achieve those goals very quickly.

Some people like to write out their goals last thing at night before they go to sleep so that their safety brains can work on them while they are sleeping. They can dream about them and remember the opportunities and solutions when they wake up. This simply comes down to personal preference. First thing in the morning or last thing at night—try both ways and decide which works best for you.

If you have between three and five goals that you are working on at any one time, that seems to be plenty. Especially if they are big, life-changing goals. I find that if I set too many goals, I do not achieve any of them very quickly because I cannot take advantage of all of the opportunities that my safety brain shows me. As well, as an Activist I get overwhelmed if I try to do too much, and then I quit all of them. Choose for yourself how many you are comfortable working with, and then do it.

4. Every day for at least 21 days; 40 days is better; 100 days is even better.

Write out each goal every day for 21 days. Do not let your safety brain talk you out of this with excuses or forgetfulness. It takes practice to perfect doing things a new way. It takes time to change a habit. Practice. How long does it take to change a habit? 21 days. Just three weeks. (Brian Tracy, Psychology of Achievement).[1] Push yourself. In three weeks you will find it easy to think of your new goal during the day. You will begin to find it easy to reach for that writing pad or a diary beside your bed and write out your goals. Every day for the next 21 days. If you miss day 10, start over at Day number one. One missed day in the 21 days is the safety brain at work. If you write them out for longer than 21 days, good for you. I will find myself writing out the same goals for two months or six months or 158 days. The longer you stick with one goal, the more deeply you are embedding it in your safety brain, and the quicker it will take shape and happen. The bigger life-changing goals require greater re-enforcement.

Changing a pattern that began when we were two years old, four years old, or 7 years old, is changing a pattern that has been deeply re-enforced. These patterns permeate many areas of our lives, not just one relationship or one situation. If this is true, it will take more time to achieve that goal—more time to change that pattern because you will have to change it in each of those different situations.

Writing out a goal for 21 days is good. Writing it out every day for 100 days is even better. Today, it is simply a Truth that I have a forever-after-loving relationship with my husband, Theode. There is no question. Almost every day one of us will comment on how good our relationship is, how much we love each other, and how great things are between us. Now, we re-enforce that goal daily and even multiple times a day simply by making those comments. And we have achieved that goal.

Start out by lying to yourself about how good life is, how wonderful you are, and how controlled, calm, and kind you are. When you look back after you have made the changes, it will seem that those wonderful lies became Truths in your life almost without your knowing it was happening.

Remember the four principles when you are setting your goals:
1. The picture has to be positive.
2. The one sentence statement is a "now" or "present" statement.
3. Write your goals down every morning, before you roll out of bed, or before you go to bed.
4. Everyday for at least 21 days; 40 days is better; 100 days is even better.

Part II: Replace the old with the new

I never packed my bags and put them beside the door when I was absolutely raging with defense-attack, but I would say, "I'm leaving." In retrospect, I realized that it was when I finally said these words that I was ready to start looking at the emotions behind the anger. These were also the words that would get my husband to start talking. As a Strategist, he was very quiet and the angrier I became, the quieter and more withdrawn he became. But, when I said, "I'm leaving," that was his cue and he would start talking about what he was feeling, as well. About two years into improving our marriage, we talked about those words. He asked me to stop using them because they were so hurtful for him. They were really hurtful for me, as well, and I agreed that I would not say that anymore. And I didn't. Not for four months. That is when we came the closest to divorce. Why?

Trying to get rid of an old pattern, without replacing it with a new one, is like having a really big area of rotten floorboards in the kitchen. You finally decide to fix the hole and you cut out the rotten floorboards and put them off to the side. But, it was late in the day when you finished and you did not take the time to go out and buy new floorboards. You still have to make meals in the kitchen. The hole in the kitchen is really big. It is so big that there is no way to get to the stove to cook dinner. You cannot jump across it. You cannot climb across the counters to get to it. There is no way get to the stove to cook the meals. So, you look around and realize that the old floorboards are sitting there. Of course, they don't fit very well any more, as you had to break them and cut them to get them up. So, you have to pile more of them into the hole, and in a pretty haphazard way, just so you can get across the hole to cook dinner.

This is exactly what we do with our patterns. If all you do is promise someone else, or yourself, that you are not going to engage in the old behavior ever again, look out! The feelings still come up. Those old situations still trigger the need for defense-attack, but for the first while you are able to hold off reacting in the old way. Within a short period of time, however, you will grab that old way of doing things and the explosion will be huge. It will be the worst that particular behavior has ever been.

That is exactly what happened when we agreed that I would no longer say, "I'm leaving." The emotions were still coming up. The need to say the words still came up, but I did not voice them. The other part of this pattern was that those words were my husband's cue to start talking. Without that cue, he stopped talking. We stopped talking and working out our various problems. We were still having the problems. We simply stopped working them out. That went on for four months, and then I piled the old floorboards back in the hole and we had the worst fight we have ever had. That time, I came very close to leaving our relationship.

Be careful. If you are going to stop an old behavior, figure out what need it is fulfilling and figure out what you are going to do instead of the old behavior. Replace the old with something new.

Another fascinating element of this pattern for my husband and me was that six months after we truly did get rid of those old words and replace them with a new pattern, my husband said, "I'm leaving." I was floored. From the day we said we were committing to our relationship while we were dating, he had assured me that he was committed for life and would do whatever it took to keep us together. Now, he was going back on a promise that he had made and that I counted on. Why would he say those words?

Every pattern that you are engaged in with one or more other people, works for both of you, that is why you both engage in the pattern. You have your reasons and needs for that pattern. The other person or people have their reasons and needs for that pattern. He needed to hear those words as much as I needed to say them. He used those words twice more before we worked out what was happening and how to change that pattern in a way that worked for both of us.

Out with the old, in with the new is essential when we are trying to change patterns and habits. The goal is never, "I don't yell at the kids anymore." Rather it would be, "I speak in a soft voice when I feel the defense-attack bubbling up."

Part III: Our comfort zones are several sizes too small

Have you ever had a really bad fight with someone? This was the worst fight you had ever had with this person. You had attacked, attacked, attacked. Hurtful things were said. After you got over the anger, you realized the relationship was still really important to you so you did something extra nice to try to repair the damage. Having that really, really bad fight took you below the floor of your comfort zone. It took you too far on this one path and your safety brain helped you become uncomfortable with what you had done. So you tried, successfully or unsuccessfully, to repair it.

We experience the other end, as well. You spend an absolutely fabulous day at the office or with your kids or with someone who was really important to you. In fact, it was such a great day that you realized how great it was, and you were commenting on it to yourself and/or the other people involved. That night, back at home, you had one of your worst fights. You attacked and attacked and attacked. You had walked too far on the path the other way. It was too good. You went above the ceiling of your comfort zone, to the point where life was so good, you were uncomfortable with it and had to do something bad to get back onto the path.

This happens in every aspect of our lives. One couple I knew made a nice living. They were both professionals, and Luc did quite a bit of investing. Within a four-month period he made and lost his first million. He made his first million on some stocks, but he had margined the stocks. Basically, he had invested $10,000 and another company lent him another $90,000. The price of these particular stocks went straight up, to the point where he was well into his first million dollars. At any point he could have sold some of the stock and paid off the borrowed $90,000. He did not. He watched the stocks go up and he watched the stocks plummet down to below their original price. Now, not only had he lost his first million, he was in debt to the lender. He still owed them $35,000, and had a really difficult time paying it off. Why? Why, being fully conversant with the stock market, knowing full well what needed to be done to protect himself and his profits, did he then watch the stocks plummet to below what he had originally bought them for? Comfort zone. He and his wife had been in debt for the 11 years that she was improving her education and readying herself for a new job. They told themselves that they did not like being in debt, but they had been doing it for 11 years. They were comfortable with it.

When it came time to solidify their profits and actually be millionaires, Luc could not take the steps he needed to make it happen. It was too good.

Know that there is a ceiling on our comfort zones. When you start making the changes and they work, and life starts to become really good, know that it can become too good and your safety brain will try to get you back onto the old path. Watch that ceiling on the good life bump up and up. Stop. Enjoy the level you are at. Then bump it up some more. When we bought our new house it was far, far outside our comfort zones. It was a wonderful house, in a wonderful neighborhood. It took us two years to repaint it and start decorating it. It took us those two years before we were comfortable enough to hang a picture on the wall.

I would spend a weekend at home after being on the road for a week or two. We would have a wonderful weekend together as a family. We would fight viciously as my husband drove me to the airport on Sunday. We would discuss the fight and work it out by Tuesday. When I got home on Friday we would start the whole pattern over again. This went on for a few months until we identified the pattern and changed it.

Have a great day with your spouse and children. Enjoy the day. Come home and make everyone take "solo time." Solo time is time spent alone, in a room, talking with no one, and doing something that is relaxing for you. Get everyone in the family doing it. We started doing this when our youngest child was three years old, after having been introduced to it by Liz Garland and Gordon Tebbut in *Love As It Can Be*.[2] The idea is that you want to protect the great feelings instead of erasing them with a negative incident.

I combined this idea of "Solo time" with something Brian Tracy says in *The Psychology of Achievement*.[3] We spend time with the people we love, that is how they know we love them. The only absolutely nonrenewable resource we have is time. A minute that has past can never be recaptured. It is gone. If this is our most precious commodity, then, by spending time with others, they know that we truly love them. Show your children you love them by spending time with them. The words "I love you" are only 7% of the message, your actions are 55% of the message. Show your spouse or significant other that you love him or her by spending time with him or her.

Do you show yourself that you love you? Do you spend time just with you, not doing chores or things that need to be done, but by doing things that you want to do? Start spending time just with yourself, and teach your spouse and your children to show themselves that they love themselves by spending time doing something by themselves that they want to do.

This is the concept behind *Solo time*. You are taking the time, following a great time, to protect the raised ceiling on the comfort zone. Instead of engaging in defense-attack with those people you just had such a great time with, become more comfortable with the raised ceiling by following it with time just with yourself, enjoying your time alone. In our family, we will set the timer for between 45 minutes to 90 minutes, depending upon the day and what is happening. When we call *solo time* everyone heads into a different room. We refuse to allow computer games or television during solo time. We are not allowed to talk to anyone else in the house until the timer sounds. We are not allowed to move to a different room, either.

We have also found that when we bicker, and it goes on for a while with no really good reason, calling *solo time* is very effective. The kids spend all day at school with people around them, and then come home and are still surrounded with people. We parents spend all day at work with people around us, and then come home and are still surrounded with people. It is too much. We need a break from other people. We need to show ourselves that we are important. We need to have quiet time, alone, to relax and unwind. *Solo time* fulfills these needs. With younger children, 30 to 45 minutes is probably long enough. Be prepared the first few times to constantly answer the question, "How much longer?"

Once everyone gets used to what *solo time* is, and how it works, you can use it in a variety of situations. Use it for everyone to calm down after their busy days. Use it when the kids are fighting a lot with each other. Use it to raise the ceiling of your comfort zones. When you have had a great day and behaved in exactly the way that makes you feel the best, call *solo time* on yourself, so that you can keep the ceiling of that comfort zone raised. Life will get better, faster, by protecting the good times with solo time.

We can push up the ceiling of our comfort zones and make life better. Simply realize that life being better, in itself, is something that will be uncomfortable. Be ready to deal with the issues that come up with life getting better.

Part IV: Take action

Listen for that little voice stating the opportunities it sees for you to start achieving you new goal, and follow through on some of those opportunities. That is what will make the difference. We can take in all of the information from this book. We can see great ideas and have incredible realizations about how we have been doing life, and how we can change. The last step is for you to take action. You have to do something different. Change just one of your current actions, using one of the ideas from this book, and you will start to get different results in your life. You will have begun the journey to becoming who you want to be, instead of who you learned to be.

Initially, the ideas in this book seem great. We have all kinds of realizations about how we can do things differently. And we start working with some of the ideas. After a few weeks or months we get tired of working with the ideas. We think, "I should be fixed by now. I should be perfect." That is the safety brain at work. After a few more months you will find yourself looking forward to the work. You begin to understand that each time you identify a pattern and each time you get rid of another emotional water balloon, each time you handle a person or situation differently than you have in the past, you are becoming more of who you want to be. Life gets better. You will like yourself more and more. You will look forward to the work. One action at a time. A little bit each day or each week, and, before long, you will not remember what it was like to be angry all the time. You will hardly remember how much you did not like your life, because you are calm, kind, and in control. Just the way you want to be.

One action at a time. Get to work. Good luck.

Bibliography

Level 1
Anger is Not an Emotion

Chapter 1

1. McKie, Robin. *Dawn of Man: The Story of Human Evolution.* (New York, NY: Dorlington Kindersley Publishing, Inc., 2000), p. 29-30, p. 47-48.

2. Aggleton, J.P. *The Amygdala.* (New York, NY: Wiley-Liss, 1992).

3. LeDoux, Joseph E. *"Emotion, Memory, and the Brain."* Scientific American. June 1994: 50-58. *"Kernel of Fear."* Discover. June 1995; 52. MAS. CD-ROM. EBSCO, 1995.

4. Perry, B.D.; Pollard, R.; Blakely, T.; Baker, W.; Vigilante, D. *"Childhood Trauma, the Neurobiology of Adaptation and 'Use-dependent' Development of the Brain: How "States" Become "Traits."* Infant Mental Health Journal. 16, (4): 271-291, 1995.

5. LeDoux, Joseph E., 1994: p. 34.

6. LeDoux, Joseph E. *24th Mathilde Solowey Lecture in Neurosciences.* National Institutes of Health. May 8, 1997.

7. Encyclopaedia Britannica, britannica.com.Inc. www.britannica.com/bcom/eb/article/9/0,5616,119939+24+110703,00.html: 1999-2000.

8. Hart, Archibald. *Adrenaline and Stress.* (Waco, TX: Word Books, 1985).

9. Goleman, Daniel. *Emotional Intelligence.* (New York, NY: Bantam Books, 1995), p. 13-29.

10. Beyerstein, B.L. *"Whence Cometh the Myth that We Only Use 10% of Our Brains?"* Mind Myths, Exploring Popular Assumptions about the Mind and the Brain. (Chichester: John Wiley & Sons, 1999), p. 3.

11. Miller, Tom. *Self-discipline and Emotional Control.* (Boulder, CO: CareerTrack, 1994).

12. Tracy, Brian. *The Psychology of Achievement.* (Niles, IL: Nightingale Conant, 1987).

13. *G.I. Jane.* Demi Moore. Directed by Ridley Scott. (Hollywood Pictures, 1997).

Chapter 2

1. Mehrabian, Albert. *Nonverbal Communication.* (Chicago, IL: Aldine-Atherton, 1972).

2. Ibid.

3. Ibid.

4. Ibid.

5. Farrell, Warren. *Why Men Are the Way They Are.* (New York, NY: McGraw-Hill, 1986).

6. Malloy, John. *New Dress for Success.* (New York, NY: Warner Books, 1988).

7. Malloy, John. *New Women's Dress for Success.* (New York, NY: Warner Books, 1996).

8. Azar, Brian. *Sales and Marketing Management.* 1992 Survey of Buying Power. (October, 1992).

9. Kasper, Jeanette. *Gain Cooperation, Not Confrontation.* Calgary, AB: Be You Inc., 2000.

10. Canfield, Jack. *How to Build High Self-Esteem.* (Chicago, IL: Nightingale Conant, 1990).

11. Tracy, Brian, op.cit.

12. Garland, Liz; Tebbut, Gord. *Love As It Can Be.* Calgary, AB; 1998.

13. Chaiet, Donna; Russell, Francine. *The Safe Zone: A Kid's Guide to Personal Safety.* (New York, NY; Morrow Junior Books, 1998), p. 20-23, 37-40.

Chapter 3

1. Matrix. Keanu Reeves. (Warner Brothers; March, 1999).

2. Ernest, Lawrence. *The 20 Minute Break.* (Los Angeles, CA; Jeremy P. Tarcher, Inc., 1991), p. 11-14.

3. Changeux, Jean-Pierre. *Neuronal Man. The Biology of the Man.* (New York, NY: Random House, 1985, p. 113.

4. Smith, T.W., Frohm, K.D. *"What's So Unhealthy about Hostility."* Health Psych. 1985; 4: 503-20.

5. Friedman, Meyer. *Type A Behavior and York Heart.* (Fullerton, CA; McGraw-Hill, 1988).

6. Kawachi, Ichiro. *"Circulation."* American Health Association Journal. Harvard School of Public Health; November 1, 1996.

7. Ibid.

8. Goleman, Daniel, op.cit.

9. Chollar, Susan. *"Exercise Can be Psychologically Beneficial."* Health and Fitness Opposing Views. (San Diego, CA: Greenhaven Press, 1985), p. 62-66.

10. Fry Jr. W.F. *"The Physiological Effects of Humor, Mirth, and Laughter.* JAMA. 1992; 267: 1857-1858.

11. Duncum, Alam; Gresty, Alec, Burden, Roger. *Logic Problems.* (London, England: British European Associated Publishers Ltd., 1998).

12. Metcalf, C.W.; Felible, Roman. *Lighten Up: Survival Skills for People Under Pressure.* (Reading, MA: Addison-Wesley Publishing Company, 1992), p.10.

13. Ibid.

14. Ibid.

Chapter 4

1. Canfield, Jack; Hansen, Mark Victor. *Chicken Soup for the Soul.* (Deerfield Beach, FL: Health Communication, Inc., 1995).

2. Canfield, Jack, 1990.

3. Waitley, Denis. *The Psychology of Winning.* (Niles, IL: Nightingale Conant, 1987).

4. Brown, R. *Words and Things.* (New York, NY: Free Press, 1958).

5. Weiskrantz, L. *Thought Without Language.* (Oxford; Oxford University Press), p. 464-484.

6. Blakeslee, Sandra. *Seeing and Imagining: Clues to the Workings of the Mind's Eye.* The Science Times Book of the Brain. (New York, NY: The New York Times, 1998), p. 19-24.

7. Belson, William A. *Television Violence and the Adolescent Boy.* (Hampshire, England; Saxon House, 1978), p. 364-383.

8. Farell, Warren, op. cit.

9. Menninger, Karl A. *The Human Mind* (New York, NY: Alftred A Knopf, 1957).

10. McLaughlin, J.; West, A.E. *The Interpreter as Listener: Effective listening for interpreting.* (New York, NY: Harcourt Brace and World Inc., 1978), p. 72-81.

11. Welsh, Richard. *Subliminal Photography.* Subliminal Dynamics, Aurora, CO.

12. Goleman, Daniel, op. cit., p. 195-196.

13. Price, John Randolph. *The Abundance Book.* (Carlsbad, CA: Hay House, Inc., 1987).

14. Armstrong, Natalie. *"Around 50 men are destined to fall in love: Study pinpoints passages in the male view of romance,"* National Post. August 25, 2000; National Edition; p. A3.

Level III
The Golden Rule Causes Conflict

Introduction

1. deLaszlo, Violet S. *The Basic Writings of C.G. Jung.* (New York, NY: Random House, 1959), p. 183-285.

2. Alessandra, Tony. *Relationship Strategies.* (Chicago, IL: Nightingale Conant, 1986).

3. Goleman, Daniel, op. cit.

Level IV
Make Them Calm Down

Chapter 11

1. Covey, Stephen. *The 7 Habits of Highly Effective People.* (New York, NY: Simon and Schuster, 1989).

2. Nelson, Noelle C. *Winning! Using Lawyers' Courtroom Techniques to Get Your Way in Every Day Situations.* (Paramus, NJ: Prentice Hall, 1997), p. 174-176.

Chapter 12

1. Paterno, Joe. *Paterno.* (New York, NY: Random House, 1989).

Level V
What Can I Do About Me?

1. Kasper, Jeanette, op. cit., p. 6.

Chapter 19

1. Kasper, Jeanette. *Frogs have it easy...They can eat what bugs them.* (Calgary, AB: Be You Inc., 2001), p. 16.

Chapter 21

1. Kasper, Jeanette, op. cit., p.33.

2. Ibid., p. 31.

Chapter 25

1. Kasper, Jeanette, op. cit., p. 5.

2. Farrell, Warren, op. cit.

3. Strauss, Murray A.; Gelles, Richard J.; Steinmetz, Suzanne K. *Behind Closed Doors.* (Garden City, NY: Anchor Books/Doubleday, 1980), p. 97-122.
4. Kasper, Jeanette, op. cit., p. 9.

Chapter 26

1. Garland, Liz; Tebbut, Gordon, op.cit.

2. Capacchione, Lucia. *Recovery of Your Inner Child.* (New York, NY: Simon and Schuster, 1991).

3. Ibid.

4. Williamson, Marianne. *A Return to Love: Refelections on the Principles of A Course in Miracles.* (New York, NY: HarperCollins, 1992).

Level VI
Lead Your Safety Brain to Change

Chapter 28

1. Tracy, Brian, op. cit.

2. Garland, Liz; Tebbut, Gordon, op. cit.

3. Tracy, Brian, op. cit.

Here's a thought...

BOOK JEANETTE INTO YOUR CONVENTIONS, MEETINGS, AND COMPANY PRESENTATIONS.

This entertaining speaker brings her unique humor, and creative insights of people, into every keynote presentation and training session. You'll not only learn solid solutions for your people problems and how to implement those solutions in everyday life—the experience will be one of pure enjoyment.

Harmonious human relations at work, home, and play

CONTACT: **Jeanette Kasper, B.A. CSO**
2428 Palisade Drive SW
Calgary Alberta Canada T2V 3V3
Telephone (403) 238 6865
Email jkasper@beyouinc.com **Website** www.beyouinc.com